Reconceptualising Professional Learning

This book presents leading-edge perspectives and methodologies to address emerging issues of concern for professional learning in contemporary society. The conditions for professional practice and learning are changing dramatically in the wake of globalisation, new modes of knowledge production, new regulatory regimes and increased economic–political pressures. A number of challenges for professional learning emerge:

- more practitioners becoming involved in interprofessional collaboration
- developments in new technologies and virtual workworlds
- emergence of transnational knowledge cultures and interrelated circuits of knowledge.

The space and time relations in which professional practice and learning are embedded are becoming more complex, as are the epistemic underpinnings of professional work. Together these shifts bring about intersections of professional knowledge and responsibilities that call for new conceptions of professional knowing.

Exploring what the authors call sociomaterial perspectives on professional learning, they argue that theories that trace not just the social but also the material aspects of practice – tools, texts, bodies, devices – are useful for coming to terms with the challenges described above.

Reconceptualising Professional Learning develops these issues through specific contemporary cases focused on one of the book's three main themes: (1) professionals' knowing in practice, (2) professionals' work arrangements and technologies and (3) professional responsibility. Each chapter draws upon innovative theory to highlight the sociomaterial webs through which professional learning may be reconceptualised. Authors are based in Australia, Canada, Italy, Norway, Sweden and the USA as well as the UK, and their cases are based in a range of professional settings including medicine, teaching, nursing, engineering, social services, the creative industries and more.

By presenting detailed accounts of these themes from a sociomaterial perspective, the book raises new questions and opens new methodological approaches. These can help make more visible what is often invisible in today's messy dynamics of professional learning, and point to new ways of configuring educational support and policy for professionals.

Tara Fenwick is Professor of Education at the University of Stirling, UK and Director of ProPEL, an international network for research in professional practice, education and learning. Her most recent book is *Emerging Approaches to Educational Research: tracing the sociomaterial*, with R.Edwards and P. Sawchuk (Routledge 2012).

Monika Nerland is Professor of Education at the University of Oslo, Norway. She has led several research projects focusing on learning and knowledge development in different professions. She recently co-edited the book *Professional Learning in the Knowledge Society*, with K. Jensen and L.C. Lahn (Sense 2012).

Reconceptualising Professional Learning

Sociomaterial knowledges, practices and responsibilities

Edited by Tara Fenwick and Monika Nerland

Routledge
Taylor & Francis Group

LONDON AND NEW YORK

First published 2014
by Routledge
2 Park Square, Milton Park, Abingdon, Oxon OX14 4RN

and by Routledge
711 Third Avenue, New York, NY 10017

Routledge is an imprint of the Taylor & Francis Group, an informa business

© 2014 T. Fenwick and M. Nerland

British Library Cataloguing in Publication Data
A catalogue record for this book is available from the British Library

Library of Congress Cataloging in Publication Data
Reconceptualising professional learning : sociomaterial knowledges,
practices, and responsibilities / edited by Tara Fenwick, Monika Nerland.
pages cm
1 Employees–Training of. I. Fenwick, Tara J. II. Nerland, Monika.
HF5549.5.T7R354 2014
378'.013–dc23
2013035118

ISBN: 978-0-415-81577-2 (hbk)
ISBN: 978-0-415-81578-9 (pbk)
ISBN: 978-1-315-81371-4 (ebk)

Typeset in Galliard
by Cenveo Publisher Services

Printed and bound in the United States of America by Publishers Graphics,
LLC on sustainably sourced paper.

Contents

List of Contributors   xi

**Introduction: Sociomaterial professional knowing,
work arrangements and responsibility: new times,
new concepts?**   1
TARA FENWICK AND MONIKA NERLAND

Introduction 1
Changing concepts, changing times 2
Sociomaterial approaches 2
Professional knowing, work arrangements and responsibility 4
Conclusion 6
References 7

**SECTION I
Reconceptualising professional knowing**   9

1 **Professional knowing-in-practice: rethinking materiality
and border resources in telemedicine**   11
SILVIA GHERARDI

Introduction 11
Knowing-in-practice as a practical accomplishment 12
Research site, research design and methodology 13
At the core and at the margins of a practice 14
Conclusions 22
Acknowledgement 23
Notes 23
References 23

2 Learning through epistemic practices in professional work: examples from nursing and computer engineering 25

MONIKA NERLAND AND KAREN JENSEN

Introduction 25
The dynamism of expert communities: epistemic objects and practices 27
Clinical procedures as epistemic objects: examples from nursing 29
Epistemic objects in computer engineering: programming patterns and project models 31
Conclusion 34
Note 35
References 36

3 The doctor and the blue form: learning professional responsibility 38

MIRIAM ZUKAS AND SUE KILMINSTER

Introduction 38
Becoming a doctor: accounting for learning 39
Researching doctors learning responsibility 44
The blue form: enacting doctors who care for the dying 45
Conclusion 48
Notes 49
References 49

4 Re-thinking teacher professional learning: a more than representational account 52

DIANNE MULCAHY

Introduction 52
What counts as professional learning? 54
A more-than-representational account 56
The project in question: data and methods 57
Learning assemblages: teacher learners at work 58
Conclusions 62
Acknowledgement 63
References 64

5 Surfacing the multiple: diffractive methods for rethinking professional practice and knowledge 67

DAVIDE NICOLINI AND BRIDGET ROE

The singular and multiple nature of professional knowledge 68
How to surface the multiple nature of professional knowledge 70

Surfacing multiplicity 72
From reflection to diffraction? 77
Conclusion: which professional will teach me today? 78
Notes 80
References 80

SECTION II
Reconceptualising professional work arrangements   83

  6 Nurturing occupational expertise in the contemporary
     workplace: an 'apprenticeship turn' in
     professional learning   85
     ALISON FULLER AND LORNA UNWIN

     Introduction 85
     Structure and agency in creative tension 86
     Apprenticeship as a model of learning 88
     Learning as apprentices in expansive environments 89
     Professional learning as a fragile endeavour 90
     Conclusion 95
     Acknowledgement 97
     References 97

  7 A technology shift and its challenges to professional
     conduct: mediated vision in endodontics   99
     ÅSA MÄKITALO AND CLAES REIT

     Introduction 99
     Visual technologies in endodontic practice 100
     Technology shifts and professional learning 101
     Re-actualizing the advent of the surgical microscope:
        an empirical case 101
     Conclusions 109
     Notes 110
     References 111

  8 Engineering knowing in the digital workplace:
     aligning materiality and sociality through action   112
     ADITYA JOHRI

     Introduction 112
     The intertwining of the social and the material in
        engineering knowing 112

Case study: newcomer participation 114
Knowing in practice through action – sociomaterial bricolage 118
Discussion and conclusion 121
Acknowledgements 122
Notes 122
References 122

9   **Interprofessional working and learning:**
    a conceptualization of their relationship and its
    implications for education   **125**
    DAVID GUILE

Introduction 125
The reorganization of work and the growth of interprofessional
    working and learning 126
Case study of interprofessional working and learning
    in a co-configured project team 128
Knowledge and the professions 130
Interprofessional working and learning and programmes
    of professional formation 133
Rethinking initial professional formation for
    interprofessional work 136
Conclusion 137
Acknowledgement 138
Note 138
References 138

10 **Arrangements of co-production in healthcare:**
    partnership modes of interprofessional practice   **140**
    ROGER DUNSTON

Preface 140
Introduction 140
Co-production – a rich but unspecified point of departure 141
Developing our investigative focus 143
What have we learned? 145
Learnings and implications 148
Conclusions – theorizing professional learning in practice 150
Notes 151
References 152

SECTION III
Reconceptualising professional responsibility   155

11   Rethinking professional responsibility:
     matters of account   157
     TARA FENWICK

     Introduction 157
     Toward a sociomaterial conception of professional
        responsibility 159
     Dilemmas of professional responsibility: the politics of materials
        and practice 163
     Conclusion 167
     References 169

12   Developing professional responsibility in medicine:
     a sociomaterial curriculum   171
     NICK HOPWOOD, MADELEINE ABRANDT DAHLGREN
     AND KARIN SIWE

     Introduction 171
     Theoretical background 172
     Empirical approach 175
     How is a sociomaterial curriculum being enacted? 176
     Conclusion 181
     Acknowledgements 182
     References 183

13   Dilemmas of responsibility for nurses in independent practice:
     knowledge, learning and innovation   184
     SARAH WALL

     Introduction 184
     A practice-based sociomaterial perspective 185
     A study of self-employed nurses 187
     Tensions, responsibilities, and emerging possibilities in nursing
     entrepreneurship 188
     New possibilities for professional work 193
     Conclusion 194
     Acknowledgement 196
     References 196

14 Putting time to 'good' use in educational work: a question of
    responsibility   198
    HELEN COLLEY, LEA HENRIKSSON, BEATRIX NIEMEYER
    AND TERRI SEDDON

    Introduction 198
    Understanding time differently 198
    Researching time orders in educational work 200
    *Finland: competing historical periods in health
        and social care education 201*
    England: clock time vs process time in youth support work 204
    *Germany: defending process time against abstract time
        in youth support work 206*
    Conclusion 209
    Acknowledgements 210
    References 211

15 Professional learning for planetary sustainability:
    thinking through Country   213
    MARGARET SOMERVILLE

    Introduction 213
    The Anthropocene 214
    Thinking through Country 215
    *Pedagogies for teacher education and professional learning
        for sustainability 220*
    Conclusion 225
    Acknowledgements 225
    Notes 225
    References 226

    Index   228

Contributors

Madeleine Abrandt Dahlgren is Professor at Linköping University within the Faculty of Health Sciences and the Faculty of Educational Sciences. Her main research interest concerns student learning in higher education. Her current research focuses on pedagogical processes within the social and material practices of health care and medical education.

Helen Colley is Professor of Lifelong Learning at the University of Huddersfield, and Visiting Professor of Adult Education at the University of Toronto. Much of her research has focused on the workplace learning of practitioners supporting disadvantaged young people, with a particular interest in the gendered nature of such work.

Roger Dunston is an Associate Professor in the Faculty of Arts and Social Sciences (FASS) at the University of Technology Sydney. His research focuses on new forms of collaboration, professional learning and practice development. His previous positions have spanned clinical practice in hospital and community health services and health services management.

Tara Fenwick is Professor and Director of *ProPEL* (Research in Professional Practice, Education and Learning) at the University of Stirling. She studies sociomateriality in practice and knowing, with particular focus on interprofessional and co-production arrangements and new digital technologies in professional work.

Alison Fuller is Professor of Education and Work, and Director of Research in the Southampton Education School, University of Southampton. Her research interests include changing patterns of young and older adults' participation in education, training and work, apprenticeship, education–work transitions and workplace learning.

Silvia Gherardi is Professor of Sociology of Work and Organization at the University of Trento where she is responsible for the Research Unit on Communication, Organizational Learning and Aesthetics (RUCOLA, www.unitn.it/rucola). Her research focuses on workplace learning and knowing.

Her theoretical background is in qualitative sociology, organizational symbolism and feminist studies.

David Guile is Professor of Education and Work at the Institute of Education, University of London, and member of the ESRC funded Research Centre 'Learning and Lifechances in Knowledge Economies/Societies'. David specializes in researching professional, vocational and workplace learning, including apprenticeship and internship, in the creative, finance and clinical sectors.

Lea Henriksson, PhD, currently works as a Senior Researcher at the Finnish Institute of Occupational Health. Her research interests in sociology of work and occupations and welfare state research focus on the politics of care and the reconfiguration of human service workforce in global, lifelong learning societies.

Nick Hopwood is a Senior Research Fellow at the University of Technology, Sydney. He has researched learning in various contexts, including secondary school classrooms, universities, workplaces, and child and family health settings. He has recently turned to sociomaterial theories to understand learning, pedagogy and curriculum in new ways.

Karen Jensen is Professor in the Department of Education, University of Oslo. She has published widely on the role of knowledge in professional education and work. Her most recent book is *Professional Learning in the Knowledge Society* (Sense Publishers, 2012), co-edited with Leif Chr. Lahn and Monika Nerland.

Aditya Johri is an Associate Professor in the Department of Applied Information Technology at George Mason University, USA. He studies the role of digital technologies in learning and knowledge sharing with a focus on cognition in informal environments. He is a recipient of the U.S. National Science Foundation's Early CAREER Award.

Sue Kilminster is Principal Research Fellow in the Leeds Institute of Medical Education at the University of Leeds and Director of the Centre for Research into Professional Education. Her research interests include transitions, responsibility, supervision and workplace learning, policy-related research, interprofessional education and gender issues in medicine.

Åsa Mäkitalo is Professor in Education at the University of Gothenburg and co-director of LinCS, conducting research on learning, interaction and mediated communication in contemporary society. She is also Head of the LETStudio, examining technologies and transformation of expertise, social organization of learning and knowing, remembering as an institutional practice and forms of participation in knowledge practices.

Dianne Mulcahy, PhD, is a Senior Lecturer in the Melbourne Graduate School of Education at the University of Melbourne. Her publications cover the three key areas of education policy, curriculum studies and educators' professional development. Presently, she is researching aspects of the spatiality and materiality of learning in schools.

Monika Nerland is Professor in the Department of Education, University of Oslo. She conducts research on knowledge practices and learning in professional education and work. Her current project examines the role epistemic practices play in inducting students in higher professional education in expert communities.

Davide Nicolini is Professor of Organization Studies at Warwick Business School where he co-directs the IKON Research Centre. His research focuses on developing a practice-based approach to study organizational phenomena and its implications for understanding knowing, collaboration, decision making and change in organizations. His latest book is *Practice Theory, Work and Organization: An Introduction* (Oxford University Press, 2012).

Beatrix Niemeyer is Acting Chair of Adult and Further Education at the Institute of Education, University of Flensburg, Germany. Her research focus is on school to work transition in Europe, educational professions and occupational boundary work between education and employment. Her recent work has examined global transformations of occupational identities.

Claes Reit is Professor of Endodontology at the Sahlgrenska Academy. His main research interests are clinical procedures, clinical decision making and dental ethics. In recent years his focus has been on factors that influence the adoption of new technology, reasons for substandard clinical performance and caries risk in root-filled teeth.

Bridget Roe is a final-year doctoral student at Nottingham University Business School, having completed her MA in Management and Organisational Analysis at Warwick Business School. Formerly a nurse and midwife, her research uses a practice-based approach to study the socialization of nurses in the context of current policy and healthcare developments.

Terri Seddon is Professor of Education at Monash University. She engages with globalisation and education by examining boundary politics and knowledge building located by adult education. Her research investigates hotspots of change where social spaces, work practices and identities are being disturbed and remade in processes that accompany global transitions.

Karin Siwe, MD, PhD, is an Assistant Professor and Senior Consultant in Obstetrics and Gynaecology at the University Hospital, Linköping, and is affiliated with the Faculty of Health Sciences, Linköping University. Her interests concern learning and tutoring in higher education, with particular reference to the development of clinical skills.

Margaret Somerville is Professor of Education and Director of the Centre for Educational Research, University of Western Sydney. Her long term collaborations with Aboriginal communities about their relationship to place has led to her abiding commitment to planetary sustainability. In *Water in a Dry Land* (Routledge, 2013) she explores thinking through country in innovative ethnography.

Lorna Unwin is Professor of Vocational Education at the Institute of Education, University of London, and a member of the ESRC funded LLAKES Research Centre. Her research interests are in the changing nature of occupational expertise and the implications for policies and practices in vocational education and training.

Sarah Wall, PhD, is an Assistant Professor in the Faculty of Nursing at the University of Alberta. Her research focuses on understanding and enabling professional nursing practice, with a particular interest in the nature of nursing knowledge and how it is applied across a range of nursing roles.

Miriam Zukas is Professor of Adult Education and Executive Dean of the School of Social Science, History and Philosophy at Birkbeck, University of London. Her research currently focuses on learning in the transition of professionals from one level of responsibility to another, particularly in relation to doctors.

Sociomaterial professional knowing, work arrangements and responsibility

New times, new concepts?

Tara Fenwick and Monika Nerland

Introduction

We were driven to begin this book by conflicting emotions. On the one hand, we have been increasingly excited by the innovative research on professionals' learning that has burgeoned in the past decade. This work has upended old orthodoxies and generated new worlds of nuance and analytic tools, working from early insights afforded through sociocultural approaches and a re-centring of practice as a significant mode for learning. The authors we have invited here represent a small portion of the many voices now reconceptualising professional learning.

But, on the other hand, we must admit to feeling some despair. Large amounts of policy and curricula for professionals' learning and assessment continue to be generated that use models long since debunked and abandoned by educationists: de-contextualized individual competency, disembodied cognitive decision-making, and de-materialized knowing and practice. Public policy in particular is notorious for responding to any new crisis of public service delivery by calling for training of individual practitioners. Professionals continue to be isolated, trained and measured, bracketing out the tangled webs of relations that constitute professionals' practice and knowing, and ignoring all the research that is now showing not only how these webs work, but also how we can trace them and work with them to facilitate learning.

While this book is unlikely to halt such regressive sorts of currents, we are hoping that it might help accelerate the more promising counter currents. In this effort, we are building on a special issue that we co-edited for the *Journal of Education and Work* (January 2012) entitled 'Reconceptualizing professional learning in a changing society'. Perhaps the different studies presented here will offer some useful language, concepts or methodological tools for those seeking to clear new paths of understanding. At the very least, we aim to affirm the work of those professional educators and researchers struggling to reconceptualise professional learning to embrace its inherent messiness, its embodied materiality, and its cultural and historical dynamics.

Changing concepts, changing times

What do we mean by professional? This is a problematic and heavily debated term (see Evetts 2011, 2013; Freidson 2001). It is problematic because it signifies status and authority accruing to a few elite occupational groups, and can easily blind us to the many practitioners who don't happen to have professional qualifications but who are significantly entangled with members of these groups in everyday work. It is heavily debated because the traditional boundaries defining what is professional have been disrupted by its many far-flung applications. Some suggest that the term professional signifies no more than a particular discourse of control (e.g. Fournier 1999). Elsewhere we have discussed in detail the definitional issues, multiple discourses and myriad shifts related to professionals and professional work and learning (Fenwick, Nerland and Jensen 2012). For the purposes of this book, we think of professionals as members of any occupational group, usually committed to public service, that defines itself as collectively sharing particular knowledge and practices, and that is publicly accountable for its service. The chapters here focus on different occupational groups ranging from doctors and dentists to creative professionals and airline pilots.

Across these groups, the enormous difficulties of continuous change are well known to anyone now involved in professional education, or who studies how professionals learn, or who is charged with regulating professionals and their learning. Obviously, the conditions for work practice are changing dramatically in the wake of globalised work, new modes of knowledge production, new regulatory regimes that audit standards of professional work, and massive funding cuts to public services. Furthermore as more practitioners are expected to work in interprofessional collaboration, or find their work becoming distributed across organizational and geographical (and virtual) boundaries, the challenges of coordination, boundaries, and continuity come to the fore. Transnational knowledge cultures are constantly pressing professionals into new practices and sometimes radically new knowledges. New digital technologies and virtual workworlds are intensifying work and creating complex new relations of space and time. The chapters in this book describe an array of specific examples of these and other changing dynamics of professionals' work.

These changes all entail learning new ways of working. Learning itself, according to the authors in this book, is inseparable from work practice. But what is meant by learning?

Sociomaterial approaches

Professional learning itself has conventionally been treated as an individual and person-centred process, related to personal experience as well as acquisition of disciplinary and problem-solving competencies in knowing what to do, how and why. Countering this individualist 'acquisitional' metaphor, situated and sociocultural views introduced some time ago a 'participational' metaphor for learning. These views emphasized the importance of environment, rules, tools and social relations; they showed that knowing is always situated in activity and therefore is particular to settings and communities.

Alongside these developments, a 'practice' turn has been heralded in social science research concerned with practitioners' knowing and learning in everyday activity (e.g. Gherardi and Strati 2013; Nicolini 2012). Practice, both as an enactment of and a medium for learning, has been argued to weave knowing together with action, conversation and affect in purposeful and regularized orderings of human activity. Increasingly, we see studies of learning in work rooted in definitions of practice as embodied human activity produced through collective practical meanings and shared tools. These studies have developed sophisticated understandings of 'practice' and 'participation' as numerous and multi-faceted and even contradictory phenomena (e.g. see Hager, Lee and Reich 2012). They also have introduced conceptions of 'knowing-in-practice' as enactments performed through assemblages that are more-than-human (Gherardi 2011).

Pushing this line of enquiry still further, a critical dynamic is materiality itself. Material forces – flesh and blood, forms and checklists, diagnostic machines and databases, furniture and passcodes, snowstorms and dead cellphone zones – are integral in shaping professional practice as a repertoire of routines as well as the particular knowing, decisions and actions that are enacted in any local instantiation of practice. Yet materiality is often overlooked or dismissed in analyses of professional practice and knowing.

In this book, the authors tend to work with sociomaterial theories. That is, they are committed to analysing the important role of materials and bodies as dynamic, fundamentally enmeshed with activity in everyday practices. Human activity, of course, also comprises the 'social': symbols and meanings, desires and fears, politics and cultural discourses. Both material and social forces are mutually implicated in bringing forth everyday activities. This is what Orlikowski (2010) describes as 'the constitutive entanglement of the social and material'. This is a core theoretical assumption across many sociomaterial theories. All things are taken to be heterogeneous assemblages, gatherings of diverse natural, technical and cognitive elements, which exercise power in producing what we take for reality. A second shared assumption in sociomaterial theories is that all things – human and non-human, hybrids and parts, knowledge and systems – are viewed as effects. They are performed into existence in webs of relations. Materials are enacted, not inert; they are matter and they matter. They *act*, together with other types of things and forces, to exclude, invite and regulate activity.

Various theoretical families examine sociomateriality in learning and practice, although each exercises particular emphases. Authors in this book draw from diverse concepts associated with activity theory, science and technology studies, actor–network theory and 'after-ANT' approaches, post-structural geographies, complexity theory (see Fenwick, Edwards and Sawchuk 2011 for an extended review), new materialisms (see Coole and Frost 2010; Dolphijn and van der Tuin

2012), and others. These approaches all tend to show how materiality is relational and distributed within webs of thought and activity, social and physical phenomena in education. They offer methods for analysing these materializing processes and their effects on particular practices, identities and knowledge. While very different in their points of departure, these approaches show how processes that we call learning are phenomena of both emergence and orderings, within and across different spaces and times. They show the interdependence of entities, revealing that learning is always more-than-human.

Professional knowing, work arrangements and responsibility

The chapters in this book are organized in three sections, the first of which focuses on ways to conceptualize the interdependent relations between professional learning, knowledge and knowing. Silvia Gherardi opens this section with an introduction to her conception of knowing-in-practice, which has become increasingly influential in studies of vocational/professional learning as well as in organization learning and change. She interprets knowledge as a situated, sociomaterial activity and as a collective practical accomplishment. In this chapter she examines a single medical practice (cardiological teleconsultation) to show not only how professional competence is enacted in different ways at the 'core' and 'margins' of practice through a mesh of learning and working, but also how technologies shape professional knowing across distances. In Chapter 2, Monika Nerland and Karen Jensen draw attention to the role that knowledge objects play in professionals' work and learning. Using concepts of epistemic objects and practices from Karin Knorr Cetina, the authors explore how professional work is embedded in dynamics of knowledge that are present within, but reach beyond, local communities. By analysing examples from nursing and engineering, Monika and Karen show how the exploration of knowledge objects in local contexts may connect practitioners with wider knowledge worlds, and how such processes may take distinct forms within different professions. Chapter 3 by Miriam Zukas and Sue Kilmister examines how young doctors in hospital settings learn to care for dying patients in ways that involve transitions from one level of responsibility to another. As such their analysis relates to a core theme in studies of professional learning. However, by employing analytical tools from actor–network theory, Miriam and Sue offer a way of understanding such transitions as emerging from sociomaterial relations in practice. In Chapter 4, Dianne Mulcahy discusses teacher professional learning from the perspective of non-representational theory. Dianne conceptualizes teacher learning as embedded in sociomaterial assemblages that make up the practical; the social, textual and material practices of knowledge production. Professional knowing in practice is therefore inevitably also professional learning, and needs to be seen as co-evolving rather than separate processes. Then, in Chapter 5, Davide Nicolini and Bridget Roe work from a case study of midwifery to open up more singular notions of knowing in practice to trace the nuances of multiplicity in professional knowing. They start from the assumption that professional *modus operandi* requires the deferral and suppression of several possible alternatives which constitute unexplored and often untapped resources for action. Drawing from Karen Barad's concept of diffraction, Davide and Bridget explain some innovative methods for how this multiplicity can actually be researched.

In the second major section, chapters show the changing dynamics and changing approaches to understanding professional work arrangements and technologies. In Chapter 6, Alison Fuller and Lorna Unwin focus on the challenges of early career professional learning in different organizations, arguing the benefits of revitalizing apprenticeship as an educational model. Alison and Lorna show how apprenticeship enables sociomaterial support structures in the workplace which may enhance individual learning as well as organizational transformation. Hence, rather than proposing new educational solutions as a response to changing work arrangements, these authors argue that historically established models have important resources to offer in our efforts to cope with new challenges. Then in Chapter 7, Åsa Mäkitalo and Claes Reit discuss the problems attending implementation of new technologies in professional practice. Their case study is dentistry, and they present a fine-grained analysis of the embodied and discursive difficulties in integrating the surgical microscope into endodontic practice. They argue that the primary shift for practitioners is in developing a 'visual re-location' into a new spatial environment, which radically alters their experiential context for learning. Chapter 8 is concerned with the impact of transnational and digital working environments, with examples from engineers and the changes to their practice. Here, Aditya Johri shows how, in the face of radical uncertainties in their everyday work, professionals learn to tinker with their social and material tools to create some sort of stability. This tinkering is what Aditya calls 'sociomaterial bricolage', arguing that this is central to professionals' knowing. In Chapter 9, David Guile focuses on the recent growth of interprofessional work and learning as well as its related educational challenges. By reviewing some significant studies and theoretical contributions within this field, he argues that we need to more rigorously analyse the ways that individuals and collectives share knowledge across professional boundaries. To address this gap, David introduces the concept of recontextualization. He distinguishes between four 'expressions' of recontextualization, and discusses how these notions can inform programmes of initial professional formation. To conclude this section, Roger Dunston critically revisits the whole question of interprofessional and 'partnership' work, which some have characterized as a new frontier of 'co-production' of knowledge and service. Roger reviews his own past studies of co-productive practice in child and family health from a sociomaterial perspective, showing the implications of these work arrangements for professional identities, contributions and knowing.

The third and final section considers issues of professional responsibility thrown up by the many changes in work. Chapter 11 by Tara Fenwick attempts to provide an overview of these issues, particularly in the growing pluralism of

professionals' obligations and the conflicts in responsibility that they must negotiate. Tara explores what it might mean to consider responsibility as material
enactments of these conflicts and compromises. Working from examples drawn
from professional work in different high-stakes, high-pressure environments
(policing, paramedics, flight pilots) she suggests that we ask, what 'responsibilities' are enacted in these sociomaterial assemblages? How do professionals negotiate the ambivalences of these complex becomings to find lines of 'responsible'
action? What matters most to professionals in these 'mattered' enactments of
responsibility? In Chapter 12, Nick Hopwood, Madeleine Abrandt Dahlgren and
Karen Siwe focus on student professionals' learning responsibility. Their study,
based in medical practice, analyses the intimate challenges of responsibility in
conducting pelvic examinations. The authors examine how particular pedagogic
guidance provided by the professional patients in this practice can engage students in a 'sociomaterial curriculum', attuning them to how bodies are a material
force as well as mediator for learning. Chapter 13 examines issues of responsibility that are generated when professionals work in independent practice. Sarah
Wall argues that these non-traditional work arrangements are increasing in public
service. Taking a practice-based sociomaterial perspective on her study of self-
employed nurses, Sarah shows the accompanying turbulent shifts in professional
knowing and responsibilities, but also the important possibilities presented by
such work arrangements. In Chapter 14, Helen Colley, Lea Henriksson, Beatrix
Niemeyer and Terri Seddon focus on the relationship between time and professional responsibility. These authors work from the assumption that time is generated through practice, rather than simply being part of organizational context. By
analysing case studies from different national contexts, the authors open up intricate relationships between models of time-use, politics and professional responsibilities. The final chapter of the book turns outwards to critical problems of
planetary sustainability, asking: How can we re-think professional learning in
relation to our responsibilities to the more-than-human world? Here Margaret
Somerville explains a pedagogical process of 'thinking through country' that she
developed through a lengthy study with Australian Aboriginal collaborators,
multi-professional teams and public stakeholders. She proposes this as a framework for ethical practice, and shows – through examples of teacher education – its
implications for professional learning and responsibility in a world of complex
planetary problems.

Conclusion

Together the chapters in this book open up new perspectives on professional
work and learning as well as new avenues for further research. Some chapters do
so by highlighting the knowledge generated through new work arrangements
using established concepts. Others employ fresh perspectives to shed new light
on enduring questions. Hence, the call to 'reconceptualise professional learning'
does not necessarily depend upon bringing new concepts to the table but can also

be about recontextualizing or revisioning more familiar understandings. But across the chapters, these authors are committed to making explicit the materialities of the phenomena they are exploring. Abstract categories tend to be eschewed in favour of tracing the particular, showing how in these particular enfleshed, emplaced encounters, knowing emerges in conjunction with persons, politics and environments. Further, as the authors bring sociomaterial approaches to their own research processes, we see how the relationship between these conceptual tools and empirical foci is also a phenomenon of emergence and orderings that become realized in practice. The way this is done, with its various sensitivities, is what matters for the production of new insights.

Throughout the chapters, we see efforts to understand changing practice both in its local instantiations and its embeddedness in cultural, historical and epistemic dynamics. Transitions are critical in these dynamics, and the analyses here illustrate how transitions emerge from dynamic relations among human and non-human forces as they come together in practical accomplishments. The authors work with different concepts to account for these aspects. Common to all, however, is a strong interest in overcoming binaries to conceptualizing these dynamic, relational and complex dimensions of professional practice, learning and change.

We started out describing general trends that contribute to changing the work environments for professionals. As the following chapters show, these developments take distinct forms in different occupational and national contexts. This points to the need for more close-up analyses of emergent practices in a range of professional settings. It is our hope that this book will inspire researchers to continue along this avenue, and that it will suggest useful questions and conceptual tools both for researchers and for professional educators seeking to understand and support professionals' learning.

References

Coole, D.H. and Frost, S. (2010) *New Materialisms: Ontology, Agency, and Politics*, Durham, NC: Duke University Press.

Dolphijn, R. and van der Tuin, I. (2012) *New Materialism: Interviews and Cartographies*, University of Michigan: Open Humanities Press.

Evetts, J. (2011) 'Sociological analysis of professionalism: Past, present, future', *Comparative Sociology*, 10(1): 1–37.

Evetts, J. (2013) 'Professionalism: Value and ideology', *Current Sociology*, online first, 12 March 2013, doi:10.1177/0011392113479316

Fenwick, T., Edwards, R. and Sawchuk, P. (2011) *Emerging Approaches to Educational Research: Tracing the Socio-material*, London: Routledge.

Fenwick, T., Nerland, M. and Jensen, K. (2012) 'Sociomaterial approaches to reconceptualising professional learning and practice', *Journal of Education and Work*. 25(1): 1–13.

Fournier, V. (1999) 'The appeal to "professionalism" as a disciplinary mechanism'. *Social Review*, 47(2): 280–307.

Freidson, E. (2001) *Professionalism: The Third Logic*, Cambridge: Polity Press.

Gherardi, S. (2011) 'Organizational learning: The sociology of practice' in M. Easterby-Smith and M.A. Lyles (eds), *Handbook of Organizational Learning and Knowledge Management* (2nd edn), Chichester: John Wiley and Sons.

Gherardi, S. and Strati, A. (2012) *Learning and Knowing in Practice-based Studies*, Surrey, UK: Edward Elgar Publishing.

Nicolini, D. (2012) *Practice Theory, Work and Organization. An Introduction*, Oxford: Oxford University Press.

Orlikowski, W.J. (2010) 'The sociomateriality of organizational life: Considering technology in management research', *Cambridge Journal of Economics*, 34: 125–141.

Hager, P., Lee, A., and Reich, A. (2012). *Practice, Learning and Change*. Netherlands: Springer.

Section 1

Reconceptualising professional knowing

Chapter 1

Professional knowing-in-practice

Rethinking materiality and border resources in telemedicine

Silvia Gherardi

Introduction

Contemporary organizational literature displays growing interest in the intersection of knowledge, work and professional practices. One reason for this interest is the potential of new information and communications technologies (ICT) and their impact on traditional ways of working, and on the competences of professional groups. Organizations now rely on various forms of work organization which presuppose groups of professionals who collaborate at a distance, creating a shared workspace. For such work at a distance, the most critical resource is knowledge and the professionals' ability to manage their knowledge interdependencies efficiently and effectively through expertise coordination (Faraj and Xiao 2006). Whence derives the renewed interest among organization and management scholars in how organizations create, transfer and apply knowledge (Argote 1999), how the design of the information and telecommunication technologies supports practical knowledge (Orlikowski 2002), how knowing is enacted and is embedded in the material and discursive context of work (Weick, Sutcliffe and Obstfeld 2005), and how professionals' learning and knowing change in such a context (Jensen, Lahn and Nerland 2012).

This field of studies raises a number of theoretical and methodological problems which I intend to discuss and illustrate here by means of an empirical study on telemedicine, my purpose being to show how collective (professional and non-professional) knowledge is performed in distance work. To this end, I shall introduce the concept of knowing-in-practice, since this will enable me to interpret knowledge as a situated, sociomaterial activity and as a collective practical accomplishment. By examining a single practice – cardiological teleconsultation – performed by two communities of professionals – general practitioners and cardiologists – supported by a group of operators in charge of the technological infrastructure, I shall illustrate the generative model that supports knowing-in-practice. Considering two interactional patterns – at the core of the practice and at its margins – I shall illustrate how professionals' competence is enacted, how learning and working are entangled, and how technological settings shape professional knowing.

Knowing-in-practice as a practical accomplishment

Study of the practical organization of knowledge, in the form of methods of talking, reasoning and acting, and the association of human and non-human elements, is one of the most important directions taken by empirical studies using the practice-based approach (Gherardi 2012a). Of central importance in this regard is practical knowledge, which is analysed from a sociomaterial and organizational perspective. The unit of analysis is activity, and the material and discursive practices that put competences to use. This perspective focuses its analysis around the concept of 'situatedness'. In fact, rather than asking what kinds of cognitive processes and conceptual structures are involved, researchers ask what kind of social engagements and material settings provide the proper context for knowing, working, learning and innovating (Brown and Duguid 1991, 2001).

This study adheres to a sociomaterial perspective and it assumes that 'the starting premise is that work activities and workspaces are mutually constituted, in ways that are structured and available for detailed understanding' (Suchman 1996:35). This assumption prompts the question: Is it possible to observe knowledge as it unfolds and describe it empirically without resorting to concepts such as the intentionality of actors, with their mental and/or linguistic representations, and without having to rely on what actors say that they think? In other words, can practical knowledge be described as a situated activity, and as an activity of joint and collaborative production between humans and non-humans, without having to attribute priority to the former, and without assuming that knowledge precedes action?

The contribution of the concept of 'knowing-in-practice' in answering these questions is that not only is it possible, it is also useful to describe knowledge as a practical accomplishment which does not require investigation of what goes on in people's minds and of what they say that they think. At the theoretical level, the entry of the concept of knowing-in-practice into the literature on practices contributes to the displacement of the mind (meanings, values or truth) as the central phenomenon in human life and to prioritization of practices over individual subjects (Schatzki 2001:2).

The area of research concerned with working practices, technology and interaction – called practice-based studies (Corradi, Gherardi, and Verzelloni 2010) – proposes a conception of 'task' that is neither cognitive (i.e. derived from specialized bodies of information and reasoning) nor the product of internalized and socially organized competencies. Rather it encompasses 'the range of practical resources that people bring to bear in the accomplishment of their work and the diverse range of interactional forms which feature in their organizational conduct' (Heath and Button 2002:159).

In fact, professionals do not usually encounter problems in understanding each other, largely because comprehension is a constant and contingent achievement which depends on their interpretive work. Understanding situated practices therefore requires understanding of how professionals successfully use indexical[1] behaviours and expressions whose meanings are constantly negotiated and renegotiated in the course of interaction. One meaning of 'situated' with reference to practices is that their performance depends on the manner in which indexicality is locally resolved. Also, social norms are indexical, with the consequence that a rule of behaviour does not have a univocal meaning outside the concrete settings where it is applied.

However, practical knowledge (knowing how to reproduce a professional practice competently) has an opaque dimension which is well illustrated in the literature with the concepts of 'tacit knowledge' (Polanyi 1958), 'art of knowing' (Duguid 2005), or *docta ignorantia* (Bourdieu 1990; Gherardi 2012b), that is, a mode of practical knowledge unaware of its own principles. The problem of this opacity is therefore well known, but it is not insurmountable from the point of view of empirical research.

In methodological terms, I propose to conceptualize knowing-in-practice as a situated accomplishment that accommodates a full range of practical resources and interactional forms according to the logic of the practice at hand, and I shall use the term *knowing-in-practice* to denote the situated activity of the community of medical and non-medical professionals which, through mediation with a material and discursive world, performs a cardiological teleconsultation.

Research site, research design and methodology

The setting of the analysis is one of the most advanced telecardiology centres in northern Italy, created in 1998. The centre uses the services of around 60 cardiologists (scattered around northern Italy) who examine electrocardiograms sent (online) by general practitioners (GPs) (numbering around 800). The general practitioner records the patient's ECG using a portable apparatus (electrocardiograph). The recordings may be made in the doctor's surgery, or at the patient's home, because the apparatus is not much bigger than a mobile phone and its memory is able to store around ten traces, which can be transmitted at a later time. The apparatus therefore allows for both synchronous and asynchronous communication. The patient's ECG is transmitted via phone or mobile phone to the telecardiological centre, which sends it to the cardiologist and, on the same telephone line, enables direct communication between the two doctors (in the case of synchronous communication). Once the call is over, the cardiologist signs the report and sends it by fax to the GP.

However, this technology changes cardiological consultation practice in significant ways:

- The cardiologist can no longer see and touch the patient or listen to his/her narrative, the consequence being that the sensory (aesthetic) abilities are lost. An impoverishment of the 'material-objective' base of knowledge should be replaced by an increase in communicative competence. The absent patient's body is represented by other means: the ECG trace and the GP's report.

- Producing a medical report becomes a cooperative activity mediated by ICT, and it takes place in a rarefied interactive field. The patient often witnesses the teleconsultation in the GP's surgery, and s/he possesses a specific and subjective knowledge base (how s/he feels, what his/her symptoms are, what is his/her illness trajectory). As the GP interacts with the patient, s/he translates the ordinary language used to express the symptoms into medically codified language.
- A technological infrastructure mediates the cooperative activity. The call centre operator interacts with the GP and cardiologist, knowing not only how to find them but also how to handle the communication technologically, how to restore it when the technical system is of no help, and how the report and the entire teleconsultation practice should be done; and the cardiologist interacts with the persons in question while following what the medical protocol, materialized and anchored in his/her computer software, requires him/her to do.

If we consider cardiological teleconsultation as 'one' practice within medical practice with an opening and a closure, we may say that the researcher is able heuristically to isolate this practice from its interconnections with the other medical practices and therefore to analyse the activities within a practice from its beginning to its end, and see how the logic of the practice takes shape. In fact, the purpose of the empirical research is to understand how local organizational constraints and resources are mobilized through discursive practices within a system of distributed and fragmented knowledge (Bruni, Gherardi and Parolin 2007). The focus of my analysis will be the discursive practices that lead to the ECG report.

The phone calls made to the centre in the course of a year were recorded and became the row material of analysis (Gherardi 2010). The analysis that follows is based on the results of listening to and analysing the transcripts[2] of all the telephone calls made in one 'typical' month (a total of 1,052 calls). Considering that the average duration of a conversation was around 2½ minutes, it was possible to analyse a considerable number of reiterations of the same practice in its natural setting.

I shall select and present here as an illustration only a few phone calls in order to discuss with an empirical example a type of interaction and/or activity. I want to stress that the aim of the analysis of discursive practices is not 'discourse' per se; on the contrary, textual data is considered as instances of 'doing things with words'.

At the core and at the margins of a practice

In order to describe the generative model guiding the logic of practice, I shall distinguish between a set of activities that take place at the core of the practice and another set that take place on its margins. The logic of the practice of cardiological teleconsultation can be characterized as two distinct but interrelated interactional models which – at the core of the practice and at its margins – mobilize the resources necessary for performing the teleconsultation. The interaction dynamic that gives unity and coherence to the knowing-in-practice is not as tidy and distinct in practice as these analytical categories may suggest, but more entrenched and closely interrelated. I begin by examining how resources are mobilized by discursive practices at the core and at the margin of the teleconsultation separately. I shall then address how the activation of border resources shapes the logic of the practice.

At the core of the teleconsultation

Knowing-in-practice at the core of the telecardiological consultation is guided by the interpretation of clues furnished by the context of interaction among the patient, the GP, the cardiologist, the call centre operator, and the technological system which connects and makes the interactions possible. The participants (human and non-human) in this local ecology interact by fashioning a choreography of resources (Whalen and Henderson 2002), mobilized in time and in space – real and virtual – as an ensemble. In doing so, they enact a competent performance which discursively mobilizes all the relevant resources available in the setting and which can be activated within it. This performance is improvised in that the logic of the practice exhibits a contingent rationality; but it is simultaneously anchored in a script consisting of the general rules on how a teleconsultation should be conducted.

A typical telephone call has the following script:

1. The GP tells the cardiologist why it has been necessary to carry out an ECG and, following a smooth alternation of questions and answers, anchored in a medical protocol and supported by a software program, the two doctors co-construct a shared knowledge space based on: the patient's details; the reason why the ECG has been carried out; the clinical history; the therapy; any previous episodes.
2. While the cardiologist is engaged in the conversation with the GP, on the screen of his computer appear the lines of the ECG (which takes 50 seconds to download), which s/he reads and then discusses with the GP.
3. When the cardiologist has concluded the conversation with the GP, s/he compiles the electronic ECG read-out file and dictates his/her report to the call centre operator, who faxes the signed clinical report to the GP.

I will now illustrate what happens at the core of the teleconsultancy practice by referring to the type of knowledge mobilized within the practice's logic, and to the logical economy that sustains it.

The generative model, which in the form of simple principles underlies the discursive practices collaboratively enacted by the two doctors, is based on the mobilization and alignment of clinical and/or instrumental knowledge. While the former kind of knowledge has its basis in medicine – the clinic – the latter is the knowledge embedded and represented in instruments, like the ECG in our case.

When clinical and instrumental knowledge reinforce each other, the two doctors' practical reasoning proceeds rapidly, and the closure of the telephone call takes place unproblematically with a system of normative accountability based on medical knowledge. Of this type are telephone calls mainly concerned with monitoring cardiopathic patients already being treated, or telephone calls in which the instrumental evidence does not match the clinical results, and the GP, after consulting the specialist, makes his/her own decision on the action to take.

I have chosen two 'extreme' cases which, with the same outcome – sending the patient to the Accident and Emergency department – illustrate the generative model determining the logic of the practice. This is based on the alternating activation of either clinical or instrumental knowledge.

Telephone call 1 (3 minutes 25 seconds): knowing-in-practice on clinical bases

(*Greetings*)

GP: He is a 82-year-old patient who's already had a cerebral vascular incident, slight cardiac decompensation.

Cardiologist (C): He's had an ictus you said?

GP: Yes, he's had an ictus this year, it didn't leave any great problems, a relatively minor thing, it's a patient with slight cardiac decompensation, he's being treated with diuretic and aspirin. Last night he had a precordial pain which radiated to the jugular and the left upper limb, and when I saw him at eight o'clock, the pain had almost completely subsided ... I wanted to do the ECG to exclude an anginal problem.

C: Did he have the pain when you did the ECG?

GP: He still had the pain but it had decreased greatly since last night, because the pain started at around three o'clock, then the relatives didn't call anybody, and it started to subside.

C: There's a slight ST-segment elevation here, but it could also be also of type ... he has a *slight ST-segment depression in the lower chamber ... should be confirmed with the cardiac enzymes* test, which means sending him to Accident and Emergency.

GP: Then I'll send him ...

CC: Seeing that he's already had these problems, it's better to send him ... also because of his age ... send him ... and then with this typical, constrictive, jugular pain ...

GP: Yes, it's quite typical ... yes, yes ... so I'll send him ... ciao.

This apparently simple telephone call[3] illustrates how the decision to send the patient to Accident and Emergency is taken on the basis of clinical knowledge, since the artifact ECG is aligned with it.

We now see the same outcome but this time in terms of a knowing-in-practice based on instrumental knowledge not aligned with the clinical.

Telephone call 2 (3 minutes 13 seconds): knowing-in-practice on instrumental base

(*greetings*)

GP: So, I've got an elderly patient notably overweight, already in therapy with (name of drug). She says that on Thursday she suddenly had a major epigastralgia, she says she felt cold, and since then she's had a constant retrosternal pain that she describes precisely as retrosternal ... and ... there's very little epigastric about it!

C: Yes.

GP: And I wanted to know what the ECG was like.

CC: Listen, it seems that the ECG got an inferior necrosis, an inferior infarct at the second or third stage with some alterations that might be specular on the lateral part. I'd send her to accident and emergency, but call the ambulance as well.

GP: Yes, ok.

C: Because if it's still symptomatic this could be a trouble!

GP: True.

C: All right?

GP: All right, I'll call the ambulance now.

(*salutations*)

This interaction is a particular case of organizing set in train by a rare case of real emergency. In this case, the instrumental knowledge is considered unambiguous, and despite the presence of clinical results that do not appear critical to the GP, the decision is taken by mobilizing the authoritativeness of the cardiologist's expert knowledge. At the same time, another rationale is at work: the decision is also taken in order to give legal protection to the profession. Professional competence, in fact, is legitimated by a dynamic between autonomy and responsibility, and it is accountable both in terms of the professional knowledge harboured by the community, and in terms of legal/institutional accountability. Activating knowledge of legal responsibility and suggesting that the GP should send the patient to hospital (this is the meaning of 'this could be a trouble') signifies closure of the teleconsultation not only on solely instrumental bases, but also using knowledge of the legal system – knowledge which may be shared by cardiologist and GP, but may also be possessed only by the former and shared only at the moment of the interaction.

In the course of telephone calls 1 and 2, one notes the activation of a diagnostic community that forms a distributed sociomaterial network which extends well beyond the two doctors to include:

- the knowledge of the patient, who not only experiences and reports the symptoms but also sets them in relation to past experience;
- the GP's clinically based knowledge; the cardiologist's instrumentally based knowledge, and his knowledge grounded on experience;
- and the absent actor – Accident and Emergency – which is virtually present and is assigned responsibility for the actual medical diagnosis. It is mobilized as a resource or a potential ally both in the care trajectory and in management of social and legal responsibility for the doctors.

Telephone calls 1 and 2 enable me to discuss the mobilization of power, status and authoritativeness in practice with direct reference to the methods widely used to manage the status asymmetry between cardiologist and GP, against the background of the more general organization of the health service and the role that it assigns to the Accident and Emergency department.

The decision to send the patient to the emergency department, or not to send him/her, or to change her/his therapy, pertains to the GP. Hence, the GP formally uses the cardiologist's specialist knowledge as a resource in the diagnostic and decision-making processes. The interactional style between the two doctors evinces the GP's status as 'somebody who ask for help' and the cardiologist's awareness of the asymmetry between those who possess the authoritativeness of expert knowledge and those who possess professional authority and responsibility. At the same time both of them try to downplay the distance by reference to a common medical community (the use of the informal 'tu' even between people who do not know each other, using a colloquial tone, indulging in a little idle conversation, trying to find out whether they have already spoken to each other in the past so that they can recognize each other as old-timers in the community of practitioners), and by enacting a deferential but friendly communicative style. For example, during most of the conversation, especially in longer and more complex exchanges where cooperation to clarify the setting is more prolonged, one notes that the cardiologist uses indirect language to suggest to the GP the action that s/he should take without being intrusive. The register that s/he uses employs expressions like: 'in my experience', 'in cases like this I'd say ...', 'what we usually do ...', 'if I were you' and similar roundabout phrases which preserve the GP's autonomy and responsibility while the solution is suggested.

In telephone call 2, one notices that the cardiologist initially assumes a consultative tone, with which he (in this case both doctors are men) suggests a line of action legitimated on the basis of experience and what he habitually does in such situations. However, then the cardiologist introduces an item of non-medical information into the interaction, in order to remind the GP of his legal responsibilities and to provide a defensive rationale for the medical profession. At this point the cardiologist leaves his consultancy role and explicitly tells the GP to send the patient to Accident and Emergency. The prosody of the telephone call, in fact, evinces hesitation in the GP's voice and surprise at the change in the cardiologist's tone. The interactive competence of the latter is apparent in what he says and what he does, and in how he does not close the telephone call until he obtains explicit assent from the GP and anchors the interaction in a materiality which associates the hospital with the course of action by sending the ECG directly to Accident and Emergency.

The interactions in these two telephone calls highlight a further element which tacitly sustains the practitioners' interactional style. In fact, clinical and instrumental knowledge represents the interoccupational jurisdiction of the two doctors. The cardiologist performs his role as a consultant who respects the authority and decisional capacity of the GP when the telephone call is conducted on the basis of clinical knowledge (more or less supported by instrumental knowledge), while he bases his authoritativeness and jurisdiction on instrumental knowledge.

In discussion of interorganizational negotiation over jurisdiction, Bechky (2003) stresses that artifacts mediate the way in which authority and legitimacy are enacted in workplace interactions. My study shows that the same artifact acquires the status of 'evidence' supporting different jurisdictions according to the type of knowledge activated in the interaction. Although the cardiologist's jurisdiction is formally expressed through his signature on the ECG, and that of the GP through his responsibility for the therapeutic action, the two doctors consult together in order to construct congruence between instrumental and clinical knowledge. In the case of doubt, they delegate the task to Accident and Emergency, activating legal accountability for their action. Instrumental knowledge is generally ancillary to clinical knowledge, and the cardiologist expresses his competence in interpreting the ECG with his cardiological knowledge; more rarely does he mobilize the ECG as an artifact supporting his jurisdiction.

At the margins of the teleconsultation

Practical reasoning at the core of the teleconsultation is focused on resolving the question of what the actors should do, and how to make what they do accountable on the bases of clinical, legal and/or bureaucratic normativity. Nevertheless, this is not the only activity performed through the discursive practices of teleconsultation. If we introduce a distinction between talk *in* practice and talk *about* practice, we shall be able to analyse the diversity of discursive practices and see how the reproduction of practice is done *in* practice.

The script of a quite typical case is when the teleconsultation in the strict sense takes place in the first turn of the conversation, when the two doctors talk *in* practice and rapidly align all the elements necessary to construct a narrative plot and to declare mutual agreement on the meaning to attribute to the situation. The cardiologist (or the GP) then gives rein to his curiosity and uses the teleconsultation as an opportunity to increase his knowledge. More often it is the GP who takes advantage of the situation in order to put questions regarding cardiology. The two doctors then talk at some length *about* medical practice. This is an interrelational mode characteristic of a good number of telephone calls, and it has a particular significance. It is not rare, in fact, for teleconsultation discursive practices to go beyond what is strictly necessary for the purpose at hand. But talk *about* practice has a very distinctive character and function.

When the two doctors discuss the pathogenesis of coronopathy and distrust risk factors, they are theorizing on their own practice and squaring experience with what they consider 'valid knowledge'. We may conclude that also theorizing about practice is a situated activity that takes place in the midst of practice and as a mundane conversation. The normative character of a practice is sustained by the discursive practices that theorize and discuss the correct ways to do things, the beliefs that inform the doing and the mutual exchange of knowledge.

This mode of interaction comprises both an instrumental function – learning in a community of practitioners – and an expressive function, the exchange of experiences and of 'war stories'. All professional communities enjoy talking about their practices, and this pleasure expresses a passion for the profession, the celebration of competence, the mobilization of reputation: that is, 'enacting a community' through the sharing of experience and participation in a discourse. Moreover, the mobilization of agreements and disagreements about practices is a specific professional practice which socially supports understanding of professional competence, of its qualitative, normative and aesthetic standards.

I often found that, when the teleconsultation *strictu sensu* had concluded, the doctors discussed the clinical validity of the ECG, declining standards in medicine, and the like, in a constant negotiation of what is considered to be 'good practice' or a 'good way to do X'. Talking about practice is simultaneously a way to theorize in/about practice, and to perform a professional self by exhibiting competent participation in a set of practices; and it is a way to stabilize them, or if necessary, adjust them to a changing context.

At the margins of the practice the production and circulation of knowledge take place in the form of a reciprocal and interwoven process of learning/teaching. This process often centres on the medical technology and the infrastructure. A large number of telephone calls begin with a question by the GP about the quality of reception. Or in the course of the telephone call numerous exchanges are concerned with the quality of the trace. These are exchanges in which, for example, the cardiologist discusses the position of the electrodes on the patient's thorax with the GP, and implicitly teaches the less-expert GP how to place them correctly.

These conversations sometimes also involve the operator at the call centre, who, in discussing the quality of the trace with the cardiologist, suggests reasons why a certain line cannot be seen clearly. One therefore realizes that the operator, having seen so many traces of variable quality on his/her monitor, has also learned to distinguish technical interferences from 'suspicious' factors. In fact, the call centre operator is an active subject in the process of knowing-in-practice, not only when s/he remains in the background of a conversational setting that s/he has activated, but also when s/he records the report dictated by the cardiologist and socializes the latter into the categories currently used to classify the reasons for telephone calls or the actions undertaken. The report dictation calls evince a particular discourse register in which cardiologist and operator use the plural form to denote the joint action which they are performing. For example, the cardiologist does not use terms like 'write' or 'put', but rather expressions like 'let's do', 'let's write', 'let's say', while the operator often gives the standard response of 'no action taken', 'programmed control', and so on. Present in the interactions is the software, which is personified in terms of what it 'requires to be done' (the fields that must not be left blank) and what it 'allows to be done'. One realizes from the dictation of the reports that the operator possesses knowledge of the software which the cardiologist does not have, and often guides the latter's responses by suggesting what to write, or how to write in a 'non-contradictory' way for the computer. Collaboratively constructed on the margins of the teleconsultation is the knowledge of the technological system that enables its use. Breakdowns in the system become occasions for mundane social occasions in which all those involved, patients included, can talk about the unreliability of technologies and their ineluctability.

I can conclude that it is at the margins of a practice that the knowledge necessary for its reproduction is performed, and that the border resources are activated.

Border resources at the interface between the core and the margins

I shall use the concept of border resources (Brown and Duguid 1994:20) to discuss the relationship between the core and the margin of the practice. The border of an artifact is that aspect given social significance by a particular community. The authors cite the example of the skeletal rattle of a keyboard. For a typist the rattle is not recognized as part of the canonical keyboard, but it may play a socially recognized role in the artifact's use. It may provide people with the useful information that a colleague is at work in the next room. Everybody invests aspects of their periphery with individual significance like this (the garbage truck noise signals that it is time to get up), but border resources are invested with socially shared rather than individual significance (Brown and Duguid 1994:8).

In the context of teleconsultation, interaction between the doctors beyond what is necessary and prescribed by the protocol may furnish border resources: that is, unintentional items of information become meaningful in the context and condition the teleconsultation.

During a long telephone call (14 minutes 30 seconds), the two doctors are on the verge of deciding not to send the patient to A&E, when:

Telephone call 3

GP: No, anyway he's single … he doesn't smoke or drink …
C: 'He's single' means he'll be at home alone tonight? I mean … if he gets sick?
GP: He's always been at home alone!

C: Right, send him to A&E! If something happens to him, he won't even be able to call an ambulance [laughs as if joking]! You know, cardiopaths are usually saved by their wives [laughs again] …

The information that the patient is single and living alone arises by chance in the conversation while the two doctors are talking about practice, but it alters the context of the interaction. The situation changes completely as a result, and so does the outcome of the teleconsultation. A commonsense rule resembling a sexist joke comes into play: 'cardiopaths are usually saved by their wives'.

Other telephone calls exhibited similar elements which arose at random but significantly changed the situation. For example, a brief exchange between doctors about their communes of residence revealed that the patient lived 50 kilometres away from the nearest hospital, and this changed the outcome of the teleconsultation.

These stretches of mundane conversation, during which 'small but important' pieces of information may occur, show how the core and the margins of the practice are interconnected in a texture of connections in action.

Conclusions

The study's primary goal was to make knowledge amenable for empirical analysis by observing/listening to what the professionals do, without having to assume as explanatory factors mental processes to which s/he does not have direct access. Every practice relies on a relatively simple generative model within which the logic of practice is expressed. This generative model is not evident to practitioners: they are not fully aware of how they go on with everyday activities, nor are they able to fully express in words all the contingencies implicit in the logic of their practices. The problem of the opacity of practices is therefore well known, but it is difficult to grasp from the methodological point of view of empirical research. Therefore, I wanted to offer a methodological contribution.

In my analysis of the empirical case of cardiological teleconsultation, I reconstruct and represent the generative model of that practice distinguishing between activities at the core of the practice (mobilizing professional authority and jurisdiction; performing accountability on professional, legal and bureaucratic bases; enacting a diagnostic community) and activities at the margins of the same practice (learning; theorizing in practice; performing of a professional self and of a community of professionals). While the former activities are oriented towards the formation of the object of practice, the latter are oriented to the reproduction of the practice itself. Teleconsultation in fact has been analysed as a collective knowledgeable doing taking place within a sociomaterial context. The practitioners' knowing-in-practice is much more than the simple 'application' of a generative model of practice to occurrences situated in time and space.

The practical usefulness of the study concerns the training of new professionals and their induction into the community of practice. A body of case studies on occurrences in natural interactive settings would be of help in the training of novices (both general practitioners and cardiologists and operators of call centres) because it could be used to develop the communicative skills necessary for distance work. Since the generative model of the practice is opaque even to its practitioners, a representation of the practice constitute a useful mirror within which the practitioners may project the rationale of what they do, negotiate the meanings of the practice, agree and disagree on the standards of the practice and collaboratively develop innovations. Reflection at work may be enhanced by re-presenting a model of practice to its practitioners and therefore an action-research approach may benefit from a re-construction and re-presentation of the model of a practice. In fact, an open discussion among practitioners involved in the same working practices often leads to negotiations and changes in habitual ways of doing things or in the way practitioners think about what they do.

Acknowledgement

A first and more elaborated version of the present chapter was published with the title '*Docta Ignorantia:* professional knowing at the core and at the margins of a practice', *Journal of Education and Work*, 25(1): 15–38.

Notes

1 The term 'indexical' was originally used in linguistics to denote expressions that are only completely comprehensible in the concrete context where they are produced and used. In ethnomethodological studies, however, the term has acquired a specific connotation to refer mainly to how individuals achieve mutual understanding.
2 The telephone calls were transcribed by a young doctor specializing in general medicine, Irene Toller, and a sociologist – Laura Lucia Parolin – a doctoral student in Information Systems and Organizations, who wrote her dissertation on this topic (Parolin 2011). I am indebted to both of them for their valuable assistance.
3 The examples provided have been translated from Italian, and unfortunately the prosody is lost in translated texts. For this reason, the transcripts do not comply with the conventions of conversational analysis. There are numerous methodological problems relative to translation from one language to another when discourse analysis is to be conducted. I do not discuss these problems here, merely pointing out that I am aware of them and that I use conversation mainly for the purpose of analysing interaction. The length of the telephone call is reported in brackets when the call is analysed in its entirety. It is not reported when only excerpts are used.

References

Argote, L. (1999) *Organizational Learning: Creating, Retaining and Transferring Knowledge*, Norwell, MA: Kluwer.
Bechky, B. (2003) 'Object lessons: workplace artefacts as representations of occupational jurisdiction', *American Journal of Sociology*, 109(3): 720–752.
Bourdieu, P. (1990) *The Logic of Practice*, Stanford: Stanford University Press.

Brown, J. and Duguid, P. (1991) 'Organizational learning and communities of practice: toward a unified view of working, learning and bureaucratisation', *Organization Science*, 2: 40–57.

Brown, J.S. and Duguid, P. (1994) 'Borderliness issues: social and material aspects of design', *Human-Computer Interaction*, 9: 3–36.

Brown, J.S. and Duguid, P. (2001) 'Knowledge and organization: a social-practice perspective', *Organization Science*, 12(2): 198–213.

Bruni, A., Gherardi, S. and Parolin, L. (2007) 'Knowing in a system of fragmented knowledge', *Mind, Culture and Activity*, 14(1–2): 83–102.

Corradi, G., Gherardi, S. and Verzelloni, L. (2010) 'Through the practice lens: where is the bandwagon of practice-based studies heading?', *Management Learning*, 41(3): 265–283.

Duguid, P. (2005) 'The art of knowing: social and tacit dimensions of knowledge and the limits of the community of practice', *The Information Society*, 21: 109–118.

Faraj, S. and Xiao, Y. (2006) 'Coordination in fast-response organizations', *Management Science*, 52(8): 1155–1169.

Gherardi, S. (2010) 'Telemedicine: a practice-based approach to technology', *Human Relations*, 63(4): 501–524.

Gherardi, S. (2012a) *How to Conduct a Practice-Based Study: Problems and Methods*, Cheltenham, UK: Edward Elgar.

Gherardi, S. (2012b) '*Docta Ignorantia:* professional knowing at the core and at the margins of a practice', *Journal of Education and Work*, 25(1): 15–38.

Heath, C. and Button, G. (2002) 'Special issue on workplace studies: editorial introduction', *The British Journal of Sociology*, 2: 157–161.

Jensen, K., Lahn, L.C. and Nerland, M. (eds) (2012) *Professional Learning in the Knowledge Society*, Rotterdam: Sense Publishers.

Orlikowski, W. (2002) 'Knowing in practice: enacting a collective capability in distributed organizing', *Organization Science*, 13(3): 249–273.

Parolin, L.L. (2011) *Tecnologia e sapere pratico nella società della conoscenza. Il caso della telemedicina in azione*. Milano: Angeli.

Polanyi, M. (1958) *Personal Knowledge: Towards a Post-critical Philosophy*, Chicago: University of Chicago Press.

Schatzki, T.R. (2001) 'Introduction. Practice theory', in T.R. Schatzki, K. Knorr Cetina and E. von Savigny (eds) *The Practice Turn in Contemporary Theory* (pp. 1–14), London and New York: Routledge.

Suchman, L. (1996) 'Constituting shared workspaces', in Y. Engestrom and D. Middleton (eds) *Cognition and Communication at Work*, Cambridge: Cambridge University Press.

Weick, K.E., Sutcliffe, K. and Obstfeld, D. (2005) 'Organizing and the process of sensemaking', *Organization Science*, 4: 409–421.

Whalen, M. and Henderson, K. (2002) 'Improvisational choreography in teleservice work', *British Journal of Sociology*, 53: 239–258.

Chapter 2

Learning through epistemic practices in professional work

Examples from nursing and computer engineering

Monika Nerland and Karen Jensen

Introduction

Work environments for professionals are changing in several ways. New technologies, new relationships with clients and new audit regimes of various kinds all contribute to altering what it takes to perform professional work. This chapter focuses on a source of change that is less often discussed, namely how knowledge is shared and developed in professional settings, and the implications for learning. One of the characteristics of today's society is that knowledge is generated from a multitude of sources and circulated rapidly across organizational boundaries. This derives not only from a growth in knowledge production within many fields but also from the emergence of agencies that specialize in verifying knowledge and synthesizing results. Examples of such agencies are the Cochrane and Campbell Collaborations in the fields of health and education and standard-setting agencies in fields such as engineering and accountancy. Many professionals thus experience a phenomenon in which new advice for their practice enters their workplaces from the outside. As may be expected in the context of the current general emphasis on science-generated knowledge, such advice often arises from research.

However, the route from research to professional practice is not straightforward. First, different studies may lead to contrasting results and therefore generate unresolved questions rather than clear advice for practice. Second, findings from research need to be translated and adapted by professionals in order to become useful in local work. Third, general advice may not represent a universal truth. For instance, even if systematic reviews lead to general recommendations for supporting children with hyperactivity disorders in school or specific groups of patients in health care, the local contexts may vary and may call accordingly for different solutions. This means that considerable local knowledge work is needed for professionals to take advantage of the resources provided and make them relevant for specific tasks. Such knowledge work may, for instance, include making decisions about what knowledge and information requires professionals' attention; exploring and assessing the validity of such knowledge and information in the context of present tasks; and further developing knowledge that 'comes from elsewhere' in their respective communities. In short, professionals become involved in epistemic practices when they face 'knowledge on its travels' and relate this to professional problems.

At the same time, these wider circuits of knowledge do not only serve to bring new knowledge into local workplaces from the outside. They also create a dynamic environment for professionals to actively approach distributed knowledge resources when they are confronted with non-routine problems. For instance, practitioners may approach journals, web-based forums or libraries to find information that can shed light on their current working tasks. In this way, knowledge is circulated and shared in extended contexts that span organizational boundaries and facilitate linkages between different sites of practice. These developments commonly invite practitioners to take part in a range of practices in which the handling of knowledge itself becomes at issue. At the same time, the current trends imply new and extended responsibilities as professionals are increasingly expected to take an active role in securing the collective knowledge underpinning work.

In this chapter, we discuss how professionals within nursing and computer engineering become involved in epistemic practices when exploring complex problems and knowledge resources at work. To conceptualize these dimensions of professional work and learning, we draw on perspectives from *Social Studies of Science*, and in particular on concepts offered by Karin Knorr Cetina (2001, 2006, 2007) and her associates. A core idea in Knorr Cetina's work is that contemporary society is permeated by knowledge processes of various kinds. Individuals engage in exploring, documenting and analysing their environments in a number of ways, often supported by technologies and by reference to some kind of expertise. Her argument goes further than the notions of reflexive modernization (Beck *et al.* 1994) or the idea that social life increasingly depends on trust in expert systems (Giddens 1991). In addition, she draws attention to the way in which people in general become involved in knowledge processes as knowledge is circulated and represented in various forms. As Knorr Cetina (2001:177) argues, the emergence of the knowledge society involves 'more than the presence of more experts, more technological gadgets, more specialist rather than participant interpretations. It involves the presence of knowledge processes themselves'. She relates this development to an emphasis on science-generated knowledge and its related logics of participation, which are now spreading to social and professional life more generally. From this perspective, it is not only knowledge that is spreading: ways of engaging with knowledge, historically associated with research communities, are spreading as well.

In the next section we introduce the concepts of epistemic objects and practices as tools to analyse the knowledge work of professionals. These concepts denote a specific path within the growing body of sociomaterial perspectives, which takes a particular interest in conceptualizing the role knowledge in its dynamic forms plays in expert practices (Engeström and Blackler 2005; Nerland and Jensen 2012; Strand and Jensen 2012; Fenwick *et al.* 2011). In this case, expert practices are not seen as isolated phenomena but rather as configurations of actions and linkages constituted by wider circuits of knowledge. To account for how professionals' epistemic practice is embedded in wider knowledge cultures, we need to 'magnify the space of knowledge-in-action' (Knorr Cetina 1999:2–3) and consider the circulation of knowledge objects in extended contexts. This allows us to discuss how the exploration of knowledge objects in local contexts may connect practitioners with wider knowledge worlds, and how such processes may take distinct forms within different professions.

The dynamism of expert communities: epistemic objects and practices

Expert communities are typically object-centred, in the sense that they are oriented toward exploring, developing and mobilizing epistemic objects (Knorr Cetina 2001, 2007). Epistemic objects can be described as complex problem–knowledge constellations around which practitioners gather and communities form. They are created in expert cultures, and then further developed and circulated as practitioners explore them in local settings. Examples from professional work settings may include computer programs and systems, procedures for medical treatment and complex representations of financial markets (Knorr Cetina and Bruegger 2000; Nerland and Jensen 2010; Moen and Nes 2012). Such objects incorporate shared knowledge in the expert community, and come with suggestions for how they should be approached or used. They are simultaneously open to different interpretations, and in a continual process of transformation. We may say that they have an unfolding ontology: new questions and opportunities arise when problems are temporarily resolved; therefore, they may simultaneously be used for specific purposes in local contexts and further developed through this very engagement. As Knorr Cetina (2001:181) describes this dynamic, 'Since epistemic objects are always in the process of being materially defined, they continually acquire new properties and change the ones they have'.

Through their unfolding and transformative character, epistemic objects may take shifting positions in expert practice. In some cases, they serve as tools for action; in others, they serve as objects of inquiry. At times, they may be opened up for exploration and investigation; at others, they may be closed or becoming (temporarily) fixed. While in some situations, they are subjected to specification and local adaption to address specific problems; in other situations, they may be developed through generalization, such as in efforts to make medical procedures valid across cases. By inviting various forms of engagement, epistemic objects generate epistemic practices when they are approached. They call upon practitioners to explore, validate, document or in other ways develop their inherent knowledge and advices for action. At the same time, it is through such practices that the objects become materialized, further developed, circulated and 'kept alive'. There is a mutually dependent relationship between epistemic objects and practices, as there is between human beings and the knowledge objects that constitute their expert practice. Furthermore, as practitioners from different sites and geographical locations group around the same epistemic objects and develop a shared sense of belonging, this dynamic interdependency lays the foundation for community formation. Such object-centred sociality is well described, for example, in hacker communities and in distributed research groups. More recently it has been identified in other types of professional work as well, such as in financial trading and in nursing (Knorr Cetina and Bruegger 2000; Jensen and Lahn 2005). We propose that increased specialization in professional work, supported by technological advances, also makes community formation around epistemic objects more common in professional contexts.

As an analytic resource, the concept of epistemic objects[1] has been used for different purposes in research on professional learning. One theme is related to the previous discussion of sociality and denotes an interest in understanding how individual professionals form more enduring relationships with objects and knowledge domains. For instance, Knorr Cetina and Bruegger (2000) investigated financial traders and their continuous efforts to understand, monitor and engage with financial markets as a matter of attachment to objects. Jensen and Lahn (2005) describe how the concept of care in nursing serves as a knowledge object with which nursing students create enduring relationships, and which subsequently leads them further into the collective knowledge and expert culture of their profession. Others have discussed how a lack of commitment to knowledge in the teaching profession may relate to an absence of shared knowledge objects (Klette and Carlsten 2012) and pointed to how attachment with knowledge objects may reduce the significance of gender differences in professional work (Rudberg 2012).

Another theme is how knowledge objects are created and negotiated in interprofessional work. For instance, Edwards and Daniels (2012) use the concept of knowledge objects to investigate how knowledge is collectively developed and 'comes to matter' in interprofessional practices around children at risk. McGivern and Dobson (2010) focus on power issues in bio-medical networks, which include practitioners from different professions and specialties, and show how the perspectives of the science-oriented practitioners in this network become more powerful in this collaboration through their ways of relating to and transforming epistemic objects. Tensions between professional communities and their knowledge orientations are also the focus of a study by Mørk et al. (2008). This study examines the different epistemic cultures at play in a medical research and development unit in a larger hospital as obstacles to interprofessional learning.

A third interest among researchers utilizing this perspective concerns the ways in which epistemic objects may stimulate work processes and learning. Ewenstein and Whyte (2009) describe how drawings and visual representations in architectural design may take the role of epistemic objects, which unfold and open up new possibilities as practitioners engage with them, hence stimulating and routing the advancing design process in a stepwise manner. In previous work, we discussed how engagement with knowledge objects generates shifts between explorative and confirmative modes of practice (Nerland and Jensen 2010) and how such engagements with knowledge more generally may stimulate a 'desire to learn' among professionals (Jensen 2007). Common to these studies is that dynamic linkages to wider circuits of knowledge in the expert culture provide materials as well as energy for the explorative actions that take place at the micro level (Jensen *et al.* 2012b).

In the remainder of this chapter, we will follow up on this theme by exemplifying how engagement with knowledge objects in professional settings involves practitioners in epistemic practices. We do so by using examples from nursing and computer engineering. These examples include practices that evolve around clinical procedures in nursing, and practices emerging in the intersection between generic programming resources and specific tasks in computer engineering. The examples are taken from the Norwegian projects ProLearn (2004–2008) and LiKE (2008–2011), in which we followed novice practitioners in three periods of time after their graduation by means of individual interviews, group interviews and learning logs (for more information, see Jensen et al. 2012b; Nerland and Jensen in press). Based on these examples, and with type of intermediaries and organization of knowledge practices in time and space as constitutive dimensions, we discuss how object-related learning takes distinct forms relative to the wider knowledge culture of the professions.

Clinical procedures as epistemic objects: examples from nursing

We mentioned earlier that professionals today are challenged to assume extended roles, which include new responsibilities for developing and safeguarding knowledge in their respective work communities. In our research on knowledge relations and learning opportunities in four professions (cf. Jensen *et al.* 2012a), this became evident in particularly interesting ways among hospital nurses. This group of professionals work in environments in which new knowledge circulates rapidly and is supported by a range of profession-specific tools and resources, such as academic journals, work technologies and advanced systems for documentation. Moreover, there is a hierarchy of expertise and organized expert roles, which brings local practices in contact with general advances in medicine. As expressed by one nurse, 'you don't have to look for new knowledge because it seems to reach you anyway. I don't feel I have to search for it because it more or less finds me'. The clinical nurse developer, who is typically assigned specific responsibilities for bringing new knowledge into the work and routines of the ward, is also important in this circulation of knowledge (Jensen and Christiansen 2012).

In the context of the previously mentioned projects, we interviewed Norwegian hospital nurses in two different periods. Learning logs and a focused study on the role of the clinical nurse developer supplemented these interviews.

In the interviews, the nurses described the development of clinical procedures as being an important site for epistemic engagement. A significant number of nurses had experience with such work when they were interviewed the second time; others described clinical procedures as an important part of their work infrastructure and as an intermediary, which brought science-generated knowledge into their practice. This was probably an effect of initiatives taken at the national level in the given period to develop more consistent and updated procedures and work descriptions. In some cases, the procedures were turned into knowledge objects that were explored, validated and further developed in local settings by way of epistemic practices. Nurses who had participated in procedure development described their engagement in terms of collecting and summarizing clinical trial reports, scoring and ranking these according to their level of evidence, or summarizing results and representing them in an easily understandable form (Nerland and Jensen 2012; Jensen and Christiansen 2012).

Through clinical procedures, nurses encounter research-based knowledge and engage in assessing such knowledge as well as in adapting it for local needs. These processes were described both in terms of monitoring new advancements and in terms of engaging oneself in knowledge development. As one nurse explained, 'We conduct some research ourselves and then adapt techniques that are highly specialized, and only taken into use in some hospitals. So, yes, I would say we build on new research when we revise procedures'. While this work is frequently organized in groups of volunteering hospital nurses who embark on an institutionally defined project, we also found examples of nurses who took extensive responsibilities for knowledge on a discretionary basis. One nurse, who at the time of the interview had only two years of work experience, described how she attended international conferences for lung specialists, such as the ones organized by the European Respiratory Society. In doing so, she gained insight into 'a lot of new knowledge'. She also met individuals with whom she established networks and exchanged experience, these contacts then formed the basis for joint procedure development at home:

> Then we have also formed a little lung group in Norway which meets regularly … doctors do not normally conduct tests themselves. So we are aiming to form our own subgroup to develop real procedures for the different tests, because I think maybe they do it rather unevenly around the country.
> (adapted from Nerland and Jensen 2012)

In this example, the nurses take responsibility for initiating collective knowledge development in the form of procedures for how lung tests should be performed. For the most part, nurses perform this task, and it is thus regarded as the nurses' responsibility to ensure the quality of this work. For the nurse who tells this story, the knowledge challenges related to the treatment of lung diseases and, more specifically, the development of procedures for medical tests, form knowledge objects with which she engages over time. Furthermore, this engagement brings her into contact with communities that reach well beyond her workplace. In this environment, the specialist communities, along with their conferences and terminologies, form important extended contexts through which knowledge objects are circulated and explored.

The development of clinical procedures in the nursing profession has the promotion of evidence-based practice in nursing as a core objective. At the same time, it forms a practice in itself through which the nurses get involved in epistemic modes of working. Researchers have conceptualized this process in different ways, such as through collective accomplishments based on the combination of different repertoires of evaluation (Moreira 2005), the creation of 'local universalities' based on the negotiation of multiple modes of knowledge (Nes and Moen 2010) and as a matter of visualizing professional work in the context of external audit regimes in ways that serve to protect the interests of an expert community (Levay and Waks 2009). What the concepts of epistemic objects and practices add to this picture is analytical tools to understand this work as a distinct set of knowledge practices that evolve around shared problem–knowledge constellations in the expert culture. Through these practices, knowledge objects are identified, explored, materialized and further circulated in the local community. Moreover, these practices are routed in specific ways along the logics and explorative pathways suggested by the objects. As Knorr Cetina (2007:365) states, objects of knowledge tend to be 'doers': 'They have powers, produce effects, may have their own internal environments, mould perception, and shape the course of an experiment'. By exploring and developing knowledge objects that are significant in their own profession, practitioners also become enrolled in the epistemic practices and strategies that define the given expert community.

Epistemic objects in computer engineering: programming patterns and project models

Computer engineers are often involved in programming tasks in which they access and utilize versatile knowledge resources available through the internet. For instance, software programmers often search for best practices and source codes on the internet and then use these to solve local tasks. Oriented towards closure, such actions lead to a preliminary solution (Lahn 2012). However, when applied as part of larger activities, such resources need to be combined and adjusted in ways that also involve analysis and exploration. Our informants described the collaborative work of identifying best practices and programming patterns to be applied in a software project as a process of negotiation and inquiry, in which the temperature could get high and the discussion quite lively (Nerland and Jensen 2010). In such phases, practitioners need to explore and validate the resources at hand, as well as create imaginary scenarios of what the different choices could imply. An engineer who worked as a software developer in a larger consultant company provides one example:

> It's not that everybody always agree [on which practice is the better]. ... But, to use the example of SUN systems again, they have a catalogue comprising the 24 most approved 'best practices', that is, for how you build a computer program. And this is an official catalogue with patterns, as we call it ... but you will also find an array of other patterns ... for very small problems, of the kind that is not that official, but where you discover that 'hey, this is really good stuff.' And then you decide, within a project, that these patterns from SUN and these smaller patterns are what we are going to use, and together they form our 'best practice.'
>
> Adapted from Nerland and Jensen 2010

In this example, the various available sources and suggestions constitute a knowledge object, which stimulated the engineers to move back and forth between confirmative and explorative modes of action. To reach a shared decision on which patterns to use, the engineers needed to engage in efforts to validate the relevance of various resources as well as in justifying their preferred solution. In this way, the object generated epistemic modes of practice. The example above also illustrates how standardized technological resources need to be recontextualized and recreated when utilized in specific settings. To become useful in concrete tasks, generalized resources need to be adapted and modified so that they, for example, are compatible with the given system. This requires creative–constructive actions and forms of local knowledge production in which different opportunities and needs are explored and aligned.

In recent years, methodological ways of working and procedural models for software development have come more to the fore in computer engineering. When re-interviewed in 2009, our informants described the shift towards agile methods and so-called test-driven development (see, for instance, Beck 2003) as a major change, which influenced their everyday work in significant ways. The key principles are that software development projects are broken down into shorter cycles in which alignment with users and the testing of functions is integrated on a regular basis. One engineer described how this also alters the purpose of testing in the development process, in which testing now serves a main function in ensuring quality as the process emerges:

> We work in cycles of two weeks, and deliver working code in the end of each period ... that the customer may take into use. Testing is integrated in these cycles. This means that ... we do not test to identify failures, as we used to. Rather we perform tests to *avoid* failures.
>
> (Computer engineer)

While agile methods are extensively described in the literature on software development and project management (e.g. Dyba and Dingsoyr 2008; Procter *et al.* 2011), our concern is what the introduction of such methods mean for the epistemic practice and learning of professionals. Our interviewees describe how the work process oscillates between developing new functionalities, and testing and documenting. Embedded in these activities are also acts of exploration, justification and validation. The engineers described an emphasis on collaborative processes based on 'continuous interaction' and sharing of knowledge, among team members as well as between developers and users. As one engineer expressed it, 'You may be very knowledgeable on technologies, but if you don't know what the customer needs to make use of it, you will not be able to create a good solution. So, this is a critical axis for communication'. To secure good opportunities for adjustment and information sharing, he had established a user group, comprising both experienced and less experienced users, in his current project. They would meet with the developer team at least once a month to review the software developed to that point and discuss future actions. In this collaboration, suggestions and solutions need to be explicated and justified. This brings transparency to the fore, both in the process as well as in the choices and justifications made.

For the engineers, such visibility and explication contribute to objectifying ideas and knowledge development. In other words, it contributes to an on-going formation and materialization of knowledge objects, which are shared in the community of software developers and their customers. Different actors may explore, use and contribute to the further development of the object in various ways, which keeps the object unfolding by oscillating between moments of closure and moments of further exploration. 'The existing is continuously driven forward', as one engineer expressed it, pointing to a change dynamism that emerges from the objects' ways of being in continuing development rather than from external innovations.

In our studies, we also observed how the methodological principles of agile software development could turn into epistemic objects themselves. Several engineers were concerned with understanding and applying these principles in their everyday work. One of them described the current situation as one of 'moulting', where the shift in methods of working generated significant attention towards managing the work process. To create a line of orderliness in the process, they needed to explore the meanings of the agile principles as well as to materialize these principles in their work context. This took, for instance, the form of creating new platforms for knowledge sharing, experimenting with new forms of collaboration by training programmers to align their ways of writing programming code with each other and developing shared routines for integrating testing in the development process. In these processes, different suggestions and ways of doing programming are explored, assessed and aligned. Although there is a relatively strong request to adjust and align practices within the team, every participant is also encouraged to bring about creative ideas and solutions. As one engineer put it, 'everybody should be creative, however it has to be some defined frames. You cannot just float out … everybody needs to adjust and work in about the same manner'.

From a wider perspective, what happens is that methodological principles and their related epistemic practices are circulated in the global community of software

developers and further developed in local work settings. Some of our interviewees seemed to relate their sense of being a professional quite strongly to these
ideas, and even followed online lectures and participated in scientific congresses
focusing on agile methods. This further illustrates how technologies and methodological scripts may take shifting functions in professional practices; sometimes
serving as intermediaries or tools for actions to be performed, and at other times
being the very object under investigation (Miettinen and Virkkunen 2005;
Østerlund 2008). We would argue that this capacity for shifting functions is an
important feature of epistemic objects and their ways of stimulating learning.

Conclusion

The examples above illustrate how nurses and computer engineers become
involved in epistemic practices when exploring knowledge objects at work. In
both professions, these practices emerge in the intersection of knowledge objects
circulated in the profession and the ways in which these objects become explored,
developed and materially defined in local work contexts. Moreover, in both cases,
procedural aspects play an important role. We will conclude by discussing how
object-related practice and learning in these examples are related to the wider
circulation of knowledge in the respective professions. The type of intermediaries
through which knowledge circulates and becomes accessible is significant in this
respect. These intermediaries may have different forms and characteristics, including human beings, technologies and various texts (Callon 1991).

In the examples from nursing, texts and documentation play a key role as
mediating instances through which science-generated knowledge and the practice of nursing become interlinked. Constructing clinical guidelines typically
includes assessing written information of various kinds. Practitioners in this group
have access to a range of textual resources specifically designed for the profession,
including manuals, intranets, reference works and textbooks (Christiansen 2010).
Nonetheless, this profession is simultaneously marked by extensive face-to-face
communication and by deliberate organization of human beings as mediators of
knowledge. For instance, the position and tasks assigned to the clinical nurse
developer represent a way of deliberately inserting a person into the organizational arrangements who is responsible for selecting and translating research-
based knowledge to make it relevant to local needs (Jensen and Christiansen
2012). Hence, while nurses have access to wider knowledge worlds in their
everyday work, the knowledge practices and settings in which they participate are
typically locally organized and have a profession-specific character.

In computer engineering, knowledge and information is largely circulated
through information technologies. These intermediaries characteristically cut
across time and space, and the content typically follows technological specialties
rather than profession-specific arrangements. The character of objects and intermediaries in this domain, and especially the capacity of technical objects to take
a role as both tools of action and objects of exploration, invites engineers to

explore and develop knowledge as part of their problem-solving activities (Nerland 2008). This serves to link practitioners with circuits of knowledge that reach well beyond their current workplace. At the same time, the need for coordination and alignment with collective ways of working, which comes with agile methods, has generated increased attention among computer engineers towards interpersonal communication.

Another significant aspect of knowledge circulation concerns the temporal organization of epistemic practices and object relations. Here we may argue that the engineers, in their investigative and knowledge-producing practices, often work within shorter time cycles than the nurses do. The introduction of agile methods has contributed significantly to this trend by regulating work sequences in a formal manner, which stimulates a dynamic interplay between explorative, evaluative and confirmative actions. It is also important to account for the simultaneity of time logics in object-related practices. Knorr Cetina (2007: 373) describes practices that evolve around epistemic objects as geared towards the future, in the sense that they 'continually open up new questions and determine new frameworks of knowing'. In the previous examples, both nurses and engineers engaged in materializing and stabilizing their current knowledge objects for specific needs, while simultaneously remaining cognizant that these objects would be subjected to future transformations. Although clinical guidelines, for instance, are based on the best knowledge available at a certain moment of time, they will need to be updated and aligned with new scientific evidence in the future. In this way, prospective scenarios may guide practitioners in their present practices. Moreover, by influencing the materialization of knowledge objects, they may also contribute to shaping the realms of future practices.

Understanding professional learning through the lenses of epistemic objects and practices implies attention towards how such objects and practices serve to link knowledge settings and communities. Epistemic objects are typically shared across sites and levels in expert cultures. While they incorporate important features of the expert culture in which they are generated, they may simultaneously be used for different purposes in local activities. Indeed, they inform local practice as this practice concurrently becomes linked with extended knowledge worlds. In this regard, object relations are important not only for learning but also for the continuation and further development of the expert culture. The circulation of and engagement with objects across organizational boundaries creates new challenges as well as new opportunities for learning and epistemic engagement. Understanding these dynamics, we argue, is important for understanding conditions for professional learning today.

Note

1 The terms 'epistemic objects' and 'knowledge objects' are both used in the literature, referring to the same type of phenomenon. Both concepts also occur in Knorr Cetina's work (e.g. 1999, 2001). Hence, we will not distinguish between these concepts in the further discussion but rather use them interchangeably.

References

Beck, K. (2003) *Test Driven Development: By Example*, Boston: Addison-Wesley Professional.

Beck, U., Giddens, A. and Lash, S. (1994) *Reflexive Modernisation. Politics, Tradition, and Aesthetics in the Modern Social Order*, Cambridge: Polity Press.

Callon, M. (1991) 'Techno-economic networks and irreversibility', in J. Law (ed.), *A Sociology of Monsters: Essays on Power, Technology and Domination* (pp. 132–161), London: Routledge.

Christiansen, B. (2010) 'Why do nurses use textual knowledge sources at work?', *Vård i Norden*, 30(4): 4–8.

Dyba, T. and Dingsoyr, T. (2008) 'Empirical studies of agile software development: A systematic review', *Information and Software Technology*, 50(9–10): 833–859.

Edwards, A. and Daniels, H. (2012) 'The knowledge that matters in professional practices', *Journal of Education and Work*, 25(1): 39–58.

Engeström, Y. and Blackler, F. (2005) 'On the life of the object', *Organization*, 12(3): 307–330.

Ewenstein, B. and Whyte, J. (2009) 'Knowledge practices in design: The role of visual representations as "epistemic objects"', *Organization Studies*, 30(1): 7–30.

Fenwick, T., Edwards, R. and Sawchuk, P. (2011) *Emerging Approaches to Educational Research: Tracing the Socio-Material*, London: Routledge.

Giddens, A. (1991) *The Consequences of Modernity*, Cambridge: Polity Press.

Jensen, K. (2007) 'The desire to learn. An analysis of knowledge-seeking practices among professionals', Oxford *Review of Education*, 33(4): 499–502.

Jensen, K. and Christiansen, B. (2012) 'New patterns of epistemic engagement among nurses. An exploratory study into the policy and practices of non-knowledge', in K. Jensen, L.C. Lahn and M. Nerland (eds), *Professional Learning in the Knowledge Society* (pp. 211–228), Rotterdam: Sense Publishers.

Jensen, K. and Lahn, L. (2005) 'The binding role of knowledge. An analysis of nursing students' knowledge ties', *Journal of Education and Work*, 18(3): 307–322.

Jensen, K., Lahn, L. and Nerland, M. (eds) (2012a) *Professional Learning in the Knowledge Society*, Rotterdam: Sense Publishers.

Jensen, K., Lahn, L. and Nerland, M. (2012b) 'A cultural perspective on knowledge and professional learning', in K. Jensen, L.C. Lahn and M. Nerland (eds), *Professional Learning in the Knowledge Society* (pp. 1–24), Rotterdam: Sense Publishers.

Klette, K. and Carlsten, T.C. (2012) 'Knowledge in teacher learning: New professional challenges', in K. Jensen, L.C. Lahn and M. Nerland (eds), *Professional Learning in the Knowledge Society* (pp. 69–84), Rotterdam: Sense Publishers.

Knorr Cetina, K. (1999) *Epistemic Cultures: How the Sciences Make Knowledge*, Cambridge: Harvard University Press.

Knorr Cetina, K. (2001) 'Objectual practice', in T. Schatzki, K. Knorr Cetina and E. von Savigny (eds), *The Practice Turn in Contemporary Theory* (pp. 175–188), London: Routledge.

Knorr Cetina, K. (2006) 'Knowledge in a knowledge society: Five transitions', *Knowledge, Work and Society*, 4(3): 23–41.

Knorr Cetina, K. (2007) 'Culture in global knowledge societies: Knowledge cultures and epistemic cultures', *Interdisciplinary Science Reviews*, 32(4): 361–375.

Knorr Cetina, K. and Bruegger, U. (2000) 'The market as an object of attachment. Exploring postsocial relations in financial markets', *Canadian Journal of Sociology*, 25(2): 141–168.

Lahn, L.C. (2012) 'The use of knowledge sources among novice accountants, engineers, nurses and teachers: An exploratory study', in K. Jensen, L.C. Lahn and M. Nerland (eds), *Professional Learning in the Knowledge Society* (pp. 109–123), Rotterdam: Sense Publishers.

Levay, C. and Waks, C. (2009) 'Professions and the pursuit of transparency in health care: Two cases of soft autonomy', *Organization Studies*, 30(5): 509–527.

McGivern, G. and Dopson, S. (2010) 'Inter-epistemic power and transforming knowledge objects in a biomedical network', *Organization Studies*, 31: 1667–1686.

Miettinen, R. and Virkkunen, J. (2005) 'Epistemic objects, artefacts and organizational change', *Organization*, 12: 437–456.

Moen, A. and Nes, S. (2012) 'Consolidating work descriptions: Creating shared knowledge objects', in A. Moen, A.I. Mørch and S. Paavola (eds), *Collaborative Knowledge Creation: Practices, Tools, Concepts* (Ch. 14), Rotterdam: Sense Publishers.

Moreira, T. (2005) 'Diversity in clinical guidelines: The role of repertoires of evaluation', *Social Science and Medicine*, 60: 1975–1985.

Mørk, B.E., Aanestad, M., Hanseth, O. and Grisot, M. (2008) 'Conflicting epistemic cultures and obstacles for learning across communities of practice', *Knowledge and Process Management*, 15(1): 12–23.

Nerland, M. (2008) 'Knowledge cultures and the shaping of work-based learning: The case of computer engineering', *Vocations and Learning: Studies in Vocational and Professional Education*, 1: 49–69.

Nerland, M. and Jensen, K. (2010) 'Objectual practice and learning in professional work', in S. Billett (ed.), *Learning Through Practice: Models, Traditions, Orientations and Approaches* (pp. 82–103), Dordrecht: Springer.

Nerland, M. and Jensen, K. (2012) 'Epistemic practices and object relations in professional work', *Journal of Education and Work*, 25(1): 101–120.

Nerland, M. and Jensen, K. (in press). 'Changing Cultures of Knowledge and Professional Learning' in S. Billet, C. Harteis and H. Gruber, (Eds.), International Handbook of Research in Professional Practice-based Learning, Part 3: Educational systems. Springer International Handbooks in Education Series. Dordrecht: Springer.

Nes, S. and Moen, A. (2010) 'Constructing standards: A study of nurses negotiating with multiple modes of knowledge', *Journal of Workplace Learning*, 22(6): 376–393.

Østerlund, C. (2008) 'The materiality of communicative practices. The boundaries and objects of an emergency room genre', *Scandinavian Journal of Information Systems*, 20(1): 7–40.

Procter, R., Rouncefield, M., Poschen, M., Lin, Y. and Voss, A. (2011) 'Agile project development: A case study of a virtual research environment development project', *Computer Supported Cooperative Work*, 20: 197–225.

Rudberg, M. (2012) 'Gender, knowledge and desire: A story of change?', in K. Jensen, L.C. Lahn and M. Nerland (eds), *Professional Learning in the Knowledge Society* (pp. 179–193), Rotterdam: Sense Publishers.

Strand, T. and Jensen, K. (2012) 'Researching the current dynamics of professional expertise: Three analytic discourses', in M. Vukasovic *et al.* (eds), *Effects of Higher Education Reforms: Change Dynamics* (pp. 59–78), Rotterdam: Sense Publishers.

Chapter 3

The doctor and the blue form

Learning professional responsibility[1]

Miriam Zukas and Sue Kilminster

Introduction

The case of junior doctors' early professional learning, specifically learning responsibility, is something of a puzzle for us. Two quotes from our research on doctors will suffice:

> It was awful and I think there was like – in the first or second day – this woman collapsed on the ward and she was actually faking it but like I think it just completely got me because it was unexpected. I didn't know what to do really and the nurses seemed to take control and the nurses expected you to be rubbish on your first couple of days.
>
> (F4)

> I was on call on my first day. It was a new hospital. Didn't really know where anything was – didn't know how to order blood tests do anything very much. I got handed the bleep, the registrar had been on nights handed me her passes for the computers – this that and the other – and I was essentially left to my own devices. I was given a tour of the admissions unit and that was about the extent of it.
>
> (S1)

As these opening extracts show, junior doctors often give frightened (and frightening) accounts of their first days in new professional roles. They talk of being overwhelmed with responsibility, whilst trying to find their bearings physically, clinically and socially (Kilminster *et al.* 2010, 2011; Zukas and Kilminster 2012a). And doctors continue to make many transitions during their postgraduate training and throughout their careers: from one place to another; from one specialty to another; from one team to another; from one level of responsibility to another. The first few transitional days and weeks form the basis for doctors' 'war' stories.

Whilst we might accept that such heightened disorientation is inevitable for the most junior doctors, for those outside clinical practice, it is somewhat disconcerting to learn that more senior doctors also describe feeling unsure, ill-prepared, out of their depth, when they move from one level of responsibility to another. There is, too, recent evidence which seems to suggest that patients are at increased risk of harmful occurrences not only during newly qualified doctors' initial days, with a small but significant increase in patient mortality (Jen *et al.* 2009), but also when more qualified doctors make transitions (Haller *et al.* 2009). The puzzle then is that, despite both professional and public concerns, there has been relatively little research on the embedded learning which is so critical during those transitions. As Teunissen and Westerman (2011) point out, Becker *et al.* (1961) showed a long time ago that the move into the clinical workplace involves a period of learning to manage relationships with clinical supervisors, nurses and others, as well as fulfilling tasks and learning from the process.

To address these transitional issues, the most common solution so far has been to focus on preparedness – that is, medical and clinical educators have expended most energy on research seeking to prepare student doctors as carefully as possible for their new positions (e.g. Lempp *et al.* 2005; Illing *et al.* 2008; Nikendei *et al.* 2008; Cave *et al.* 2009). This presupposes that learning and work can be separated, and that the actual sociomaterial conditions of work involve second-order or context/background learning.

However, we believe that theoretical understandings of doctors' learning have to include both material and broader social aspects of clinical work as primary-order learning; the preparedness research is therefore conceptually and practically insufficient and may even contribute to the conditions that increase the risk to patients outlined above. In line with the general theoretical orientation of this book, we seek to interrupt the individualistic and human-centred understandings of responsibility and learning in medical education. Such an account is not only more satisfactory in understanding doctors' learning, but it also helps us rethink pedagogies of responsibility. The chapter will thus briefly explore dominant explanations for doctors learning in transition before coming to actor–network theory (ANT). In order to understand the puzzle we initially described, we consider the assemblages of human and non-human actors which enact junior doctors, and introduce Michel Callon's (1986) analysis. Touching briefly on the research underpinning our approach, we will expand this argument through an example of the enactment of the doctor as someone who comes to be able to take 'life and death' decisions.

Becoming a doctor: accounting for learning

In the UK, where our research is situated, doctors' preliminary medical qualifications are taken in medical school. Once qualified, doctors are provisionally registered with the General Medical Council and enter a compulsory two-year Foundation (F1 and F2) programme designed to provide general clinical experience which includes different specialties; the doctors rotate between different posts. Subsequently, doctors apply for entry to specialist training (ST) and undertake a series of paid posts. Each stage of training has a structured programme with formalized requirements. At foundation level, these include explicit expectations that trainees will have clinical training in a range of practices and procedures and regular, formal educational sessions. Trainees are also required to have a designated educational supervisor, to sign a training/learning agreement at the start of each post and to maintain a logbook and/or a learning portfolio relevant to their current programme, which they discuss with their educational supervisor (or representative).

Acquisitive perspectives

A number of implicit assumptions about learning emerge from this brief outline of the pedagogic support for doctors, and from our discussion earlier about preparedness. First, learning tends to be understood mainly as an individualized, cognitive process (Sfard 1998; Saljö 2003; Mason 2007). Second, context is seen as separate from the learner with the learner enveloped by context (Edwards 2009). Issues of work organization, power and wider social and institutional structures are generally excluded from consideration (see for example Unwin *et al.* 2009). This critique may be taken one step further: because learning is seen as an individualistic, internal and mostly cognitive process, people and artefacts (the sociomaterial world, in other words) are also separated from the learner and learning/knowledge-making processes (Nespor 1994; Knorr Cetina, 2001; Fenwick and Edwards 2010a, 2010b). This not only ignores learning as an embodied process with practical, physical and emotional aspects as well as cognitive ones: as we shall discuss, it also fails to take account of the network or assemblage of actors implicated in learning.

The response to doctors' difficulties with transitions from the field of medical education is almost always to call for more and better 'preparedness' (assumed to be a characteristic of the doctor in question). One reason for the persistence of the concept of preparedness lies in the attribution of difficulties in transition to incomplete learning by doctors. Attributions range from claims concerning deficits in knowledge *about* practice to ones suggesting that the problems lie in learning and knowing *in* practice. The preparedness discussion derives, on the whole, from the former – i.e. that there is a deficit of knowledge *about* practice.

Even in the case of those seeking to unite learning and practice more closely together through, for example, exercises in reflective practice, it is generally assumed that learning derives from patients and/or knowledge and/or practice. Pedagogical interventions such as simulations and role plays, early clinical experience, peer practice, bedside teaching, collaborative team working and problem-based learning are all channelled through a focus on the patient. All other aspects of the workplace (social and material) fade into the background (context).

Sociocultural perspectives

In contrast, socially derived understandings of learning within the work environment emphasize practice as the basis for learning. Many different versions of these socially derived understandings exist (cf. Hager *et al.* 2012), but within the context of medical education, Lave and Wenger's (1991) work on situated learning is most frequently cited (for example, Bleakley 2005; Dornan *et al.* 2005). Learning is viewed as engagement in legitimate peripheral participation under the guidance of experienced practitioners. Learning is thus understood as a form of 'becoming' in which knowledge, values and skills are not separate from practice. However, there are immediate problems in employing these concepts in relation to doctors' transitions and learning.

First, the transition itself is not an apprenticeship; there is frequently a disjunction between one level of responsibility and another. For example, overnight, upon qualification, doctors acquire the responsibility to prescribe. Second, responsibility does not necessarily increase progressively through transitions and over time; levels of responsibility may vary between settings and specialities and a trainee may find they have less, rather than more, independence in some settings than others. Third, legitimate responsibility may change significantly depending on other factors such as the time of day (or night) and/or who else is present – if there are no experienced practitioners around, trainee doctors have to act as full members, rather than legitimate, peripheral practitioners.

There are other aspects of practice which do not fit Lave and Wenger's characterization. Clinical teams (to which doctors belong) are not stable communities because the structure of much clinical practice involves shift working and other changing work patterns. The transitional workplace is often populated by intersecting – even competing – communities of professionals (doctors, nurses, pharmacists, other healthcare workers). There may also be competing values and practices between old-timers and newcomers, as newcomers bring changing practices with them. Finally, practices themselves transform constantly, because of changes in policy and regulation, technological transformation or responses to evidence; the notion therefore of what we mean by an old-timer in relation to these new practices may also be questionable. This critique also has resonance for practice in other professions where service demands on newcomers require high levels of performance and responsibility.

Sociomaterial perspectives

Other theoretical perspectives exist which are concerned with the interplay between the individual and the social world. For example, Hodkinson *et al.*'s (2008) cultural theory of learning and theory of learning cultures which responds to some of the dualisms (for example, mind/body and individual/social) of learning theories and takes a situated approach in which learning is understood to be practical, embodied and social. However, the human, the social and the cultural are foundational: the non-human, the technical and the material are present but still in the theoretical background, as it were. And yet, in doctors' reports from the field, and the empirical research we have described elsewhere, doctors in transition seem constantly to be battling with a series of trivial but nevertheless highly inconvenient hurdles: passwords, security passes, machines that analyse blood, chest drain kits and patients' notes which seem to travel through wards on journeys of their own.

For this reason, we have drawn on theoretical understandings which resist the separation of the non-human (material and textual) from the human constitution of the workplace. Whilst a range of theoretical possibilities are available, including complexity theory and cultural–historical activity (summarized by Fenwick 2012), we have approached our research question with what might be called a 'set of sensitivities' (Mol 2010) in mind: actor–network theory (ANT).

To use such a term is contentious, even for those who have become most associated with it. The oft-repeated quote from Bruno Latour that 'there are four things that do not work with actor–network theory: the word actor, the word network, the word theory and the hyphen! Four nails in the coffin' (Latour 1999:15) suggests that he feels it has outstayed its useful life. The publication of Law and Hassard's collected edition, *Actor Network Theory and After* (1999) also suggests that actor–network theory's time might be up, not least because it is not a theory. Mol (2010) summarizes the debate about its theoretical standing neatly: ANT is not a theory because there is no attempt to look for laws of 'nature–culture'; it does not offer causal explanations; it does not suggest a consistent method. However, Mol also proposes that it might be considered a theory if 'a "theory" is something that helps scholars to attune to the world, to see and hear and feel and taste it. Indeed to appreciate it.' (Mol 2010:262). In their overview of the contribution of ANT in education, Fenwick and Edwards (2010a) entitle their first chapter 'A way to intervene, not a theory of what to think' to indicate that ANT is more akin to a sensibility or, rather, loosely connected sensibilities. By attuning ourselves (Mol 2010), ANT enables us to 'tell cases, draw contrasts, articulate silent layers, turn questions upside down, focus on the unexpected ...' (262).

So what might these sensibilities be? For the purposes of this chapter, a good deal will need to be assumed. What is outlined here is only what might be needed to understand the gist or direction of our own interests: others (for example Fenwick *et al.* 2012; Mulcahy 2012) have written much more extensively about the origins, diverse associations and meanings, or disciplinary work to which actor–network theory and allied ideas have been put in education.

First – we were drawn to an ANT sensibility because of the attention ANT gives to actors – actors (artefacts, people, texts) who do something that makes a difference. But – and this is crucial – ANT is interested in the effects of these actors and their activities – and not in their goals or ends. Take, for example, a new hospital doctor's security pass: such a pass opens doors; it enables those who carry it to move freely between the corridor and the ward without having to ask others (usually via a bell) for admittance; it legitimizes pass holders as people who have the right to come and go. And, by reflecting on what happens when new doctors do not have passes or whose passes fail to work (a nearly universal theme in junior doctors' reports of working in UK hospitals), we can see that passes – or more accurately security pads and passes – also contribute to particular kinds of working practices in which the landscape of professional relationships are both sustained and disrupted. It seems that answering the door – both to let others in and/or to establish legitimacy – is the work of nurses on many wards. Whoever answers the door is likely to be in the middle of something else – perhaps attending to a patient, or to paperwork, or preparing something in the sluice room. The admission of another is therefore disruptive of certain kinds of work, and entails an act which is simultaneously gate-keeping (or door-keeping more accurately) and servicing.

In thinking about doctors in transition, passes and keypads as well as nurses are actors – their effect is, in a small way, to legitimate certain people as doctors. Others have noticed such effects in other arenas – for example, Fenwick's (1998) work on teachers' lives also drew attention to the ways in which keys (to classrooms, lockers and so on) did something – they 'exerted important effects on how people felt about their work, themselves and each other' (Fenwick and Edwards 2010a:7). The effect of not having a pass is that junior doctors do not feel themselves to be legitimate and autonomous.

Second, and as is customary in ANT explanations, we need to attend to what is meant by network. As Mol (2010:257) points out, following de Saussure, in the same way as words do not point directly to a referent but form part of a network of words, so too do actors depend on others around them – that is, they are embedded in a network which enacts them. This needs unpacking with an example. Whilst we usually think of doctors as individuals with certain attributes (knowledge, skill, particular attitudes) who are able to move freely amongst patients in their care, 'applying' their knowledge, etc., when we look carefully, doctors depend on security passes, passwords, other doctors' notes, medicines, nurses, patients, beds to practise – to doctor. In other words, from an ANT point of view, being a doctor is not a given status conferred by passing one's exams (as so many junior doctors know): the doctor is an effect of a network of immense complexity: patients, passes, notes, nurses, other doctors, instruments, drugs, hospital wards and much more. The ANT way to speak of this is as an 'assemblage': 'a process of bundling, of assembling … in which the elements put together are not fixed in shape, do not belong to a larger pre-given list but are constructed at least in part as they are entangled together' (Law 2004:42). Thus, passes and nurses in the example above are part of the assemblage of the doctor in transition; but assemblages or networks – webs of relations – are fluid, ever-changing, interdependent and co-existing – with actors (nurses, passes, doctors) associated with many different networks.

Given that we wish to explore the enactment of a doctor which, from this perspective is fluid, unstable, entangled and messy, we have returned to an earlier use of the ANT concept of translation. By translation, ANT theorists mean 'what happens when entities, human and non-human, come together and connect, changing one another to form links' (Fenwick and Edwards 2010a:9), thus becoming enrolled as part of the network or assemblage. For us, the concept is helpful because it enables us to trace the formation of linkages with learning as an effect, rather than as an acquisitive or sociocultural process.

Although sometimes criticized for the ways in which others have employed them, Callon's (1986) concepts of 'moments of translation' are particularly helpful in making explicit how some networks become stabilized and powerful across time and space, whilst others fail. These 'moments of translation' are not chronological; nor do they imply a linear, progressive framework, as has sometimes been understood (Fenwick and Edwards 2010a). In brief, Callon proposed that networks entail *problematization* in which something attempts to become an 'obligatory passage point' – a framing of problems or ideas and the like. The moment of *interessement* describes how entities are brought to or bring themselves to the network, whilst other entities are excluded. In other words, *interessement* involves strategies to stabilize actors defined through problematization. Actors are *enrolled* into the network through 'multilateral negotiations, trials of strength and tricks that accompany the interessements and enable them to succeed' (Callon 1986:211). When the actor network stabilizes, that is, when actors are transformed into manageable entities that can be transported through space-time, Callon referred to this as *mobilization*.

We will return to these moments of translation in the enactment of a doctor as someone who comes to be able to take 'life and death' decisions when we look closely below at a specific example, taken from our empirical research. But before that, we explain the background to our study.

Researching doctors learning responsibility

Fuller accounts of the methodology, ethical procedures, method, participants and analysis of the study informing this chapter are given elsewhere (Kilminster *et al.* 2010, 2011),[2] together with the broad findings. In short, in our original study, *Learning responsibility? Exploring doctors' transitions to new levels of medical performance* Roberts (2009), we sought to understand better from a learning perspective the transitions which are such a major feature of doctors' careers: ward to ward, specialty to specialty, level to level. We concentrated on doctors working in elderly medicine because this specialty involves complex patient care pathways and decision making. In order to investigate learning in transition, we focused on two main points of transition: from medical student to foundation training (F1); and from foundation training or generalist training to specialist clinical practice/specialist training (ST). We investigated aspects of transition at four regulatory levels – the individual, their clinical team (and the site in which they were located), their employer, and the regulatory and policy context. We drew on documentary evidence and interviews with a range of clinical team members (consultants, pharmacists, senior nurses, physiotherapists and so on). But our key participants were F1 and ST doctors who we interviewed twice – once at the point of transition and once more, two to three months later. We asked participants if we could observe them at work on the ward, near the beginning of the transition we were investigating, and following the first interview. The case below is taken from an observation of an F1, undertaken by the first author of this chapter.

The blue form: enacting doctors who care for the dying

> When I come on the ward, the consultant is behind the desk with the matron and the specialist trainee. The consultant discusses the treatment of a dying patient and gives F13 an instruction to stop treatment – F13. asks if she should fill in the 'blue form' and the consultant goes through the form, showing which sections she needs to fill in. She asks again about stopping all treatment and the consultant says yes, so she goes to find the patient's file, tells the nurse that they are stopping everything and brings them back to the desk. She returns to the 'blue form' throughout the evening, switching backwards and forwards between the patient's thick file and the 'blue form', sometimes reading and sometimes writing.
>
> (Observation notes)

The 'blue form' refers here to a specific protocol in the UK entitled the 'Liverpool Care Pathway (LCP) for the Dying Patient' which is intended to 'improve the care of the dying in the last hours/days of life'. Once it is agreed that a patient is on the LCP and therefore that they are being cared for as someone who is dying, a form is completed to this effect. But, rather than understanding this as a bureaucratic process, in which humans are privileged and complete forms, we have considered this from the vantage point that things (bodies, texts, passes) are all assumed to be capable of exerting force and joining together to form networks across time and space. A point to repeat from above, therefore: a junior doctor (this junior doctor) does not pre-exist when he or she passes their exams. Instead, she is an effect of blue forms, dying patients, consultants – these entities connect with one another and with other actors as an assemblage network that enacts a doctor.

The LCP and the blue forms are also enactments of knowledge that came into being through networks at a distance both temporally and spatially (*Liverpool* refers here to a place as well as an approach). They could be regarded as delegates of other networks (Fenwick and Edwards 2010b) or 'immutable mobiles' (Latour 1987), moving into new spaces (wards, other clinical settings in this case) to draw together the network. This 'network of knowledge' (Fenwick and Edwards 2010a:17) of the blue form acts in a number of ways: bureaucratically in the requirement that actions be recorded; pedagogically in the ordering and framing of the treatment of a dying person for a new doctor; epistemologically in the gathering together of 'best practice' in the care of the dying; and clinically in the actions brought about, such as the withdrawal of treatment.

To return to Callon's (1986) 'moments of translation' as outlined above. Decisions on how best to treat dying patients within a variety of care settings (e.g. hospitals) are framed as a process in which excellent care can be transferred from site to site:

> The LCP affirms the vision of transferring the model of excellence for care of the dying from hospice care into other healthcare settings. We have demonstrated a process that inspires, motivates and truly empowers the generic workforce in caring for the patient and their family in the last hours or days of life.
>
> (LCP 2010)

Thus the LCP/blue form frames the problem (the *obligatory passage point*) as how to acknowledge and care for someone who is dying using 'the model of excellence' generated in places which are not hospitals (*problematization*).

The moment of *interessement* involves strategies to stabilize actors defined through problematization. Actors are invited into this framing – not only hospice workers but doctors, nurses, the multi-disciplinary team (MDT), patients' families, patients, drugs, other treatments, organizations, and so on, to become *enrolled* as caring for the dying. Some entities are excluded in this process – presumably curative treatments are amongst them. The network relations of the LCP are *mobilized* when care of the dying is transformed into a manageable entity that can be transported through space-time. Thus, in this analysis, the form is an actor with the effect of enacting a doctor who cares for dying as well as sick patients.

I asked F13 about filling in the blue form in the follow-up interview three months later. In response, F13 said: 'I've got better at recognizing patients who are dying and maybe just benefit from palliative care and then just deciding when it might be appropriate to start that and then discussing that with a senior'. The blue form is therefore part of an assemblage which has 'done' several things: it has assisted F13 in 'recognizing patients who are dying'; it has enrolled F13 as someone who is able – in theory at least – to practise palliative as well as therapeutic care; and it has enacted F13 as a responsible junior doctor who is able to decide (albeit in consultation with a senior) on matters – literally – of life and death.

This is, but one example: many others have had the insight that texts are actors. Specifically in relation to clinical practice, Berg (1996:499), for example, analyses the ways in which medical records figure as 'a fundamental, constitutive element of medical practice'. He argues that medical records enter 'into the "thinking" processes of medical personnel and into their relations with patients and with each other'. They 'help to shape the form the patient's trajectory takes' and also transform the body into 'an extension of the hospital's routines' (520) whilst they are continually altered and worked on by the very individuals whose work practices they transform. The additional insight we offer is that texts and other material enactments are fundamental in understanding learning as well as practice.

In presenting this example and other empirically-derived sociomaterial analyses to colleagues, we have been asked – why focus on the blue form when it is the medium of transmission of cultural practices, rather than an 'agent' in itself? Critics have argued that the form does not do anything by itself, and that to suggest that it does is to project human capacities onto a text (or object, or other inanimate objects). The response to this long-standing criticism of ANT is summarized crisply by Fenwick (2012:71) in terms we discussed above:

> the concept of agency has traditionally been limited by its human-centric definitions associated with intention, initiative and exercises of power … Agency [in ANT] is understood as a distributed *effect* produced in material webs of human and non-human assemblages.
>
> (Italics in the original; content in brackets added)

But such assemblages are not random and are not sustained without 'interest' – defined by Mol (2010) as a verb (that is, to interest). Assemblages are, as she says, 'hard work' (259), if they are to succeed. In thinking of how to speak about what sustains a network, one of her suggestions is to talk of 'logics' since this 'stresses that what makes up a distinct network/logic and what belongs to another, partly depends on what makes sense in the terms of the network/logic at hand' (259). In her work on professionalism, she contrasts the logics of choice and care which she sees operating in clinical practice (Mol 2008). A logic of choice presupposes that care practices are linear – measures are taken, instruments are used, facts are presented, patients are given information after which they are able to evaluate their choices and come to a decision. However, care practices are not linear:

> Facts do not precede decisions and activities, but depend on what is hoped for and on what can be done. Deciding to do something is rarely enough to actually achieve it … Caring is a question of 'doctoring': of tinkering with bodies, technologies and knowledge – and with people too.
>
> (Moll 2008:12)

We have worked through instances of doctors' workarounds or tinkering (Zukas and Kilminster 2012b) and argued that doctors are educated within a logic of choice (for example, seeking consent for medical intervention so that a patient knows what their 'choice' might be), but come to learn to work within a logic of care based on 'what can be done'. Nevertheless, the logic of 'choice' prefigures educational and public discourse, and some of the changing conditions for professional practice (for example as outlined by Fenwick *et al.* 2012).

Conclusion

The analysis here has focused on the translation involved in enacting a responsible junior doctor who is able to decide (albeit in consultation with a senior) on matters of life and death. Since the fieldwork reported here was completed and an earlier version of the paper was presented at a conference in 2011, substantial controversy has erupted in the UK about the ways in which decisions are taken to put patients on the LCP. A variety of claims have been made, including that: patients' relatives were not informed or consulted; decisions were taken inappropriately; and, in a few instances, care was cruel because patients were deprived of pain relief and water (this is not advised in the LCP). As we write, each day brings fresh debate in the newspapers and on websites as to what should be done. A change to the National Health Service (NHS) constitution has been proposed by the current Government in which patients and their families would be given a legal right to be consulted on all decisions about end-of-life care. The rights would mean that patients and relatives could sue the NHS if the requirements are not met, and doctors could be struck off the register if they fail to consult properly. New networks are forming – at the top of the list of a web-based search on the LCP is a paid advertisement from a legal firm claiming to specialize in cases involving the LCP, particularly where relatives were not consulted, and seeking to collect enough evidence to bring forward a collective case for compensation. Put differently, whilst 'best practice' in the care of dying patients is still framed through the LCP in the current debate, the actors invited into this framing (*interessement*) are expanding. This is a stark reminder, if one were needed, that actor–networks are unstable, complex and dynamic as well as fixed and durable, coming into being through interest and 'hard work'. It is clear too which logic is legitimized in this discussion.

Having made the case that the theoretical resources for understanding doctors' learning in transition need to be expanded if doctors are to be enabled to make smoother transitions (and patients are to benefit), we have argued through a single example for a sociomaterial approach. Following in the tradition of Callon's early work, we have analysed the translation of the LCP (the blue form) network which enacts doctors who care for the dying. Such an approach turns on its head the 'preparedness' research, cited at the start of this chapter.

Our struggle to understand doctors' learning (in transition or otherwise) through an ANT sensibility is, as Mulcahy (2012) puts it so acutely, an attempt to conceive of learning as 'a matter of seeing double': 'In a socio-material account of learning, we are impelled to give attention, at one and the same time, to its *socialities* and *materialities* ... Seeing double is a matter of taking associations or connections or relations into account.' (125; italics in the original). Pedagogies of responsibility generally, and doctors' learning in transition specifically, require us to review those transitions, to trace the assemblages which enact junior doctors, to describe more precisely the significance of seemingly trivial impediments to doctors working (passwords, passes, machines, record-keeping and form-filling). Most importantly, we need to understand better the relations or connections with patients, disease, other professionals involved in patient care, protocols, employers, legislation – the list could go on. We believe that an ANT sensibility offers one way forward.

Notes

1 An earlier version of this paper was given at the 7th International Conference on Researching Work and Learning. East China Normal University, Shanghai 2011.
2 This research was funded by the Economic and Social Research Council and the General Medical Council in the UK (ESRC RES-153-25-0084).

References

Becker, H.S., Blanche, G., Hughes, E.C. and Strauss, A.L. (1961) *Boys in White: Student Culture in Medical School*, Chicago: University of Chicago Press.

Berg, M. (1996) 'Practices of reading and writing: the constitutive role of the patient record in medical work', *Sociology of Health and Illness*, 18(4): 499–524.

Bleakley, A. (2005) 'Stories as data, data as stories: making sense of narrative inquiry in clinical education', *Medical Education*, 39(5): 534–40.

Callon, M. (1986) 'Some elements of a sociology of translation: domestication of the scallops and the fishermen of Saint Brieuc Bay', in J. Law (ed.) *Power, Action and Belief: A New Sociology of Knowledge?*, London: Routledge and Kegan Paul.

Cave, J., Woolf, K., Jones, A. and Dacre, J. (2009) 'Easing the transition from student to doctor: How can medical schools prepare their graduates for starting work?', *Medical Teacher*, 31(5): 403–8.

Dornan, T., Scherpbier, A., King, N. and Boshuizen, H. (2005) 'Clinical teachers and problem-based learning: a phenomenological study', *Medical Education*, 39(2): 163–70.

Edwards, R. (2009) 'Life as a learning context?', in R. Edwards, G. Biesta and M. Thorpe (eds) *Rethinking Contexts for Learning and Teaching: Communities, Activities and Networks*, Abingdon: Routledge.

Fenwick, T. (1998) 'Managing space, energy and self: beyond classroom management with junior high school teachers', *Teachers and Teacher Education*, 14(6): 619–31.

Fenwick, T. (2012) 'Matters of knowing and doing: sociomaterial approaches to understanding practice', in P. Hager, A. Lee and A. Reich (eds) *Practice, Learning and Change: Practice–Theory Perspectives in Professional Learning*, Dordrecht: Springer.

Fenwick, T. and Edwards, R. (2010a) *Actor–Network Theory in Education*, Abingdon: Routledge.

Fenwick, T. and Edwards, R. (2010b) 'Reading educational reform with actor network theory: Fluid spaces, otherings, and ambivalences', *Educational Philosophy and Theory*, online first, DOI: 10.1111/j.1469-5812.2009.00609.x

Fenwick, T., Nerland, M. and Jensen, K. (2012) 'Sociomaterial approaches to conceptualising professional learning and practice', *Journal of Education and Work*, 25(1): 1–13.

Hager, P., Lee, A. and Reich, A. (eds) (2012) *Practice, Learning and Change: Practice–Theory Perspectives in Professional Learning*, Dordrecht: Springer.

Haller, G., Myles, P.S., Taffe, P., Perneger, T.V. and Wu, C.L. (2009) 'Rate of undesirable events at beginning of academic year: retrospective cohort study', *British Medical Journal*, 339: b3974.

Hodkinson, P., Biesta, G. and James, D. (2008) 'Understanding learning culturally: overcoming the dualism between social and individual views of learning', *Vocations and Learning*, 1: 27–47.

Illing, J., Morrow, G., Kergon, C., Burford, B., Spencer, J., Peile, E., Davies, C., Baldauf, B., Allen, M., Johnson, N., Morrison, J., Donaldson, M., Whitelaw, M. and Field, M. (2008) *How prepared are medical graduates to begin practice? A comparison of three diverse UK medical schools: Final summary and conclusions for the GMC Education Committee*, London: General Medical Council.

Jen, M.H., Bottle, A., Majeed, A., Bell, D. and Aylin, P. (2009) 'Early in-hospital mortality following trainee doctors' first day at work', *PLoS ONE*: 4(9): e7103.

Kilminster, S., Zukas, M., Quinton, N. and Roberts, T. (2010) 'Learning practice? Exploring the links between transitions and medical performance', *Journal of Health Organization and Management*, 24(6): 556–570.

Kilminster, S., Zukas, M., Quinton, N. and Roberts, T. (2011) 'Preparedness is not enough: Understanding transitions as critically intensive learning periods', *Medical Education*, 45: 1006–15.

Knorr Cetina, K. (2001) 'Objectual practice', in T.R. Schatzki, K. Knorr Cetina and E. Von Savigny (eds) *The Practice Turn in Contemporary Theory*, Abingdon: Routledge.

Latour, B. (1987) *Science in Action*, Cambridge, MA: Harvard University Press.

Latour, B. (1999) 'On recalling ANT' in J. Law and J. Hassard (eds) *Actor Network Theory and After*, Oxford: Blackwell Publishers.

Lave, J. and Wenger, E. (1991) *Situated Learning: Legitimate Peripheral Participation*, Cambridge: Cambridge University Press.

Law, J. (2004) *After Method: Mess in Social Science Research*, Abingdon: Routledge.

Law, J. and Hassard, J. (eds) (1999) *Actor Network Theory and After*, Oxford: Blackwell Publishers.

LCP (2010) *What is the LCP? (Healthcare Professionals)*, Liverpool: Marie Curie Palliative Care Institute.

Lempp, H., Seabrook, M., Cochrane, M. and Rees, J. (2005) 'The transition from medical student to doctor: Perceptions of final year students and preregistration house officers related to expected learning outcomes', *International Journal of Clinical Practice*, 59(3): 324–9.

Mason, L. (2007) 'Introduction: Bridging the cognitive and sociocultural approaches in research on conceptual change. Is it feasible?', *Educational Psychologist*, 42(1): 1–7.

Mol, A. (2008) *The Logic of Care: Health and the Problem of Patient Choice*, Abingdon: Routledge.

Mol, A. (2010) 'Actor–network theory: sensitive terms and enduring tensions', *Kölner Zeitschrift für Soziologie and Sozialpsychologie*, 50(1): 253–269.

Mulcahy, D. (2012) 'Thinking teacher professional learning performatively: a socio-material account', *Journal of Education and Work*, 25(1): 121–39.

Nespor, J. (1994) *Knowledge in Motion: Space, Time and Curriculum in Undergraduate Physics and Management*, Philadelphia: Falmer Press.

Nikendei, C.B., Kraus, B., Schrauth, M., Briem, S. and Junger, J. (2008) 'Ward rounds: how prepared are future doctors?', *Medical Teacher*, 30(1): 88–91.

Roberts, Trudie (2009). Learning responsibility? Exploring doctors' transitions to new levels of medical responsibility: Full Research Report ESRC End of Award Report, RES-153-25-0084. Swindon: ESRC.

Saljö, R. (2003) 'From transfer to boundary-crossing', in T. Tuomi-Gröhn and Y. Engeström (eds) *Between School and Work: New Perspectives on Transfer and Boundary-crossing*, Amsterdam: Elsevier.

Sfard, A. (1998) 'On two metaphors for learning and the dangers of choosing just one', *Educational Researcher*, 27(2): 4–13.

Teunissen, P.W. and Westerman, M. (2011) 'Junior doctors caught in the clash: the transition from working to learning explored', *Medical Education*, 45: 968–970.

Unwin, L., Fuller, A., Felstead, A. and Jewson, N. (2009) 'Worlds within worlds: the relational dance between context and learning in the workplace', in R. Edwards, G. Biesta and M. Thorpe (eds) *Rethinking Contexts for Learning and Teaching: Communities, Activities and Networks*, London: Routledge.

Zukas, M. and Kilminster, S. (2012a) 'Learning to practise, practising to learn: doctors' transitions to new levels of responsibility', in P. Hager, A. Lee and A. Reich (eds) *Practice, Learning and Change: Practice–Theory Perspectives in Professional Learning*, Dordrecht: Springer.

Zukas, M. and Kilminster, S. (2012b) 'Doctors in transition: conflicting responsibilities in practice', contribution to symposium on *Practices that 'matter': Material enactments of professionals' conflicting responsibilities*, given at the Propel (Professional Practice, Education and Learning) International Conference, Stirling, Scotland.

Chapter 4

Re-thinking teacher professional learning

A more than representational account

Dianne Mulcahy

Introduction

New socioeconomic conditions have resulted in significant reconfiguration of professional learning and professional education (White *et al.* 2010; Groundwater-Smith and Mockler 2009). Increased demands created by more economistic and managerial pressures characterize the current educational environment in a number of countries, including Australia. 'Education in Australia over the past decade has been dominated by concerns associated with issues of quality and, in particular, ways in which quality learning outcomes can be produced, measured and assured' (White *et al.* 2010:181). Styling education reform along the lines of these concerns serves to strengthen discourses of the centrality of the teacher (Larsen 2010) and enlarge the idea that the key to educational success lies with the teacher. Challenging the established individualized, psychological perspective, where learning is primarily seen in terms of the intrinsic capabilities or potentialities of people, and the learner in terms of the self-knowing, reflective subject, the argument made in this chapter is that it is *practices* that produce learning and learners, practices that involve agencies of an ontologically diverse kind.

It is assumed from the outset that social practice as a medium for learning is intricately entangled with material practice; thus, teachers learn not only in association with each other but in association with material phenomena such as texts and technologies, spaces and places that actively bring their learning into effect. 'Practices of knowing cannot be fully claimed as human practices' (Barad 2003:829). Accordingly, my guiding questions for the inquiry are:

* How might thinking teacher professional learning from a perspective that acknowledges practices of knowing other than human practices, and agencies other than human agencies, change the ways in which this learning is thought, authorized and enacted?
* What does the process of practising teacher professional learning look like when material practice and its non-human participants (texts, technologies, affects, spaces, places) are taken into account?

In my attempt to re-think teacher professional learning and gain a more material, theoretical purchase on it, I turn to two bodies of theory, non-representational theory (Thrift 2008; Anderson and Harrison 2010) and actor–network theory (Latour 2005; Law 2009) which share a concern for material practices and a philosophic commitment to thinking the human (subject) world and the non-human (object) world together, while respecting their irreducible difference. This shared concern and commitment serves as an analytical resource for the analysis and discussion that follows. Set respectively within the fields of human geography and science and technology studies, concepts from these theories are increasingly being taken up in education (Fenwick and Edwards 2010; Saito 2010; Sorensen 2009; Mulcahy and Aberton 2008; Macknight 2011). Pioneering the development of non-representational theory (NRT), Nigel Thrift (2008:112) refers to a non-representational style of work as

> both anti-cognitivist and, by extension, anti-elitist since it is trying to counter the still prevalent tendency to consider life [and one might add learning] from the point of view of individual agents who generate action by instead weaving a poetic of the common practices and skills which produce people, selves, and worlds.

Actor–network theory (ANT), in turn, constitutes itself *as*/in/for practice. As one of its originators, John Law (2007:145), explains:

> (I)t is the practices (including the people) that come first. It is their materiality, their embodiment, their diurnal and organizational periodicities, their architectural forms, that are central. And these practices are often pretty obdurate. In this way of thinking, practices make the world.

The account of teacher professional learning put forward here is a 'more–than-representational' one. Proposing the term more-than-representational as an alternative to the term non-representational, Lorimer (2005:84) claims that what matters most in the 'more-than' is 'multifarious, open encounters in the realm of practice'. In the context of this inquiry, a more–than-representational account of teacher professional learning accommodates traditional, human-centred views of knowledge whereby individuals are thought to mentally process symbols or representations (the image of the 'reflective teacher' might be brought to mind) *and* poses a challenge to these views by emphasising the participatory role that material entities such as objects and affects play in knowledge production. It affords a practice-based perspective on professional learning in which both people and materials *participate* and through this participation create effects (e.g. knowledge, learning).

The chapter is organized into three substantive sections. In the next section, I draw largely on the educational literature to sketch some modes of understanding teacher professional learning as a field of study. I follow this sketch with a summary of two broad patterns of this learning, termed here the representational and the relational. These patterns derive from the theoretical vocabulary of NRT and ANT and from empirical data collected on processes of teacher professional learning. As Sorensen (2012:719) has it, 'practice research implies a very specific theoretically guided methodology, which, like any other approach, contributes to shaping its findings'. In the section Learning Assemblages: Teacher Learners at Work, a national empirical study tracing the relationship between the development of professional standards for teaching geography in Australian schools and teacher professional learning is outlined, and details describing the empirical methods used to collect data for it are given. Two empirical examples of practices of teacher knowing and learning apparent in the key contexts in which the study was set, and the patterns that form in these practices, are presented. In the Conclusions, the implications of these examples for re-thinking teacher professional learning are drawn out and the significance of the contribution of thinking learning along more than representational lines is discussed.

What counts as professional learning?

Tale 1 – Learning as growth in representational knowledge

Learning can be defined minimally as 'growth in knowledge' (Sorensen 2009). According to cognitivist approaches to professional learning, this growth is located in the *individual* professional, or prospective professional. Knowledge has a definite form (e.g. theory, standards of professional practice) that is substantially independent of and prior to the mental ability used by this professional to acquire it. 'Knowledge is understood as mental, and practice is irrelevant for knowledge achievement' (Sorensen 2009:177–178). This model of professional learning comes out of a *representational* epistemology wherein 'knowledge is understood to represent or "stand for" aspects of a reality that is somehow separate from the knowledge "itself". This applies regardless of whether knowledge is understood as a "picture" or a "construction" of reality' (Osberg 2009:v). Professional learning is taken to involve 'the acquisition of something, such as a particular skill, fact, competency, or capacity or its internalization (something external is brought within the individual) (Lattuca 2002:718).

Tale 2 – Learning as participating in the practices of a social group

My second tale defines learning as increasingly skilled participation in the practices of a social group. Teacher learning involves the construction of new knowledge through the interaction of what teachers already know and believe and the ideas, events, and activities with which they come in contact. 'It is the interactive co-construction of knowledge between teachers reflecting on their own practice, in relation to existing knowledge/research, which is considered most valuable' (Hardy 2010:716). Going beyond traditional psychological perspectives of mind, this *situated* or *sociocultural* approach to learning takes thinking and learning to be mediated and distributed – 'not contained within individual minds, but rather distributed across persons, tools, and learning environments' (Leander *et al.* 2010:330). It represents the contemporary view of teacher professional learning which, in the educational literature, centres on human individuals coming together in community by means of: practitioner inquiry and teacher research; shared sense-making and collaborative engagement; peer networks; and inquiry communities and professional learning communities (DuFour and Eaker 1998; Levine 2010; Campbell and Groundwater-Smith 2010; McArdle and Coutts 2010; Cochran-Smith and Lytle 2009; Stoll and Seashore 2007; Berry *et al.* 2006). The focus of inquiry shifts from the individual to individuals-in-context.

The notion of learning as skilled participation in the practices of a social group assumes that learning is an outcome of social interaction and that the practice of participation is an exclusively human one. In line with Tale 1 above, a *representationalist* view of the world informs this account of (teacher) learning. While learning is mediated by material tools and learning environments, and material tools are constitutive parts of learning, the assumption is made that meaning and matter are separate. 'Mediational means ... are developed and used by individuals and groups for different purposes. ... We appropriate them so that we may participate in the particular practices of our culture' (Lattuca 2002:715). Material mediation (here, tools and representations), *supports* human problem-solving (Katic *et al.* 2009). Altogether, knowledge and learning are confined to a human/social world.

Tale 3 – Learning as assemblages of knowledge practice

In this, the final and more sociomaterial tale, knowledge and learning demonstrate the characteristics of an *assemblage*. As Anderson and McFarlane (2011:125) claim, 'the most obvious reference points for assemblage as a concept include an "after" actor–network theory literature (Latour 2005; Hetherington and Law 2000) and the emphasis in Deleuze and Guattari on the event of agencement' – 'a process of *connecting*, gerund rather than noun' (Bradley *et al.* 2012:142, original emphasis). In an actor–network rendering, the term assemblage is often used to emphasise emergence and indeterminacy, rather than fixed arrangements. Thus, Law (2004:42) describes the concept of assemblage as 'a process of bundling, of assembling ... in which the elements put together are not fixed in shape, do not belong to a larger pre-given list but are constructed at least in part as they are entangled together'. In any assemblage account, attention is given at one and the same time to sociality – for example, the social negotiation of meaning and knowledge that teachers enter into when engaged in professional learning – and materiality – the specific relationships between bundled entities, for example, how the spaces and places in which this negotiation takes place act on and *participate in* this learning. For Anderson and McFarlane (2011:124), 'assemblages are composed of heterogeneous elements that may be human and non-human, organic and inorganic, technical and natural'.

Thinking in an assemblage frame, we are impelled to give attention to heterogeneous elements and *how* they assemble, reassemble and disassemble, as relations take hold, or not. A *relational* view of the world informs this account of (teacher professional) learning. The focus is not on the learning subject (teacher professionals) as a result of an *a priori* assumption of a separation of matter from meaning, the object from the subject (Edwards 2010); it is on *associations*, or *connections*, or *relations* through which matter and meaning, object and subject co-emerge. This co-emergence is well illustrated in the example of new arrangements of teacher learning (e.g. learning to team teach) that are discernible in new arrangements of learning environments (e.g. open, 'flexible' spaces in architecturally re-modelled schools) (Mulcahy Forthcoming). Teacher learning achieves its form as a consequence of the relations in which it is located and enacted; here, in and through relations among teachers, their take-up of the pedagogic potential of new learning spaces and these spaces *qua* spaces. The scholarly focus shifts away from 'the human as a natural source of agency' (Schraube and Sørensen 2013:8).

A more-than-representational account

In a more-than-representational account of learning, it is assumed that what learning *is* depends on how participants in it accomplish it as a practice. After the work of Pickering (2008) and Emirbayer (1997), I call upon two disparate styles of reasoning, termed here 'representational' and 'relational', towards arguing that radically different, but not necessarily competing, versions of professional learning exist and that, while in the educational literature, a representational framing predominates, this learning can, with profit, be thought relationally. In a *representational* rendering of knowledge, the assumption is made that knowledge is produced exclusively by human agents and that these agents have the ability to separate themselves from the world such that 'the material, embodied and quality-full' nature of it can be ignored (Macknight 2011:457).

Grounded in a *relational* view of knowledge and learning, the broad commitment of this chapter is to relational reasoning or, as Thrift (2004:59) has it, a different model of what thinking is. It takes its inspiration from the shared concern in NRT and ANT with material practices. Each is characterized as *relational materialism*, that is, non-dualist: material and social relations are not naturally different in kind. An ontology that is relational (rather than essentialist) is in play affording the possibility of researching 'the human as relationally configured with whatever is present together with her or him in specific situations' (Sorensen 2013:127). Reasoning in a relational frame allows one to grasp disparate categories such as human and non-human, meaning and matter and representational practice and non-representational practice 'together', without erasing one or the other. Each of these categories is taken to be implicated in the other. Allegorically, it is 'like the silence that is the necessary background to speech but which also withdraws when speech expresses itself and yet is always present as a supportive absence' (Cooper 2005:1692). While not refusing representation *per se*, this reasoning challenges the idea of representation as mediation (see again Tale 2); rather, representations *take part* in events. What this means for present purposes is teacher learning is not a matter of what a teacher learner does but what provides this learner with their learning, what puts it into effect – among other things, representational practice (e.g. reflections on practice) and non-/more-than-representational practice (e.g. bodily and material processes such as affective encounters in practice). All in all, under NRT and ANT, teacher learning is the performance (practice, doing) of a specific learning assemblage.

The project in question: data and methods

Funded under the Australian Research Council Linkage Grant scheme, the study from which the data described below are drawn was concerned to trace the relationship between the development of professional standards for teaching geography in Australian schools and teacher professional learning. The first empirical phase of the project entailed studying what accomplished geography teaching *is* by documenting what geography teachers, who are deemed accomplished, *do*. Data were sourced from teachers and students via video-recordings of accomplished teaching, with identification of accomplished teachers being made by way of purposeful sampling, using various criteria, including reputation for accomplishment within the disciplinary field. The video recordings of classrooms were supplemented with post-lesson video-stimulated interviews with students and the teacher. Altogether, 11 case studies (22 lessons altogether) were conducted in eight schools (government and non-government; metropolitan and non-metropolitan) in three major Australian states. The second empirical phase of the project sought to study the process of developing a set of standards for the accomplished teaching of school geography and the teacher learning of the teachers who took part in this development. It involved the conduct of teacher panel meetings (focus groups) in five Australian states. Here, panels of practising geography teachers (64 teachers altogether) reviewed video excerpts from the video-recordings made in the first phase of the project and a sub-sample of these teachers (41 altogether) responded individually to a series of semi-structured interview questions designed to elicit their experience of standards development work and any professional learning that formed part of this work.

The data 'worked' below are drawn from the *two key empirical contexts* of the study, teacher panel meetings and school classrooms. Initially, a composite account is made of the 41 interviews conducted with teachers regarding their learning as a result of their participation in the *project panel work*. Subsequently, processes of professional learning *as classroom teaching* are traced. I acknowledge that should other contexts of the study (e.g. the project website on which materials are available for purposes of teacher professional learning; see: http://www. geogstandards.edu.au/), or other instances of this learning (e.g. other case material) be selected for analysis, other forms of learning assemblage would, in all likelihood, present.

Learning assemblages: teacher learners at work

Enactment 1 – Learning as reflecting: 'If one doesn't reflect, one doesn't learn'

Teacher learning in the context of geography teachers getting together in a small (focus) group as part of a research project is a matter of assembling knowledge through *sharing* experiences, ideas and feelings about accomplished teaching and *reflecting* on these. Critically, this exploration occurs away from the classroom, or, more materially, is channelled through images of fellow teachers' classrooms (video case material). Accordingly, and as I go on to argue, teacher learning presents as *about* practice. A *representationalist* patterning of learning appears with representations presenting as *reflections* on an *a priori* order of teaching practice. A small number of responses to the interview question, 'What learning took place as a result of working with colleagues at the panel meetings? Can you identify three things that you learned?', has been selected to give a sense of the participating teachers' views:

Firstly it's great just to be working with other Geographers, the passion they actually have. … It's great just to listen, because a lot of the time you're thinking 'I do this, I do that, but how can I get that to work?' and it's those little things that really help, and I suppose it's more the enthusiasm to keep on going for it as well.

It's been great just to reflect on all the various aspects of what it is to be an accomplished teacher; often you just don't sit down and think about it, as I was saying before, so that's been good. Whether I have gone away and actually changed anything as a result of these meetings, I may have done it subconsciously, but I haven't gone away thinking I must do that now because of what I remembered, that hasn't happened. But it may have happened on a different level; I may have been more aware of doing things better because of what I have been doing here.

You always learn that other ways and approaches of doing things just get mentioned almost incidentally.

Nearly all Geographers get on together, there's something about Geographers, that we have this perspective, although there is not many degrees of separation between us which is a starting point, but we are all kind of interested in the world and interested in travel and interested in other people and what's going on, so even though we may not be the world's best friends, there is always plenty to talk about and plenty of common ground and I kind of like that about Geographers.

I think viewing the video clip and X's lesson, that provided a lot of opportunities for me to think about what I do in the classroom, and the discussion that occurred after, even more so, in terms of my reflecting on learning, and the fact that, at the end, he was reflecting on his teaching, on his lesson, what the kids learnt, or didn't learn. Because I would say that's a critical element of teaching; if one doesn't reflect, one doesn't learn.

I think it really reinforced the collaborative and collegiate nature of this subject when you get a group of passionate Geography teachers, you get a group of people that want to keep learning and that want to share their ideas, and so for me personally, I just enjoy bouncing ideas off other Geography teachers and hearing what particularly young Geography teachers are doing, seeing their ideas and hearing about it. That's something that you could never get sick of doing I think as a teacher.

Commonality of understanding of Geography and Geography teaching I think is really important; it's been very reinforcing. The breadth of experience of other teachers, just listening to their ideas and the way that they've approached things, I think is also really important and that's why networks are also absolutely vital. And the importance of professional development in creating a better teacher. I think those would be the three things.

I always enjoy talking about what we're doing with different people. Again with that reflection, I guess being with people who are at all different stages of their career as well was really good and learning how to use a meta language a little bit more.

The most useful thing for me was to meet with some other key Geographic professionals that think about the sorts of issues that we're all dealing with in our teaching every day, and trying to grapple with what Geography is and what makes a good Geographer, and that's been great.

There was an affirmation I think in terms of what we do, you know, accomplished teaching in geography, anyway.

I always enjoy talking about what we're doing with different people. Again with that reflection, I guess being with people who are at all different stages of their career as well was really good and learning how to use a meta language a little bit more.

> Commonality of understanding of Geography and Geography teaching I think is really important; it's been very reinforcing. The breadth of experience of other teachers, just listening to their ideas and the way that they've approached things, I think is also really important and that's why networks are also absolutely vital. And the importance of professional development in creating a better teacher. I think those would be the three things particularly.

Whether an imagined or actual community, it is clear from the comments that teacher learning is a matter of teachers getting together and having 'plenty to talk about and plenty of common ground'. The labour of teacher learning appears to lie within teachers as a collective group, reflecting the contemporary view of teacher professional learning which is framed in terms of participation in the practices of a social group (see in particular McArdle and Coutts 2010). 'The most useful thing for me was to meet with some other key Geographic professionals'. Teacher learning is a matter of immersion in and engagement with the geographic community through manifestly *human* processes of *meaning-making* – reflection, thinking, talking and listening: 'I just enjoy bouncing ideas off other Geography teachers'. It involves the construction of new understandings, or the extension of existing understandings, through the interaction of what is already known and believed about accomplished geography teaching with the ideas and activities proffered at the panel meetings.

Epistemologically, this means that 'the "action" is *not* in the bodies, habits, practices of the individual or the collective (and even less in their surroundings) but rather in the ideas and meanings cited by and projected onto those bodies, habits, practices and behaviours (and surroundings)' (Anderson and Harrison 2010:5, original emphasis) – 'I think viewing the video clip and X's lesson, that provided a lot of opportunities for me to think about what I do in the classroom, and the discussion that occurred after, even more so, in terms of my reflecting on learning'. In these data, the discourse and practice of reflection is paramount: 'If one doesn't reflect, one doesn't learn'. A teacher learning assemblage is in place and this assemblage works to make representational practices (reflection, viewing, discussion) a priority.

Enactment 2 – Learning as encountering: 'Something pretty big has happened and I couldn't ... not talk about it today'

My second data story concerns a video-recording of *classroom teaching* within a secondary school in which a Year 8 geography class is being introduced by its teacher, Simone, to river processes. Here, teacher learning presents, without prior notice, *from* practice. The trope 'learning as encountering' is used to refer to processes of professional learning that are unplanned, uncertain and indeterminate. In line with non-representational theories, the term encountering is 'marked by an attention to events and the new potentialities for being, doing and thinking that events may bring forth' (Anderson and Harrison 2010:19, original emphasis). Introducing the lesson thus: 'We're going to start looking at river landforms and the way rivers work in erosion, deposition and transportation', Simone's stated intention for it is to build (representational) knowledge about the workings of rivers in preparation for a forthcoming field trip to a river. Five or so minutes into the lesson however, she stops and says: 'Before I start though ... something pretty big has happened and I couldn't ... not talk about it today'. Showing a digital image of Burma, she proceeds to hold an extended class discussion about the impact of a tropical cyclone, Cyclone Nargis, which, as reported worldwide earlier in the day, has devastated southwestern Burma. Referring to this discussion as 'my little quick introduction', she concludes it thus:

> I just couldn't come today and not talk about this ... it's a big deal. Sixty thousand people, that's a bit of a big deal and Australia is currently tossing up (as to) how much support we should provide. ... That was just my little quick introduction; 'cos we couldn't live without that.

Affected by the scale of the event and the fact that it has occurred in a poor country – 'You live in Burma ... you're a farmer and you don't have much money' – Simone's (seemingly psychological) desire to talk about it means taking a departure from her 'teaching text'. In consequence, I posit, she is learning professionally – learning to enact alternatives to the established representational knowledge practice of school geography – 'looking at river landforms and the way rivers work' – and learning to 'be' somewhat differently as a geography teacher. At the post-lesson interview, Simone comments:

> The first thing I decided to do this morning was to talk about the cyclone. I added that to the (lesson); that to me was important. Because one of the things I have been talking to them about is current events in geography. So, I thought I have to talk about this. ... Talking about the cyclone, that was unexpected for me. I, I, that was just something, I just thought this morning, I've got to talk about this because I get excited. That was for me, a lot of them had not put that all together before. And, you can tell with that class when most of them are listening because they lean forward. There's a few boys in there specially who used to lean right forward and that sort of thing and get involved.

Cyclone Nargis does not serve as a *sign* or a *signal* for Simone to teach differently as perhaps 'hearing what particularly young Geography teachers are doing, seeing their ideas and hearing about it' (Enactment 1) could be claimed to do; rather it puts learning into effect through the 'push' of an unsettling event. This push concerns affects. 'Defined as the property of the active outcome of an encounter', affect 'takes the form of an increase ... in the ability of the body and mind alike to act' (Thrift 2008:178).

For Anderson and Harrison (2010:16–17), 'it is often through affect that relations are interrupted, changed or solidified'. In the case under consideration, these changed relations are a matter of multiple and contradictory practices – teacher decision 'to talk about the cyclone', unexpected talking about the cyclone, the planned conduct of a geography lesson, the unplanned teaching into a geographic event, other geographic events, teacher excitement, listening students, bodies leaning forward and getting involved, and so on. While styling the decision to talk about the cyclone as a matter of *rational* curricular *choice* – 'I added that ... because one of the things I have been talking to them about is current events in geography' – something other than the individualized subject-of-will (Davies 2010) – is in play. The felt intensity and hesitancy of: 'I've got to talk about this', and, cos we couldn't live without that', and, 'I, I, that was just something, I just thought this morning ... , and the distinction drawn between talking about the cyclone and the lesson 'proper' – 'That was just my little quick introduction' – imply a rupture and a change (learning) of some kind.

Albeit providing a reflective account on learning in the post-lesson interview – 'The first thing I decided to do this morning was to talk about the cyclone. I added that to the (lesson); that to me was important' – the practice of professional learning in which Simone is caught up is not largely a reflective one. The ties that bind are affective: 'I've got to talk about this because I get excited'. Difficult to describe in words, this learning emerges 'from the very matter-ings in which (Simone) engage(s)' (Edwards 2012:532) and which engage her, the 'pretty big' happening of Cyclone Nargis, affects such as excitement at the prospect of teaching into this event and sadness for those whose lives and livelihoods have been lost through it, student involvement in learning through discussion and the material process of bodies leaning forward as well as of digital technologies. Teacher professional learning is co-produced amid a disparate mix of elements.

Conclusions

Established accounts of teacher professional learning tend to rely upon a version of representation in which the world and the learner are held apart. A more-than-representational account, by contrast, puts learner and world back together, making each available to the other. As Carolan (2008:412) has it, while having a story to tell, 'representations tell only part of the story'. Teacher professional learning occurs in 'the thick of things, in the intersection of the human and the nonhuman' (Pickering 2008:3). This is clearly the case in Simone's story in which a pedagogic event and a cyclonic event 'collide'. Teacher learning (and student learning too) emerges through practices that *entangle* meaning and matter: 'I just couldn't come today and not talk about this (cyclone)'. It is also the case in the first data story; however, here, the socio-material reality of knowledge production is blackboxed (Sorensen 2012:733). Thus, the samples of work brought along by teachers to the panel meetings are not 'matter-ings' in which these teachers engage; they are products of human endeavour: 'It was really good to see the two colleagues that produced the sample work from their classrooms'.

Teacher learning primarily concerns the practical: contingently composed of social, textual and material practices of knowledge production, different practices *do* this learning and, indeed, *are* this learning. Along with other entities such as established discourses of teacher learning (reflective practice), the teacher panel meetings of the first data story bring a *representational* reality of teacher learning into effect. This learning is learning *about* teaching. It does not necessarily take teacher learners close to teaching practice – 'Whether I have gone away and actually changed anything as a result of these meetings, I may have done it subconsciously, but I haven't gone away thinking I must do that now because of what I remembered, that hasn't happened'. These learners emerge as reflective practitioners, albeit engaged collaboratively in learning. In the classroom setting of the second data story whereby a practising teacher is imputed to be enacting both teaching and learning, this learning presents as *materialized*; as *co-affective* and *co-embodied* – 'You can tell with that class when most of them are listening because they lean forward'. Importantly, it is also of consequence (matter-able): "cos we couldn't live without that'. Far from a reflective practitioner, the teacher-learner emerges as interventionist; acting *with* and *from* events; looking ethically, and perhaps politically, to shape the course of events: 'Sixty thousand people, that's a bit of a big deal and Australia is currently tossing up (as to) how much support we should provide'. Ethics is immanent to the concrete practices–matter-ings – that comprise *relational* learning. I posit that this version of teacher professional learning provides an enlarged sense of who it serves and what it stands for. It is an accomplishment that binds people (teacher, students) and the thing world (Thrift 2008:10), making each available, and also answerable, to the other: 'I just couldn't come today and not talk about this'. To examine how teacher learning is accomplished through the concrete practices of relationality is to 'orient toward new conceptual, and, with this, ethical territories of inquiry' (Michael and Rosengarten 2012:13). It is also to challenge the self-evidence of perspectives on this learning which characterize contemporary education and perhaps, the socio-political context for education in which matters of fact and metrics appear to rule. It raises questions about the limitations of those forms of teacher learning that have been focussed rather too tightly on the symbolic (e.g. teacher shared sense-making, teaching standards) and calls for acknowledgement of the constitutive role that material practice (e.g. bodies, bodily mobility, affective encounters, teachers' practical engagement in learning events) plays in this learning.

Acknowledgement

This chapter is based on a 2012 article 'Thinking teacher professional learning performatively: A socio-material account', *Journal of Education and Work*, 25(1): 121–139, which has been extensively revised.

References

Anderson, B. and Harrison, P. (2010) *Taking-Place: Non-representational theories and geography*, Farnham: Ashgate Publishing Ltd.

Anderson, B. and Mcfarlane, C. (2011) 'Assemblage and geography', *Area*, 43: 124–127.

Barad, K. (2003) 'Posthumanist performativity: Toward an understanding of how matter comes to matter', *Signs*, 28: 801–831.

Berry, A., Clemans, A. and Kostogriz, A. (2006) *Dimensions of Professional Learning: Professionalism, practice and identity*, Rotterdam: Sense Publishers.

Bradley, B., Sumpsion, J., Stratigos, T. and Elwick, S. (2012) 'Baby events: Assembling descriptions of infants in family day care', *Contemporary Issues in Early Childhood*, 13: 141–153.

Campbell, A. and Groundwater-Smith, S. (eds) (2010) *Connecting Inquiry and Professional Learning in Education: International perspectives and practical solutions*, London: Routledge.

Carolan, M. (2008) 'More-than-representational knowledge/s of the countryside: How we think as bodies', *Sociologia Ruralis* 48: 408–422.

Cochran-Smith, M. and Lytle, S.L. (2009) *Inquiry as Stance: Practitioner research for the next generation*, New York, Teachers' College Press.

Cooper, R. (2005) 'Relationality', *Organization Studies*, 26: 1689–1710.

Davies, B. (2010) 'The implications for qualitative research methodology of the struggle between the individualised subject of phenomenology and the emergent multiplicities of the poststructuralist subject: The problem of agency', *Reconceptualizing Educational Research Methodology*, 1: 54–68.

Dufour, R. and Eaker, R. (1998) *Professional Learning Communities at Work*, Alexandria, VA: Association for Supervision and Curriculum Development (ASCD).

Edwards, R. (2010) 'The end of lifelong learning: A post-human condition', *Studies in the Education of Adults*, 42: 5–17.

Edwards, R. (2012) 'Theory matters: Representation and experimentation in education', *Education Philosophy and Theory*, 44: 522–534.

Emirbayer, M. (1997) 'Manifesto for a relational sociology', *American Journal of Sociology*, 103: 281–317.

Fenwick, T. and Edwards, R. (2010) *Actor–Network Theory in Education*, London: Routledge.

Groundwater-Smith, S. and Mockler, N. (2009) *Teacher Professional Learning in an Age of Compliance: Mind the gap (professional learning and development in schools and higher education)*, Dordrecht: Springer.

Hardy, I. (2010) 'Teacher learning: A call to complexity', *Discourse: Studies in the Cultural Politics of Education*, 31: 713–723.

Hetherington, K. and Law, J. (2000) 'After networks', *Environment and Planning D: Society and Space* 18: 127–132.

Katic, E.K., Hmelo-Silver, C.E. and Weber, K.H. (2009) 'Material mediation: Tools and representations supporting collaborative problem solving discourse', *International Journal of Teaching and Learning in Higher Education*, 21: 13–24.

Larsen, M.A. (2010) 'Troubling the discourse of teacher centrality: A comparative perspective', *Journal of Education Policy*, 25: 207–231.

Latour, B. (2005) *Reassembling the Social: An introduction to actor–network-theory*, Oxford and New York: Oxford University Press.

Lattuca, L.R. (2002) 'Learning interdisciplinarity: Sociocultural perspectives on academic work', *The Journal of Higher Education*, 73: 711–739.

Law, J. (2004) *After Method: Mess in social science research*, London and New York, Routledge.

Law, J.(2007) 'Pinboards and books: Juxtaposing, learning, and materiality', in D. Kritt and L.T. Winegar (eds) *Education and Technology: Critical perspectives, possible futures*, Lanham, MA: Lexington Books.

Law, J. (2009) 'Actor–network theory and material semiotics', in B.S. Turner (ed.) *The New Blackwell Companion to Social Theory*. 3rd ed. Chichester and Malden, MA: Wiley-Blackwell.

Leander, K.M., Phillips, N.C. and Taylor, K.H. (2010) 'The changing social spaces of learning: Mapping new mobilities', *Review of Research in Education*, 34: 329–394.

Levine, T. (2010) 'Tools for the study and design of collaborative teacher learning: The affordances of different conceptions of teacher community and activity theory', *Teacher Education Quarterly*, 37: 109–130.

Lorimer, H. (2005) 'Cultural geography: The busyness of being "more than representational"', *Progress in Human Geography*, 29: 83–94.

Macknight, V. (2011) 'Maths teaching methods: Relational abstracting as a hidden metaphysics', *Science as Culture*, 20: 455–470.

Mcardle, K. and Coutts, N. (2010) 'Taking teachers' continuous professional development (CPD) beyond reflection: Adding shared sense-making and collaborative engagement for professional renewal', *Studies in Continuing Education*, 32: 201–215.

Michael, M. and Rosengarten, M. (2012) 'Introduction – Medicine: Experimentation, politics, emergent bodies', *Body & Society*, 18: 1–17.

Mulcahy, D. (Forthcoming) 'Re/assembling spaces of learning in Victorian government schools: Policy enactments, pedagogic encounters and practical politics', *Discourse: Studies in the Cultural Politics of Education*.

Mulcahy, D. and Aberton, H. (2008) Embodied practices: Enacting experiential learning in classroom and community settings. Available: http://services.eng.uts.edu.au/userpages/brucem/public_html/icel2/1/icel/Papers/78_Paper.pdf

Osberg, D. (2009) '"Enlarging the space of the possible" around what it means to educate and be educated', *Complicity: An International Journal of Complexity and Education*, 6: iii–ix.

Pickering, A. (2008) 'New ontologies', in A. Pickering, and K. Guzik (eds) *The Mangle in Practice: Science, society, and becoming*, Durham and London: Duke University Press.

Saito, H. (2010) 'Actor–network theory of cosmopolitan education', *Journal of Curriculum Studies*, 42: 333–351.

Schraube, E. and Sørensen, E. (2013) 'Exploring sociomaterial mediations of human subjectivity', *Subjectivity*, 6: 1–11.

Sørensen, E. (2009) *The Materiality of Learning*, Cambridge: Cambridge University Press.

Sørensen, E. (2012) 'The mind and distributed cognition: The place of knowing in a maths class', *Theory & Psychology*, 22: 717–737.

Sørensen, E. (2013) 'Human presence: Towards a posthumanist approach to experience', *Subjectivity*, 6: 112–129.

Stoll, L. and Seashore, L.K. (2007) *Professional Learning Communities: Divergence, depth and dilemmas*, Maidenhead: McGraw-Hill/Open University Press.

Thrift, N. (2004) 'Intensities of feeling: Towards a spatial politics of affect', *Geografiska Annaler: Series B, Human Geography*, 86: 57–78.

Thrift, N. (2008) *Non-representational theory: Space, politics, affect*, London and New York: Routledge.

White, S., Bloomfield, D. and Le Cornu, R. (2010) 'Professional experience in new times: Issues and responses to a changing education landscape', *Asia-Pacific Journal of Teacher Education*, 38: 181–193.

Chapter 5

Surfacing the multiple

Diffractive methods for rethinking professional practice and knowledge

Davide Nicolini and Bridget Roe

In this chapter, we argue that professional knowledge is necessarily singular and multiple. We add that this is an inherent characteristic of professional knowledge heightened by recent developments. Our point of departure is that practical knowledge is over-determinate by nature: multiple and often dissonant causes, forces, histories intersect at the point where practice is accomplished. In the process, the adoption of a given *modus operandi* leads to the deferral and suppression of all the possible alternatives. In this sense, the ideal of professional practice as a stable, coherent, bounded phenomenon is largely a myth and a convenient fiction that is part and parcel of the process of normalization and disciplining that is inherent in professionalization. To become a professional means both expanding and constraining one's repertoire of conducts. This is because on the one hand, becoming a professional allows one to expand the possibilities of action (i.e. 'what to do next') by tapping into the repertoire of actions developed by former members and sedimented in the professional community's collective experience. On the other hand, joining a profession means observing certain canons and norms and submitting to the profession's authority – something that automatically limits what is do-able, say-able and often thinkable (Foucault's disciplinary project).

This unexplored multiplicity has particular implications for the identity formation of the novice practitioner who could wonder what is being transmitted during interactions with role models and mentors. Tapping this multiplicity therefore poses both a theoretical and practical problem. Finding a way to expand the possibility of action is in fact a critical step towards realizing the 'post-modern professional' (Scanlon 2011a).

In this chapter, we suggest that one way of doing so is through the process of self-confrontation generated by the 'Interview to the Double' (ITTD) technique. The ITTD is a methodological device that helps practitioners come up with a rich description of their own practice with which they can then be confronted. The process of generating an ITTD and feeding it back to professionals exposes the inherent multiplicity of practice so that it can be appreciated by the practitioners themselves. The process is thus a powerful research tool but is also a way to generate diffraction and, under the right conditions, support the expansion of the practical understandings and options for action. A diffractive methodology is useful as it draws attention to difference in what might be otherwise conceived to be homogeneous practice. Our argument is illustrated by examples drawn from a study conducted among midwife mentors in the UK.

The singular *and* multiple nature of professional knowledge

Stanley Fish once argued that relativism is a position that one can entertain but not occupy (Fish 1980:319). In real life, faced with urgent and pressing problems, practitioners must enact a specific course of conduct and perform a specific action. In other words, faced with the practical concern of 'what to do next', practitioners – unlike academics and other detached observers – cannot escape making choices. Practice is thus inherently singular at the moment (or point) of its accomplishment.

The argument of course is not new and has been made before. Heidegger (1929/1996), for example, uses the expression 'ready-to-hand' (*zuhanden*) and 'present-to-hand' (*vorhanden*) to contrast these two modes of encountering the world. *Ready-to-hand* describes the condition of practitioners immersed in a world of immediate and present practical concerns, i.e. things that they care about and they want to take care of. By contrast, *present-to-hand* captures the detached observer's 'view from nowhere' that is enshrined in traditional philosophy. One of Heidegger's main concerns in his writing was to recover and reaffirm the precedence of the former over the latter. Bourdieu (1980:82) also emphasized the unitary nature of real-time action when he suggests that the practitioner's view is fundamentally different from that of the spectators given that the latter can survey things in their totality. Practitioners in fact act 'on the spot, in the twinkling of an eye, in the heat of the moment, that is, in conditions that exclude distance, perspective, detachment and reflexion'. In Schatzki's view, practices 'inexorably' constitute conditions of life and worlds (1996:115).[1]

This view – which suggests that real-time practice is inherently singular at the point of accomplishment – co-exists with another view that characterizes practical action (and specifically professional activity) as inherently multiple. The latter is implicit in the work of scholars who studied the process whereby practitioners in general – and professionals in particular – are socialized in their activity. Building on Mead's intuition that individuals develop their identity and acquire mastery through interaction with a number of significant others (Mead 1934), authors such as Markus and Nurius (1986), and Ibarra (1999) suggest that becoming a professional entails experimenting with a variety of possible, provisional professional selves. Possible selves direct attention to certain role models, help newcomers to choose what to do in certain situations and set tacit standards against which they judge their own conduct, for example, 'Did I act like the person I want to become?' (Markus and Nurius 1986). Provisional selves, on the other hand, are new and makeshift identities that newcomers use, especially during career transitions (Ibarra 1999). These are rehearsed and refined with experience until they consolidate as the main way in which people define themselves in their professional role (Ibarra 1999:767). In both cases, becoming a professional entails developing and putting to the test a repertoire of actions that set the horizon within which actual activity is accomplished.

While entertaining and experimenting with possible selves has been typically associated with socialization and role transition, a growing number of scholars suggest that this condition applies to all practitioners all the time and does not stop when socialization has ended. The point has been comprehensively elaborated by Clot (1999) and the French school of the 'Clinique de l'activité'. Clot builds on Vygotsky's (1997) view that 'At every moment the individual is full of unrealized possibilities' and that action requires resolving the conflict between multiple possible actions at the crossroads of multiple conflicting horizons (70). Clot argues that Vygotsky's view requires that we distinguish between the activity that is realistically possible (*le réel de l'activité*) and the activity that is actually carried out in a specific situated scene of action (the realized activity or *activité réalisée*). The latter is in fact only a subset of the former. The activity that is realistically possible also includes 'what is not done, what one tries to do without succeeding … what one wanted to do or could have done, what one thinks it is possible to do somewhere else. To this must be added – a frequent paradox – what one does to avoid doing …' (Clot *et al.* 2001:18).

The real-time accomplishment and realization of professional work thus takes place at the intersection of: a) impersonal prescriptions, routines and rules that define expectation of the organization in terms of task; b) transpersonal influences that carry the historical memory of the practice (often framed in discursive terms) under the guise of a specific professional genre; and c) interpersonal interactions and dialogues with other professionals (Clot and Kostulski 2011). While these conditions frame a specific site for the practitioner to act, they also bracket, suspend or suppress other possibilities: 'the development of the activity that came to dominate is governed by conflicts between concurrent activities that could have accomplished the same task at other costs' (Clot and Kostulski 2011:685). Professional activity is thus inherently singular and multiple. Indeed 'activities which are suspended, thwarted or hindered, and even counter-activities, must be included in the analysis' if we are to make sense of both professional effectiveness and well-being (Clot *et al.* 2001:19).

This Vygotskyian view, which is rooted in a psychological view of professional work, resonates with the work of social scientists from other traditions who also put forward the idea of the plural nature of professional knowledge and identity. Abbot (1988) and Freidson (2001), for example, suggest that professionalism is fundamentally a disciplinary project which – while granting a given group of individuals jurisdiction over a certain body of knowledge and action – also constrains the group's repertoire and discourse. Thus on the one hand, becoming a professional entails expanding the scope of action as a result of socialization and mastery acquisition. On the other hand, it entails eliminating other possible selves to fit in with professional canons. Yet alternative possible selves remain available to practitioners, if only in terms of examples not to be emulated (the 'alter' of the professional ego).

According to other authors, this inherent multiplicity of professional knowledge is amplified by the current historical conditions. Franzak (2002) and Scanlon (2011a), for example, suggest that we increasingly live in a world of negotiated identities where we must continually construct and revise visions of self (Scanlon 2011a:16). This is all the more true for professionals of all sorts. To the extent that professions are faced with the temporalization and relativization of their knowledge base, the weakening of their truth claims, and the 'rebellion of the clients' (Pfadenhauer 2006:568 in Scanlon 2011a), being a professional requires nurturing a repertoire of possible individual identities that need to be not only consciously entertained and nurtured but also carefully and skillfully managed. Developing possible and provisional selves is thus not the preserve of novices and professionals in transition but rather the permanent condition of the post-modern professional (Scanlon 2011a).

In short, while professional practice is inherently singular when it is accomplished (*in actu*, as the Romans used to say), it is also inherently multiple *in potentia*. Producing a coherent and accountable course of action and maintaining a coherent and accountable professional self therefore constitute special types of work. The questions are: how can such multiplicity be unearthed and made visible? How can we capture such work and what are the practical effects and benefits of doing so?

How to surface the multiple nature of professional knowledge

The task of surfacing the inherent multiplicity of professional knowledge poses several methodological and practical problems.

For one thing, work in the early 21st Century requires presenting and sustaining a unified self that meets the legal requirements of accountability. Displaying an unstructured or uncertain or mutable identity is seen as a sign of weakness and even of mental illness. Identity work (that is, the work that goes into creating the appearance of stable and well-bounded identity) thus by definition produces an erasure of multiplicity and transforms the on-going process of identification into a reified image – an identity as something that we possess (Jenkins 1996). Observation alone is thus ineffective as from the 'outside' we can only appreciate the result of the process. In order to unearth this 'parliament of professional selves' and the unrealized possibilities of action that lay behind the activity accomplished in a specific scene of action, we need to produce some form of interruption or breakdown that allows the underlying process to become visible. This can be achieved through some form of self-confrontation, a process that interrupts the continuity of the process of identification by creating distance between practitioners and their perceived 'self-in action' (Clot *et al.* 2001). The process requires a protected (i.e. construed and negotiated) situation or setting where the expectations of modern work conditions are consensually suspended. Presenting the image of a coherent stable and authoritative self is in fact something that is expected as a matter of fact in modern workplaces. Interrupting this process in natural settings is extremely difficult as it generates strong resistance and can cause very strong reactions as Garfinkel's student quickly discovered (see Garfinkel 1967).

Finally, even when practitioners are convinced of the benefits of perceiving themselves as post-modern professionals, the problem is that such multiplicity is usually invisible to practitioners. Switching between possible professional selves is a form of tacit knowledge that practitioners may acknowledge but seldom articulate. As Suchman (1987) convincingly argued, work becomes invisible with distance and members systematically disregard the type of work they do not see or that they take for granted. Practitioners understand and apply the term 'work' in relation to their professional activities in a very selective manner and hence try to tap into the plurality of their expertise through their accounts by undertaking a specific selection and deletion process. In other words, practitioners cannot see what they are blind to and asking them to take an introspective stance and look harder 'inside themselves' may be ineffective, frustrating and even seen as an utter waste of time.

The interview to the double

One method that has shown promise in overcoming the issues discussed above is the 'interview to the double' technique (Oddone and Briante 1977; Gherardi 1995; Nicolini 2009). Originating in the 1970s, the interview to the double (ITTD) is a projective technique rooted in the Marxist tradition (Nicolini 2009) which was first developed by the Italian work psychologists Oddone and colleagues in 1977. During training workshops in a factory setting, the ITTD successfully helped to uncover some of the more hidden aspects of local practices that were being transmitted to novice workers. Whilst helping workers to increase awareness of their own expertise and its bargaining value vis-à-vis the management (Oddone and Briante 1977:127), the ITTD also allowed the workers to reflect upon and enhance the understanding of their own practice, uncovering new possibilities of action that were available to them (Nicolini 2009). The developmental aspect of the technique was later advanced by a group of French ergonomists (Clot 1999; Clot et al. 2001; Clot and Faita 2000) who employed it as a method of changing and improving work practices within the approach of the Activity Clinic (Nicolini 2009).

Rather than focusing on the person introspectively, the ITTD encourages participants to position themselves 'outside of their body'. This is achieved by instructing the double (the researcher) to take their place at work, on a day when mentoring a student and in particular, to avoid being found out (Nicolini 2009:196). In practice, the ITTD requires interviewees to imagine that they have

a double who will stand in for them at work on the following day. The inter-
viewee-instructor is then asked to provide the necessary detailed instructions
which will ensure that the interviewer-double is not unmasked. This approach
helps practitioners to 'observe' their own practice (Nicolini 2009) and to establish a dialogue with themselves which renders their own personal experience alien.
In so doing, alternative forms of signification can emerge, and the normative
constraints that imprison professional thinking are lifted, so that new possibilities
of action and new ways of being a competent practitioner can emerge.

According to Nicolini (2009), the ITTD is particularly effective in surfacing
the normative dimension of practice, that is, the imperatives behind activity, the
rules and conventions, and moral justifications upheld within a specific local
occupational community. Rather than offering an insight into a presumed inner
self, the ITTD thus brings to the fore the main 'normative and technical regimes
of conduct' (Du Gay 2007:11) regulating the production of professional selves
displayed for all practical purposes. In so doing, it offers the opportunity for practitioners not only to think 'outside the box' but also to appreciate the nature of
the box itself.

Nevertheless there is an important caveat about the use of the ITTD. Although
originally developed to capture practical knowledge in the workplace, it should
not be used as a stand-alone technique (Nicolini 2009). This is due to a need to
build up trust (for this more demanding type of interview) and avoid misunder-
standings over the wording of the monologue. Further, using a 'toolkit' approach
avoids interpreting the phenomena from an *etic* or an outsider's view (Nicolini
2009). The ITTD has thus recently achieved more success by contributing to a
richer understanding during ethnographic studies (e.g. Gherardi 1995; Nicolini
2009, 2011, 2012).

Surfacing multiplicity

In this section, we illustrate the capacity of the ITTD to surface the multiple
nature of professional knowledge and provide insight into the unexpressed professional selves that all practitioners carry with them. We do so by reporting the
results of a study conducted among English midwives. Midwifery constitutes an
interesting case as the profession is located at the intersection of different and
often conflicting world views and some of the 'grand dichotomies of Western
thought' (Weintraub 1997:1).

Reflection at work has become increasingly important for midwives and has
been an integral part of continuous professional development and education
since the 1980s (Philips *et al.* 2002). Indeed, reflection is an implicit requirement
for the annual supervisory meeting and engaging with the process of Post-
Registration Education and Practice (PREP). Learning and socialization could
therefore be argued to be dependent upon reflection. It is expected that midwives
should, after deep reflection, pass on their expertise to novices during supervisory
practice. Yet midwives, when acting as supervisors and mentors, are also expected

to project a very specific professional self that complies with the image of their work carefully nurtured by their professional association. So it may be asked, what is transmitted during novice supervision? How is identity revealed and what is the role that student midwives learn from? What is the specific social scene of action that constitutes their novice supervision?

Method

In our small exploratory study, eight midwives with ten years or more experience were interviewed by the double (the researcher), taking the specific activity of mentoring of student midwives as a focus. Each interview took roughly an hour and yielded a monologue from the participant which was sporadically interspersed with prompts from the 'double' when seeking clarification. Prompting the participant is an important feature of the ITTD, as it encourages the interviewee to instruct in the second person, thus maintaining distance and encouraging reflection throughout the interview (Nicolini 2009). Whilst instructing the double, the midwives frequently closed their eyes when trying to instruct in the second person so that they could better concentrate on articulating their tacit knowledge. This projection serves to stop them merely parroting the instruction manual and avoiding a particular version of events (Nicolini 2009). The ITTD was followed up by a second reflexive interview where the instructions gleaned from the ITTD were discussed. This second self-confrontation interview also lasted between 40 and 60 minutes. Both interviews were tape recorded and transcribed verbatim. The data were analyzed using thematic analysis and any sub-themes were seen as an extension to the analysis, and the data were re-interrogated (Lincoln and Guba 1985).

Instructing the double

The ITTD helped the midwives to articulate their concerns around the transmission of practice during mentoring. The midwives provided a plain description of their work that although not comparable to that of a professional ethnographer (as discussed earlier), is nevertheless much denser than one obtained through traditional semi-structured interviews. Here is an example:

> We have got to the ante-clinic, and you will need to set up your room ... you will find that there is ... there's a trolley with antenatal records, information leaflets ... blood forms, and you will need to wheel that into the room. You will need to set up your equipment to enable you to do your examinations and then if you can, organize your paperwork and your bottles ahead of time for blood taking. Now the student midwife can help you with this but you need to remind her what the bottles are for ... And she will need to be reminded, in case she forgets that a urine sample is always taken and sent off for microscopy.

The ITTD gave an insight into how the midwives have come to be who they are at work. Many of their concerns appeared to be linked to authoritative knowledge and indeed, the technical and power regimes they had moved through during their careers. For example, the following excerpt reveals the concerns with following correct procedure:

> I am meticulous about writing records *correctly*, that's always been a point that other people have made. I got pulled up once for not ticking a box, even though there was a great long story about the situation, all the correct protocol was followed …

In general, the responses to the ITTD where characterized by a strong moral tone and there was some evidence that accounts were partially idealized to portray a more harmonious description of the mentoring process. Students for example were often instructed to 'work as a team', although the midwives were clear that the mentoring is strongly unequal and therefore conflicts and incidents like the one described above are very common.

Heroic images of the profession were also often used for the novice's consumption:

> Community midwives don't stop for a break on their way to the visits, in-between and if possible you could maybe pull the car over in a layby for 2 mins to unwrap your sandwiches. It's not ideal [but] … I always do this

One aspect that emerged clearly from the ITTD is that the instruction given to student midwives goes far beyond just clinical practice. Indeed, they learn how to act as midwives and the normative skills involved. Thus, the double was often instructed how to look and act like a midwife, often from the moment of leaving home. An example of this was when one of the midwives asked the double to wear little make-up for work. After prompting, she revealed that this does not reflect local policy but is rather a concern and habit she picked up when a former mentor taught her not to show her sexuality when dealing with vulnerable people.

Overall, the results of the ITTD constituted a rather optimistic and glorified account of practice. While accounts of conflict occurred in the reflective interviews, the general tone was quite assertive. The midwives had presented to the interviewer what they expected a novice should have heard. One in particular gave a strongly normative version of what a midwife should be. This, however, was expected from the ITTD and instead of being seen as a weakness, the very constraints of the ITTD can be used as a platform for producing diffraction (Nicolini 2009). This can be obtained by feeding back the usually stern view of the profession given during the ITTD to the practitioners.

When the microphone goes off

As soon as the voice recorder was switched off, the midwives immediately began to reflect on what they had spoken about. The midwives recognized the stylizations of their accounts, whilst also finding the reflective potential of the ITTD useful and enlightening as a lens through which to zoom in on their tacit practical knowledge. As one of the midwives put it:

> I was quite shocked actually, yes, yeah, because I was amazed how much I talked, and then it got me thinking, I was thinking about what did I say and I didn't say this and I didn't say that … [laugh]

The midwives also recognized how difficult it is for practitioners to speak about their own job and how much of their work becomes invisible to themselves.

> Yes it did because when you, you've been doing a job for a long time you do it almost with your eyes closed and you have your own way of doing things it is sometimes good to have students; students challenge you and you have to explain what you are doing and I always like having a student for that reason.

The mention of the importance of having a student is critical as it reiterates that any form of self-confrontation leads to critical scrutiny. It also suggests that reflection carried out alone is likely to fail as one cannot see what one cannot see.

The self-confrontation

The most interesting aspects of the process emerged when the ITTD was fed back to the interviewees.[2] Once they had got over their surprise and bafflement, the midwives started to recognize that their narratives could have been different and yet still be perfectly plausible:

> I was just really aware that you know, that some things I thought of, I thought I could have said that and I didn't say …

> I thought, then I came back into the car … and I didn't say that and I was just looking at things that I did and I was thinking you just carry on in your own merry way.

The midwives also openly recognized how much their professional identity and practice was speaking through them, without them being fully aware of it:

> No, [laugh] …… no what did I say?

> I'm not aware of [having said it], and part of it was maybe that that was how I was mentored

As soon as they became aware of what identity had spoken through them during their mentoring activity, the midwives were able to articulate different and alternative conducts open to them and to the novices. In the following extract, a midwife, who had previously bowed to authoritative and medicalized knowledge, performs the alternative identity of a more autonomous midwife:

> Do not assume the doctor has got the information … because they don't do any maternity care anymore … they need to be advised of the changes in practice that occur … in fact you will find if you can do this with the student, she can see the importance of a midwife's knowledge base. So she can see it is quite alright for the midwife to discuss on a professional level with the GP, her point of view, for care of the pregnant lady, that's something I have always done.

In another example, after emphasizing the importance of following the protocols during the interview (see the first extract above), the *same* nurse went on to suggest students follow their 'inner voice', a course of action that clearly reflects a form of knowledge that belongs to a very different paradigm of what it means to be a midwife: 'I say to them, listen to your inner voice, you've got that thing that, I call it my 'hum', if I'm going 'hum' I'm not sure, there's something not quite right, listen to that and then act.'

In general, during the self-confrontation all of the midwives openly discussed alternative professional ways of doing and being. This ranged from references to other midwives who they did not wish to emulate – expert midwives from both current and historical contexts – to alternative models of midwifery. Jen, one of the interviewees, talked about her fight to be the holistic type of midwife she had always identified with and her wish not to become '*a clone*' of the medical model of obstetrics. This was voiced through her concerns regarding the spread of the medical model that she hears in students' language and discourse.

Anchoring identity to artifacts

Interestingly, the midwives anchored possible recognizable practices (and professional identities) to objects and artifacts. Three of the midwives mentioned the preferential use of the Pinard stethoscope (a traditional tool, also known as a Pinard[3] horn or fetoscope), a choice which they confirm is driven by a commitment to practising holistic midwifery. One of the midwives explicitly linked the use of this traditional tool (rather than electronic Doppler) to fear of midwives losing the very skills that underlay their professional identification. Another midwife said that she always buys a Pinard stethoscope for her students to remember her by but also because: 'It's yours, it's the tool of the trade and actually says that you know one of the oldest professions going … you're very proud of being a midwife, you tell everybody that you're a midwife'.

Indeed, the above statement suggests that the Pinard stethoscope appears to be a symbolic instrument through which midwives manage their identity as a member of a traditional and expert profession and through which they hope to perpetuate the activity. Although other midwives were more than happy to use the electronic stethoscope to listen to the baby's heart, they knew that the fact that they could also use a Pinard stethoscope made them (and the novice) feel different and unique.

From reflection to diffraction?

Summarizing from the above, professional knowledge-abilities and identities were openly switched during the 'interviews to the double' and a variety of ways of being a midwife (and mentor) became increasingly detectable as result of the self-confrontation. This multiplicity brought to the surface through ITTD-based self-confrontation was visible to both the researcher and the practitioner. As a result, the midwives started narratively performing different professional selves and progressively expanded (at least verbally) the horizon of possible conducts open to them and to their ideal novice. This did not escape the midwives, who clearly explained what happens when one is presented with a representation of one's work: 'I think it made me look ... at what I did and what I'm doing now and I just was thinking – Oh, is that what I do?'.

On the surface the above observation made by the midwife would suggest that the ITTD triggered some form of reflexive practice or reflexive learning (Cotter and Cullen 2012). Reflexive learning is an internally experienced, actively subjective process in which things become apparent as we are 'struck' (Cunliffe 2003:36) and thus 'moved to change our ways of being, talking and acting'(ibid.). As a practice, it entails entering a dialogue with others and 'periodically stepping back to ponder the meaning to self and to others in one's immediate environment about what has recently transpired' (Raelin 2001:11). The aim of different forms of reflexive practice is to provide time and space for 'indwelling' (Cotter and Cullen 2012:234).

We suggest, however, that the ITTD triggers a different, albeit related phenomenon. The self-confrontation does not produce reflection so much as diffraction. As Barad put it: 'A diffractive methodology [is] a practice of reading insights through one another while paying attention to patterns of difference' (including the material effects of constitutive exclusions) (Barad 2011:3).

While the end of both reflexivity and diffraction is to help 'participants unpick the underlying assumptions of the organized contexts in which they manage and work' (Cotter and Cullen 2012:231) this is achieved following two divergent strategies. Reflection and reflexivity are in fact inclined towards articulating the unexplored meanings that are inherent in the practice itself. This attitude stems from the phenomenological origin of the approach, which facilitates the dialogical search for new meaning through 'digging deeper' into what people already do. Diffraction, on the other hand, is 'more attuned to differences' (Haraway 1992:299) and more interested in bringing out the fundamental divergence of practices over time. Diffraction is thus attuned to widening possibilities rather that articulating meaning. The elaboration is dispersive; it multiplies what a practice may be rather than trying to reveal its inner core. In this sense 'diffraction moves from identifying what was present and contained within an interaction to analyzing intra-actions as a process of producing differences' (Keevers and Treleaven 2011:509). The self-confrontation triggered by the ITTD is designed to produce multiple perspectives by introducing a copy that interferes with its original. The diffraction is thus a result of the difference between two representations that should be the same. The shift is not from one stable way of being a midwife to another; rather the multiplicity is left hanging so that it can become a resource for future action. Learning is obtained by grasping multiplicity. Equally, the critical reflexive effect – that is, the appreciation of the social, political and cultural context and the discourses that saturate practice (Cunliffe and Jun 2005)– are obtained from *within* the practice. The distinction between medicalized and non–medicalized discourses in the modern practice of midwifery are manifest in two competing modes of justification, which become transparent to midwives and from which they can learn (Jordan 1989).

Conclusion: which professional will teach me today?

A multiplicity of competing knowledge and abilities co-exist in uneasy tension behind the authoritative normative accounts produced to support the myth of a coherent and bounded professional practice (and practitioner). Acceptance of this fact raises a number of issues and challenges for the process of professional learning.

First, one needs to recognize that the process of mentoring in particular and instruction in general are necessarily situated activities and performances in both the agential and theatrical senses of the term. Teachers, mentors and instructors selectively choose which identity they play out and communicate to novices, although such choice is tacit and often invisible to them. This however presents a further conundrum. Absorbing a practice requires one to accept the authority of certain standards against which one's performance may be judged. One cannot be initiated into a practice without accepting the initial incapacity to judge correctly. As McIntyre put it: 'If, on starting to play baseball, I do not accept that others know better than I when to throw a fast ball and when not, I will never learn to appreciate good pitching (or to hear good music, or to recognize a nice building) let alone pitch' (MacIntyre 1981:190). Performing a univocal, coherent and bounded professional identity for the novice may thus be a myth but this is to some extent a necessary one or at least one that serves a purpose. On the other hand, producing 'clones', as one of our informants put it, is dangerous not only ethically but also practically. Learning to replicate the mentor's habits means that when a student moves into a new context, her practice may not be legitimized by other midwives.

Acknowledging that practice is inherently multiple on several grounds thus requires dealing creatively and often explicitly with these two opposite requirements.

Interestingly enough, we found that some of the midwives in our study were painfully aware of the need to address this issue as well as the problems it spawns. This is because midwives already live in a world of competing bodies of knowledge and fragmented identities. For example, Jen, the midwife mentioned above, cautioned the novice against becoming her clone; indeed she instructed the double thus: 'Say to [the novice] you're not going to try and become a little Jen'. She then proceeded to encourage the novice to adopt fragments of practice from the various experts she would work with and to be selective in terms of whom she may choose to emulate. Susie, another of the interviewees, asked the double to tell the student to adopt her own habits, which are indeed very set patterns of practice justified by her belief about what is right and good. But she also cautioned that midwifery mentors are seen as 'next to God' and therefore asked that the student be explicitly warned not to worry as there are 'no set patterns of practice'; then paused to say that she was aware that the student may feel anxious about contradictory teaching and reflected on the stress and confusion that this may generate. Both midwives thus struggled to combine an awareness of multiplicity with the need to perform univocality. Neither they nor we have a solution on how to strike a balance but our discussion and their comments suggests that the search for the post-modern professional cannot be divorced from the search for the post-modern mentor or instructor.

Second, our discussion and research emphasize the active and proactive role that novices perform and must play as authors of their own socialization. This idea, which is implicit in the notion that novices experiment with provisional selves Ibarra (1999), adds a further layer of complexity to our understanding of the process of professional socialization. While for the (reflexive) teacher the issue is: 'What identity will I perform today?', for the learner the question is: 'Which professional identity will be performed for me today?'. This poses a question that is specular to that discussed above, that is, how and to what extent can novices be exposed to multiplicity without affecting their learning process (and confidence)? How can novices be helped in taking both relativist and non-relativist approaches? Creating the post-modern professional will thus also require delving into the nature of what one might term 'the post-modern novice'.

Third and last, attempting to grasp professional practice in a way that goes beyond individuals' discretionary decision-making, beyond stable communities and given knowledge draws attention to the critical role of tools and materials in both anchoring and displacing professional identity as a stable, coherent and univocal phenomenon.

As we have shown in the foregoing discussion, symbolic and material artifacts often operate as powerful anchors of professional identities (Swidler 2001). While mediating the scene of action, a universe of knowledge and histories of use (Kaptelinin and Nardi 2006), Pinard stethoscopes and *robozos*[4] (and of course classes and books) foster the performance of one specific genre of practice, which in turn is linked to a specific professional identity.

However, tools can also derail, interfere and surface the co-existence of different professional identities. As we have seen, tools such as the ITTD not only reveal the plurality of professional self to the researcher but also act as a diffractional tool for the practitioner. Tools such as the ITTD and other techniques such as video-reflection and the use of movies in the process of socialization (Scanlon 2011b) subvert normative readings and accounts of our everyday practices and thus render one or more alternative courses of action plausible.

Finally, tools may also help to address some of the issues raised above. If handling competing identities in discourse is difficult (after all, we live in a society which still abhors dissonance and conflict) maybe we should turn towards tools. Deliberately equipping novices with tools carrying different identities may help individuals come to terms with professional alternatives and contradictions more effectively than merely exposing them to different discourses.

Notes

1 Of course these authors do not discuss professional knowledge but it is safe to assume that to the extent that professional workers are also practitioners (of a special kind), these principles apply to them as well.
2 In our case, for reasons of time the interview was transcribed and given to the nurses. Clot *et al.* (2001) suggest going through an intermediate step whereby the practitioners are asked to transcribe their interview as this constitutes a powerful trigger for reflection.
3 Named after the Adolphe Pinard, the French physician who invented it in 1895.
4 Note: in Mexico a *robozo* is a shawl or scarf used for various midwifery tasks.

References

Abbot, A. (1988) *The System of Professions*, Chicago: University of Chicago Press.
Barad, K. (2011) 'Erasers and erasures: Pinch's unfortunate 'uncertainty principle', *Social Studies of Science*, 41(3): 1–12.
Bourdieu, P. (1980) *Le Sens Pratique*, Paris: Minuit.
Clot, Y. (1999) *La Fonction Psycholgique du Travail*, Paris: Presses Universitaires de France.
Clot, Y. and Faita, D. (2000) 'Genres et styles en analyse du travail. Concepts et methodes. *Travailler* 6: 7–42.
Clot, Y. and Kostulski, K. (2011) 'Intervening for transforming: The horizon of action in the clinic of activity', *Theory and Psychology*, 21(5): 681–696.
Clot, Y., Faïta, D., Fernandez, G. and Scheller, L. (2001) 'Entretiens en autoconfrontation croisée: une méthode en clinique de l'activité', *Education permanente*, 146: 17–25.
COTTER, R., & CULLEN J 2012. Reflexive Management Learning: An integrative Review and a Conceptual Typology. Human Resource Development Review, 11, 227–253.
Cunliffe, A. L. (2003) 'Reflexive inquiry in organizational research: Questions and possibilities', *Human Relations*, 56(8): 983–1003.
Cunliffe, A. and Jun, J. (2005) 'The need for reflexivity in public administration'. *Administration and Society*, 37(2): 225–242.
Du Gay, P. (2007) *Organising Identity: Persons and organizations after theory*. London: Sage.
Fish, S.E. (1980) *Is There a Text in This Class?: The authority of interpretive communities*, Cambridge, MA and London: Harvard University Press.

Franzak, J.K. (2002) 'Developing a teacher identity: The impact of critical friends practice on the student teacher', *English Education*, 34(4): 258–280.

Freidson, E. (2001) *Professionalism, the Third Logic: On the practice of knowledge*, Chicago: University of Chicago Press.

Garfinkel, H. (1967) *Studies in Ethnomethodology*. Englewood Cliffs, NJ: Prentice Hall.

Gherardi, S. (1995) 'When will he say: "Today the plates are soft"? The management of ambiguity and situated decision-making', *Culture and Organization*, 1(1): 9–27.

Haraway (1992) The Promise of Monsters: a Regenerative Politics for Innapropriate/d Others in Grossberg, L., Nelson, N., Treicler, P. *Cultural Studies*. Routledge New York.

Heidegger, M. (1929/1996) *Being and Time*, Albany: SUNY Press.

Ibarra, H. (1999) 'Provisional selves: Experimenting with image and identity in professional adaptation', *Administrative Science Quarterly*, 44(4), 764–791.

Jenkins, R. (1996) *Social Identity*, London: Routledge.

Jordan, B. (1989) 'Cosmopolitcal obstetrics', *Social Science and Medicine*, 28(9): 925–944.

Kaptelinin, V. and Nardi, B. (2006) *Acting with Technology: Activity theory and interaction design*, Cambridge, MA: MIT Press.

Keevers, L. and Treleaven, L. (2011) 'Organizing practices of reflection: A practice based study', *Management Learning*, 42(5): 505–520.

Lincoln, Y.S. and Guba, E. (1985) *Naturalistic Inquiry*, London: Sage.

MacIntyre, A. (1981) *After Virtue: A study in moral theory* (1st ed.), London: Gerald Duckworth and Co Ltd.

Markus, H. and Nurius, P. (1986) 'Possible selves', *American Psychologist*, 41(9): 954–969.

Mead, G.H. (1934) *Mind, Self and Society*, Chicago: University of Chicago Press.

Nicolini, D. (2009) 'Zooming in and zooming out: Studying practices by switching theoretical lenses and trailing connections', *Organization Studies*, 30(12): 1391–1498.

Nicolini, D. (2011) 'Practice as the site of knowing: Insights from the field of telemedicine'. *Organization Science*, 3(22): 602–620.

Nicolini, D. (2012) *Practice Theory, Work and Organization: An introduction*, Oxford: Oxford University Press.

Oddone, I., Re, A. and Briante, G. (1977) *Esperienza Operaia, Coscienza di Classe e Psicologia del Lavoro*, Turin: Einaudi.

Pfadenhauer, M. (2006) 'Crisis or decline?' *Current Sociology*, 54(4): 565–578.

PHILLIPS, D., FAWNS, R., HAYES, B. 2002. From Personal Reflection to social positioning: the development of a transformational model of professional education in midwifery. Nursing Inquiry, 9, 239–249.

Raelin, J. (2001) 'Public reflection as the basis for learning', *Management Learning*, 32(1): 11–30.

Scanlon, L. (2011a) 'Becoming' a professional', in L. Scanlon (ed.), *'Becoming' a Professional. An interdisciplinary analysis of professional learning* (13–32), London: Springer.

Scanlon, L. (2011b) 'White coats, handmaidens and warrior chiefs: the role of filmic representations in becoming a professional', in L. Scanlon (ed.), *'Becoming' a Professional. An interdisciplinary analysis of professional learning* (109–127), London: Springer.

Schatzki, T. (1996) *Social Practices: A Wittgensteinian approach to human activity and the social*, Cambridge: Cambridge University Press.

Suchman, L. (1987) *Plans and Situated Action: The problem of human machine interaction*, New York: Cambridge University Press.

Swidler, A. (2001) 'What anchors cultural practices', in T.R. Schatzki, K. Knorr-Cetina and E. von Savigny (eds) *The Practice Turn in Contemporary Theory* (74–92), London: Routledge.

Vygotsky, L.S. (1997) *The Collected Works of L. S. Vygotsky: Problems of the theory and history of psychology*, New York: Plenum Press.

Weintraub, J. (1997) 'The theory and politics of the public/private distinction', in J. Weintraub, J. and K. Kumar (eds), *'Public and Private in Thought and practice: Perspectives on a grand dichotomy'* (1–42), Chicago: University of Chicago Press.

Section II

Reconceptualising professional work arrangements

Chapter 6

Nurturing occupational expertise in the contemporary workplace

An 'apprenticeship turn' in professional learning

Alison Fuller and Lorna Unwin

Introduction

If the use of the term 'apprenticeship' in a book about professional learning seems odd, this is because apprenticeship tends to be regarded as an institutional component of national education and training systems. Yet, its original conceptualization as a model for developing and refining occupational expertise (through work-based practice) explains why references to apprenticeship still form part of the vocabulary used by many professionals to describe the way they learn (Fuller and Unwin 2010a, 2010b, 2013). In this chapter, we argue that research in and the organization of and support for early career professional learning would benefit from an 'apprenticeship turn' to enable the development of more overt and robust forms of socio-material support for professionals in contemporary workplaces.

As a model of learning, apprenticeship is formed by the interrelationship of pedagogical, social and institutional characteristics which provide the affordances to enable the apprentice to grow as an individual through contributing to and benefitting from the collective endeavour of the workplace. Thus, apprenticeship embraces the concepts of individual agency and identity, without losing sight of the equally important dimension of context. Using apprenticeship as a lens enables questions to be raised about the extent to which the important role that maturation and socialization play in the formation and refinement of professional expertise is being undermined in two ways. First, early career professionals are entering workplaces where work is increasingly organized as a response to efficiency and competitive imperatives emanating from the wider productive systems within which the workplaces sit. Second, the continued emphasis on a front-loaded model of education and training ignores the need for scaffolding structures within the workplace to support continued professional development.

An 'apprenticeship turn' aligns with the concept of the 'practice turn', which, as Boud (2010:29) has argued, 'gives new respect to and also problematises practice' at a time when long-standing assumptions about the relatively stable nature of professional practice and professional identity need to be challenged. Boud identifies three reasons for the 'practice turn':

a) the acknowledgement that professional work is a collective endeavour (and reflected in the call for a 'relational turn' in professional work as advocated by Edwards 2010);

b) because 'high-level demanding work is not held together by professions or disciplines but by the nature of work itself' (ibid:31), many professionals work in and across multi-disciplinary and often trans-disciplinary groups that are formed and reformed to meet the needs of the work in question; and

c) because professionals now often co-construct goods and services with 'clients', the identity of the professional as the expert is becoming unsustainable (see also Bishop *et al.* 2009.)

In the midst of this turbulent activity, early career professionals need to find firm ground on which to stand whilst they develop their (multi-faceted) expertise. As Fenwick *et al.* (2012:3) argue:

> a core challenge for professionals is to maintain continuity in professional work. This requires stabilisation of knowledge and practice. An emerging question is thus how stability is achieved in practices characterised by multiple knowledge sources, strategies and concerns, while enabling innovation.

The chapter draws on case study research to argue that apprenticeship offers a potential way forward in providing a supportive scaffold for early career professionals to enable them to develop their expertise.

Structure and agency in creative tension

Studies of professional learning are now more likely to acknowledge the importance of context and the impact on professional identity and autonomy of new forms of managerialism, particularly in the public sector. Evetts (2002) has highlighted the shift away from the notion of the professional as a fully autonomous expert to one who seeks ways within the structures in which they operate to find opportunities to exercise discretion (see also Beckett and Hager 2002). In their research on nurses, Nerland and Jensen (2012), building on the Foucauldian approach of Tobias (2005), argue that it is through being deeply embedded in their epistemic practices and the associated epistemic networks that they can avoid being constrained by structures.

Whilst these arguments are important, they may perpetuate the stereotype of the professional as 'hero' battling the system. We argue that a more holistic approach is required, one that brings together the agency of individuals and the relational process of learning and working with colleagues and clients in what

Cook and Brown (2005) have called a 'generative dance' with the organizational structures in which professional work takes place.

During research in a wide range of occupational sectors in the UK, we drew on the economic concept of the productive system as an analytical tool for examining how organizations of all shapes and sizes are affected by the structures and stages of production governing their activities (see Felstead *et al.* 2009, for a detailed analysis). The structures of production form the vertical axis of the productive system. An automotive manufacturing plant making doors and wheels for cars in one country, for example, might be owned by an organization in a different country and hence, there will be structural layers above the workplaces where the doors and wheels are produced. The extent to which the engineers, managers and supervisors can exercise discretion in the way work is organized and conducted in the factory will be subject to pressures exerted from far up the structural axis. In contrast, an employee-owned architectural practice may sit at the top of its structural axis, though it will be subject to and very mindful of regulatory requirements imposed by bodies sitting to the side of the axis. Even the freelance professional will be affected by the productive systems of the client organizations for whom they work. These structural frameworks determine the nature of the employment relationship for full-time, part-time and project-based practitioners (see Rainbird and Munro 2003).

The stages of production form the horizontal axis of the productive system and encompass the flow of work and materials for processing, whether patients in a hospital, students in a university, cases in a law firm or raw materials in a manufacturing plant. In professional work, the management of the stages of production determines the extent to which individuals and teams have sufficient time and resources to complete their part of the overall process to a standard they believe to be right. When timescales are squeezed, often due to pressures being exerted in the vertical axis, professionals come under stress and the effects are felt throughout the whole system, including in the relationships with clients (see Jewson *et al.* 2008). Early career professionals can be caught in the crossfire as the productive system buckles, leaving them insufficient time and space for the maturation process that is central to the development of expertise.

Creating the appropriate conditions for early career professional learning needs to begin with an understanding of the productive system in which that learning takes place. By exposing the characteristics of the productive system, it becomes possible to identify the points at which early career professionals will need to be given greater or lesser amounts of support, and afforded more discretion to take on more responsibility and be subject to great risk. We have argued (Fuller and Unwin 2003) that the positioning and treatment of apprentices in an organization provides a valuable window on its understanding of the workplace as a learning environment. This is because the very presence of an apprentice necessitates that attention be paid to the creation of a programme of activities both inside and outside the workplace that will enable the apprentice to grow into becoming an expert in their own right. The central tension rests in finding the right balance between engaging the apprentice in productive work and allowing time for reflection and the learning of theories and concepts that underpin occupational practice. The trick here is to create a programme that takes account of each individual's capacity whilst providing a framework of support that can weather the worst storms emanating from turbulence inside the productive system, thus achieving the stability advocated by Fenwick *et al.* (2012).

Apprenticeship as a model of learning

There are four dimensions to the apprenticeship model of learning which resonate strongly with the needs and experiences of early career professionals:

1. *Pedagogical dimension* – the workplace views the work and development of the apprentice through a pedagogical lens. A workplace curriculum is constructed, made visible and enacted through the apprentice's participation in authentic and relational work with colleagues (and clients). Feedback and the modelling of the career trajectory are central to the manager/supervisor's role. In addition, to use Wenger's (1998) terminology, apprentices also 'disengage' with the workplace, to acquire knowledge beyond the immediate needs of the job and/or scope of the organization and develop a critical capacity leading to individual transformation (see Guile 2010; Engeström 2001).

2. *Occupational dimension* – the apprenticeship functions to initiate the individual into an occupational community, defined by the solidarity formed around shared knowledge, skills, values, customs and habits. In the case of early career professionals, it is this dimension that is critical for providing a sense of stability. The pedagogical dimension, as described above, ensures that stability does not restrict the innovative capacity of the apprentice or early career professional.

3. *Locational dimension* – apprenticeship is an outward symbol of an organization's commitment to providing opportunities for skilled employment supported by substantive training for young people living in the same area as the employing organization. Whilst recruitment, management and the carrying out of the work itself have all become less spatially specific, most work activity still has a locational dimension, even in cases of workplaces governed by multinational organizations. In the case of organizations providing professional services (e.g. hospitals, law and accountancy practices, and schools, colleges and universities), this locational and civic dimension gives rise to obligations which underpin their reputation and socio-economic standing in the community. For individuals who are less locationally anchored, professional networks and associations can provide a means of staying connected to the dispersed occupational community, enabling them to reach their potential within the spatial configuration of wherever the work takes place, including in the home or on the move (see Felstead *et al.* 2005).

4. *Social dimension* – the quality of its apprenticeships is one of a number of litmus tests of an organization's public image (locally or globally). Recent negative reports in the British media about organizations running unpaid and exploitative internships highlight the strength of feeling among members of the general public when they suspect that young people striving to enter the labour market are being mistreated (Wood 2011; see also Grugulis and Stoyanova 2012). At a time when corporate social responsibility matters to organizations in both the public and private sectors, being able to demonstrate a commitment to supporting the next generation brings rewards.

These four dimensions complement the productive system concept by connecting the pedagogical and occupational characteristics of apprenticeship to the organization's position within the society or societies in which it is physically, virtually and operationally located. In the next section, we illustrate how this relationship works to the advantage of all stakeholders when apprenticeship is organized along what we have elsewhere conceptualized as 'expansive' lines (Fuller and Unwin 2003, 2004, 2010b).

Learning as apprentices in expansive environments

Through our research across a range of workplace and sectorial settings, we developed the concept of the 'expansive–restrictive continuum'. Organizations that regard workforce development as a vehicle for aligning the twin goals of developing individual and organizational capability create expansive learning environments. Due to the nature of their productive systems, however, sustaining and enhancing such environments is challenging, regardless of the size or nature of the organization and, hence, all organizations (and/or workplaces within them) move within the continuum. Apprentices who find themselves in organizations closer to the expansive end of the continuum will find their apprenticeship is underpinned by a number of key features not found in organizations closer to the restrictive end. These features include:

- The apprenticeship is embedded within the broader business plan of the organization;
- The organization protects the identity of the apprentice as learner and worker throughout the apprenticeship;
- The apprenticeship reifies time for disengagement from productive work and for apprentices to cross work boundaries;
- The apprenticeship has a clear end point signified by the achievement of some form of certification to mark that a recognized level of expertise has been reached and that the apprentice can move to the next stage of development.

One of the organizations in which we have carried out research runs an apprenticeship programme that epitomizes these expansive features. It is a medium-sized company (around 700 employees) manufacturing bathroom showers. Here, we met Peter, a young man in his early twenties who had completed an apprenticeship in engineering and was given a permanent job in the company's special projects department as an 'ancillary project engineer'. Peter was working with five colleagues on a project to redevelop one of the company's 'power shower' models. He reported to the project team leader and underwent a monthly performance review and development session with his line manager. In addition, he had been given sole responsibility for reclassifying the parts of the previous power shower model as 'old spares' and for moving these to a 'spares cell'. When showers are superseded by new versions, it is company policy to make spare parts available to customers for a period of 10 years after the line has been discontinued.

Peter told us how his career progression in the company and in the wider labour market was dependent upon three interconnected and formalized elements of his programme of development, starting with the apprenticeship and now post-apprenticeship: a) gaining increasing work experience; b) proving his ability at each level; and c) gaining further nationally and occupationally recognized higher level qualifications (to degree level) to signal his growing knowledge base beyond that established through the apprenticeship. At each stage, from the beginning of the apprenticeship through to the point when we met him, when he was seen as an early career professional, Peter had been guided by more experienced colleagues, who monitored his progress and formally recorded how and when he should be given more responsibility.

Professional learning as a fragile endeavour

We now contrast Peter's experience with a group of early career researchers in the fields of biological, experimental and social sciences in an English elite university whom we interviewed and observed over a period of two years. We begin by describing where the researchers sit in the university's productive system. The university is governed by a Royal Charter and so is technically an institution independent of government, though partly funded by government. Since the 1980s and, in particular, since the 2004 Higher Education Act, universities have become subject to more intense monitoring and accountability regimes exercised by central government and its agencies. The university has complex managerial structures which are extended and hierarchical. The early career researchers we studied sit near the bottom of the institutional hierarchy. Above them sit lecturers, professors, department and faculty heads, and senior university level management. Like their thousands of counterparts in the British higher education system, these researchers are paid from externally funded research grants and, hence, are known as 'contract researchers'. They are employed on fixed term contracts determined by the length of the project. In 2006, there was a major jolt to the productive system when the European Commission introduced new legislation to reduce the use of fixed term contracts, thus forcing universities to pay much more careful attention to the career and employment prospects of this highly vulnerable category of staff. This led to the creation of 'open-ended' contracts, which mean that, if a project is coming to an end and a researcher has been employed for at least four years, then alternative work should be found, for example in another department.

The university in our study was making considerable efforts to use the new legislation as a catalyst for improving the employment conditions of contract researchers because it realized that there were business advantages in trying to solve a personnel problem. The Human Resources director told us:

> if we can get it right then we will be able to both attract and retain very good people which is just absolutely critical to the future of the institution ... however brilliant the PI [Principal Investigator] is, they need to be surrounded by really really good researchers because actually it's the dynamic of all that that works

Other studies of contract researchers (see, inter alia, Roberts 2002; Allen-Collinson 2003) have highlighted the problems they face. As well as job insecurity and a sense of being seen as 'second class' as compared to their colleagues in established posts, these researchers complain strongly about the lack of robust structures to enable them to develop their careers. When we began our study, we became acutely aware of how much the plight of these researchers resembled that of apprentices we had studied in a range of restrictive environments. We now turn to the four dimensions (pedagogical, occupational, locational and social) presented earlier in the chapter to examine how far the contract researchers could be said to be supported by any form of apprenticeship-style framework and to what extent the managers of the researchers are able or willing to exert agency within the productive system of British higher education.

Pedagogical and occupational dimension

The starkest evidence of the restrictive nature of the researchers' professional environment relates to the way in which many of the researchers we interviewed and observed were positioned in a 'master–servant' style relationship with the colleague who controlled the research grant. Known in the British higher education system as the 'Principal Investigator' and referred to colloquially as the PI, the grant holder is in a position of considerable power.

It is here that the importance of having a productive system analysis needs to be asserted. A personnel officer in the university, who was attempting to encourage PIs to pay more attention to the career development needs of their researchers, said:

> I can think of one department where the researcher just has to do the work: [the supervisor asks], 'what do you mean look at their future career?' 'What do you mean give them time to go to a workshop? ... Well that's crazy who's going to do the project?' You know it's almost a factory mentality.
>
> (Personnel Officer)

This encapsulates the pressures facing the PIs who, on the one hand, have to ensure they meet the demands of the funders of their research as well as other demands related to the performance measures that impact on British universities, whilst, on the other hand, being expected to accept responsibility for the career development of their junior colleagues. Many of the PIs will themselves have once been contract researchers or post-doctoral research assistants and so will know only too well what it was like being in the 'servant' category. Some PIs will have experienced expansive forms of a researcher apprenticeship, but many will be modelling the restrictive practices that they experienced. It should also be stressed that some PIs will have only recently ended their apprenticeship and taken the leap from servant to master.

Although the blame for the PIs' behaviour might be laid fully at the door of the productive system, there are, however, questions to be asked about the way universities allow that productive system to fashion the way work is organized and managed within their institutions. For example, whilst many universities will have personnel guidelines that stress the importance of PIs (as line managers) taking responsibility for the career development of their researchers, they could do far more to support the PIs in achieving this. Although the researchers in our study ranged in age and experience (as would be the case across higher education in Britain), they are positioned as apprentices in occupational terms. The goal they all strive to achieve and that marks the end of their apprenticeship is to conceive and submit research proposals in their own name to funding bodies. This signals that they have made the transition from being apprenticed to being autonomous, independent professionals with the necessary expertise to be trusted by their managers. As Fox (1974) has argued, it is much harder to generate a trusting environment in workplaces where power is unequally distributed. Generating trust requires managers to afford individuals and teams the discretion to conceptualize, carry out and evaluate their work tasks, and it is this affording of responsibility that is both a hallmark of the professional workplace and also central to the way in which professionals continue to develop and refine their expertise.

The contract researchers in our study commented on the limited amount of discretion they had and the lack of opportunity to move beyond the stage of carrying out tasks assigned to them, as illustrated in this quotation from a scientist:

> Well because I'm contract staff ... I have to do what I'm told. So in terms of research, well my boss specifically is very sort of hands-on ... So it's a question of going to her and asking exactly what you're going to be doing in the experiment that day

We did find evidence of PIs who afforded their researchers considerable levels of discretion, but this required working against the grain of the productive system of higher education, as illustrated by this comment:

> So we're going to put this [proposal] in ... I told my ex-boss about this, you know said, this guy wants me to be on it ... and I was like well it's completely

my project anyway ... but he rang up my colleague in this other institution and said that if [researcher's name] goes on that grant then I'm pulling the plug on this whole thing ... So my name gets scrubbed off and his name got put on it

In occupational terms, universities are faced with a curious dilemma in their approach to contract researchers. On the one hand, they need some of these apprentices to become autonomous experts to build the next generation of PIs, but, on the other hand, they also need a substantial army of operatives to ensure projects are completed. This leaves many contract researchers in the difficult position of being perpetual apprentices, as this quotation illustrates:

> they put your CV in a box a year or so before your contract's due to end and then they try and find you an alternative position within the department to avoid making you redundant ... but it's difficult to do that because people that work in a particular group obviously have particular specialities and it's, I mean skills are definitely transferable, but it's still going to take a lot of training up for some postdocs to shift from one lab to another ... So it's really not as easy as kind of transferring from one lab to the other ... it's nice to learn a brand new technique within your own field, but to go into somebody else's field completely unknown, that you've never worked on before at all, and then just effectively start from scratch again

The university was clearly aware of this problem and had introduced training programmes and improved careers guidance to help the contract researchers with their occupational development. Ironically, however, and in contrast to an apprenticeship-style approach, this activity was largely regarded by researchers as a means to help them gain jobs in other universities. This perception was underpinned by the fact that the training and careers advice were delivered by staff who worked in a separate area of the university from the academic departments. This relates to the point made above about the absence of an official duty of care on the part of PIs to take direct responsibility for nurturing the career trajectory of their researchers. The resources for and attention to the generic aspects of career development are certainly present in the university, but they are divorced from the actual workplaces within the university where staff develop their specific expertise. This creates a fracture between the organizational goals of the university and the way work is organized.

Locational and social dimension

Due to its history, the university has a civic identity in the city in which it is located, but as an elite research-intensive English university, it also sees itself a global player. Like other elite universities, it has to manage the potential tensions between maintaining a civic identity and its global ambitions. The danger with the latter is that they can encourage universities to prioritize the global over the local and, therefore, to downplay their physical and historical foundations (see Goddard 2009). The contract researchers are very aware that they will have to be prepared to move if they want to pursue not just an autonomous academic career, but also to sustain their employment as a contract researcher. This is particularly true for researchers in the natural, experimental and biological sciences where it is expected that researchers will spend time with different research groups in a range of institutions. In this, they are different to the classic apprentice who is regarded as being a central part of the future of the organization in which they work. As we saw in the previous section, the university provides resources to help contract researchers manage their careers and encourages them to attend training courses, but the emphasis is on moving to another organization. Moreover, and again in contrast to an apprenticeship model, the separation of professional development from organizational goals (from the locational dimension) means that the university does not have a strategy for moving its early career professionals on from the status of, in Lave and Wenger's (1991) terms, legitimate peripheral participants.

Mobility was central to the medieval concept of apprenticeship. On completion of their initial training, an apprentice became a 'journeyman' who could now sell their expertise without being beholden to their master, though they would still be part of their occupational community of practice (the guild). Thus, apprenticeship was the vehicle for sustaining and expanding the craft or trade as a whole. As the patterns and organization of work changed through industrialization and bureaucratization, apprenticeship became the vehicle for embedding individual development within organizational strategies for sustainability and growth. Some professional communities reflect both this transition to an organizational approach whilst also maintaining a strong sense of being a community of individual experts, as in the case, for example, of small-scale accountancy, architectural and legal practices that are found in towns and cities in many countries.

There are still, of course, examples of the journeymen of the past, such as the freelancers in the media, design and consultancy sectors. Our concern here is with early career professionals who work within organizations that can and should have a responsibility of care for their career progression. In the case of the contract researchers, our evidence suggests that they are in a vulnerable position because their employers have not sufficiently thought through how to combine the local and social dimensions that make the apprenticeship model of development so robust. When attention is paid to these dimensions, employees in a transitional category (e.g. apprentices, interns, graduate trainees and early career professionals) are regarded as being in transition in an occupational rather than an organizational sense. In other words, they are treated as if they are going to stay with the organization even if the reality is they will move on at some point. As such, they will reflect well on the organization and enhance its local civic, and sectoral (and in the case of some organizations even their international) reputation.

For many early career professionals, the expectation of mobility clashes with their personal and social aspirations, as well as the lived reality of their social characteristics. Gender, ethnicity and family circumstances are important here, and, given the extended nature of the transition from education to the labour market that is now a common feature of advanced economies, age has also become a factor challenging the concept of the mobile professional. In our study, both male and female researchers were particularly concerned about their capacity and/or willingness to buy into the mobility game, and were fearful that they faced years of short-term contracts which would impede their chances of putting down roots and having children.

Our evidence suggests that there are weaknesses in the ability of existing approaches and practices to scaffold individuals beyond the last (post-doc) stage of their apprenticeship and into the role of independent researcher generating their own projects. Part of the problem is that there is a shortage of the sort of research posts that allow holders to make their own applications. However, there are two further questions relating, first, to whether PIs recognize that the ability to generate ideas and translate them into fundable research proposals is a skill that their researchers need support to develop; and, second, to the extent to which PIs have been trained and encouraged by institutions to provide their researchers with the professional development they need to make the transition from 'post-doc'. A goal of renewing and strengthening universities' local social and civic missions would be one way of helping to generate the sort of underpinning organizational culture likely to generate a more expansive approach to the development of early career professionals and the workforce as a whole.

Conclusion

Despite their initial professional skill formation through completion of undergraduate and postgraduate programmes, the contract researchers discussed in this chapter still entered the workplace needing mentoring, training and ongoing support and commitment from the organization and its experts to complete their transition to independence. As novices, researchers need help, but they find themselves in an asymmetric power relationship with the PI. Their ability to integrate into the established academic community and progress toward autonomy is closely tied to the willingness and capacity of the PI to take on this responsibility by, for example, building researchers into their networks. Conceptualizing and articulating the relationship between a PI and a contract researcher in terms of 'expert–apprentice' rather than 'master–servant' is more likely to invoke an apprenticeship pedagogical approach where teaching is an integral and accepted part of the managerial role and reflected in the social relations of producing research. Whilst the structures and stages of production in the contemporary higher education sector in the UK help explain the fracture between organizational goals of the university and the way research work is organized and distributed, utilization of an (expansive) apprenticeship approach would help repair that fracture by reducing the likelihood of variable and even exploitative practice.

We have argued that the pedagogical and occupational dimensions of apprenticeship could provide a framework of support for new professionals that was lacking for the contract researchers, and we referred to the experience of Peter, the early career engineer, as an example. Elsewhere, we have discussed at more length another case which explored how a company deliberately set out to create a stable environment within which to develop and nurture the expertise of its newly recruited and novice software engineers (Fuller and Unwin 2010b). Key to this was the way the social relations of production were organized to ensure that newcomers were incorporated into project teams as part of their planned trajectory over time to project leader status. Coupled with this, an apprenticeship approach to teaching and mentoring was articulated and practised as core aspects of the manager's role and responsibility for less experienced staff. The organization's competitiveness was associated with its system for generating high level technical competence and also creative and innovative ideas and solutions. Interestingly, the founders of the organization had introduced a model of employee share ownership which they believed created and supported a stable and high trust organizational environment in which they could grow their own highly skilled and innovative workforce. The software engineers we spoke to made the link between their ability to be creative professionals and their sense of feeling 'safe' in the organizational culture.

In conclusion, therefore, we propose that apprenticeship, when viewed as a model of learning and support for the development of occupational expertise, is as relevant to early career professionals as it is to intermediate or technician level workers. This is not to suggest, of course, that all apprenticeships provide high quality teaching and learning experiences; or that they all allow individuals to make gradual and effective transitions to skilled status and constitute a platform for ongoing education, training and career progression. The concept of the expansive–restrictive continuum provides a tool for analysing the highly variable forms of apprenticeship experienced by individuals in different organizational contexts. Identifying the pedagogical and organizational features that give apprenticeships their more or less expansive character offers a lens through which to think more generically about how the development of expertise for the professions can be supported in contemporary institutional and occupational scenarios.

In considering these issues, we have tried to respond to Fenwick et al.'s important question about how the necessary stability for 'maintaining continuity in professional work' can be achieved by suggesting that an apprenticeship approach is part of the answer. Writing over twenty years ago, Streeck (1989:99) pointed out that:

> 'pre-modern' institutions with their higher mutual interpenetration of functions and social arenas often seem to perform better in a period of change and uncertainty than 'modern', functionally differentiated institutions.

Apprenticeship has proved itself to be a resilient model of learning that has continued to adapt from its 'pre-modern' origins in response to changes in work and the way it is organized, as well as to social and cultural change. As a labour market institution, to use Streeck's term, apprenticeship could provide a more robust model for supporting the development of occupational and professional expertise, particularly now given the volatile nature of many professional settings. As we noted at the start of this chapter, an apprenticeship approach does underpin the way professional expertise is developed, particularly in fields such as medicine, law, teaching and music, though this tends to be implicit rather than explicit. An 'apprenticeship turn' in relation to the development and support of early career professionals would bring both the individual and organizational dimensions of the apprenticeship model into play, thus effecting workplace as well as individual transformation.

Acknowledgement

This chapter was written with the support of the ESRC funded LLAKES Research Centre – grant reference RES-594-28-0001.

References

Allen-Collinson, J. (2003) 'Working at a marginal 'career': the case of UK social science contract researchers', *The Sociological Review*, 51(3): 405–422.

Bishop, D., Felstead, A., Fuller, A., Jewson, N., Unwin, L. and Kakavelakis, K. (2009) 'Constructing learning: adversarial and collaborative working in the British construction industry', *Journal of Education and Work*, 22(4): 243–260.

Beckett, D. and Hager, P. (2002) *Life, Work and Learning: Practice in postmodernity*, London: Routledge.

Boud, D. (2010) 'Relocating reflection in the context of practice', in Bradbury, H., Frost, N., Kilminster, S. and Zukas, M. (eds) *Beyond Reflective Practice*, London: Routledge.

Cook, S.D.N. and Brown, J.S. (2005) 'Bridging epistemologies: the generative dance between organisational knowledge and organisational learning', in Little, S. and Ray, T. (eds) *Managing Knowledge*, 2nd edn, London: SAGE.

Edwards, A. (2010) *Being an Expert Professional Practitioner: The relational turn in expertise*, Dordrecht: Springer.

Engeström, Y. (2001) 'Expansive learning at work: Toward an activity theoretical reconceptualisation', *Journal of Education and Work*, 14(1): 133–155.

Evetts, J. (2002) 'New directions in state and international professional occupations: Discretionary decision-making and acquired regulation', *Work, Employment and Society*, 16(2): 341–353.

Felstead, A., Jewson, N. and Walters, S. (2005) *Changing Places of Work*, Basingstoke: Palgrave MacMillan.

Felstead, A., Fuller, A., Jewson, N. and Unwin, L. (2009) *Improving Working for Learning*, London: Routledge.

Fenwick, T., Nerland, M. and Jensen, K. (2012) 'Sociomaterial approaches to conceptualising professional learning and practice', *Journal of Education and Work*, 25(1): 1–13.

Fox, A. (1974) *Beyond Contract: Work power and trust relations*, London: Faber.

Fuller, A. and Unwin, L. (2003) 'Learning as apprentices in the contemporary UK workplace: Creating and managing expansive and restrictive participation', *Journal of Education and Work*, 16(4): 406–427.

Fuller, A. and Unwin, L. (2004) 'Expansive learning environments: Integrating personal and organisational development', in Rainbird, H., Fuller, A. and Munro, A. (eds) *Workplace Learning in Context*, London: Routledge.

Fuller, A. and Unwin, L. (2010a) 'Change and continuity in apprenticeship: The resilience of a model of learning', *Journal of Education and Work*, 25(5): 405–416.

Fuller, A. and Unwin, L. (2010b) "Knowledge workers' as the new apprentices: The influence of organisational autonomy, goals and values on the nurturing of expertise', *Vocations and Learning*, 3(3): 201–222.

Fuller, A. and Unwin, L. (2013) (eds) *Apprenticeship as an Evolving Model of Learning*, London: Routledge.

Goddard, J. (2009) 'Reinventing the civic university', *Provocation 12*, London: Nesta.

Grugulis, I. and Stoyanova, D. (2012) 'Social capital and networks in film and TV: Jobs for the boys?', *Organization Studies*, 33(1): 1311–1331.

Guile, D. (2010) *The Learning Challenge of the Knowledge Economy*. Rotterdam: Sense Publishers.

Jewson, N., Unwin, L., Felstead, A., Fuller, A. and Kakavelakis, K. (2008) 'What is the vision for this profession?: Learning environments of health visitors in an English city', *Learning as Work Research Paper, No. 14*, Cardiff: Cardiff University.

Lave, J. and Wenger, E. (1991) *Situated Learning: Legitimate peripheral participation*, New York: Cambridge University Press.

Nerland, M. and Jensen, K. (2012) 'Epistemic practices and object relations in professional work', *Journal of Education and Work*, 25(1): 101–120.

Rainbird, H. and Munro, A. (2003) 'Workplace learning and the employment relationship in the public sector', *Human Resource Management Journal*, 13(2): 30–44.

Roberts, S.G. (2002) 'SET for success. The supply of people with science, technology, engineering and mathematics skills', *The Report of Sir Gareth Roberts' Review*, London: HM Treasury.

Streeck, W. (1989) 'Skills and the limits of neo-liberalism', *Work, Employment and Society*, 3: 89–105.

Tobias, S. (2005) 'Foucault on freedom and capabilities', *Theory, Culture & Society*, 22(4): 65–85.

Wenger, E. (1998) Communities of Practice: Learning, Meaning and Identity, Cambridge, Cambridge University Press.

Wood, W. (2011) 'Unpaid internships are exploited by the wealthiest in the creative industry', *The Guardian*, November 30th: http://www.guardian.co.uk/culture-professionals-network/culture-professionals-blog/2011/nov/30/internships-unpaid-arts-culture.

Chapter 7

A technology shift and its challenges to professional conduct

Mediated vision in endodontics[1]

Åsa Mäkitalo and Claes Reit

Introduction

To become a professional dentist one needs to develop medical knowing and skills by working with the relevant materials and instruments and by enacting them in relevant circumstances guided by instructors with specific expertise. Professional discourse usually guides such practices when categorizing and distinguishing features of importance for the profession to recognize. As Goodwin (1994, 1997) has shown in his empirical cases of archeologists and geochemists, professional vision is accomplished through such interaction, shaping both action and perception by highlighting and articulating specific features of the relevant social and material environment. In the area of dentistry, students are oriented to spatial relationships, particular manners of moving the body and manoeuvring the instruments, when instructed how to perform treatments through careful, skilled and fine-tuned actions. They are also guided to distinguish and recognize auditory and tactile experiences in the immediate context of pursuing specific procedures (Weddle and Hollan 2010). Learning for the purpose of entering this professional field accordingly implies understanding and articulating what one can see and feel, how one can proceed during a treatment, and how to manage one's body so as to align with the design of the instruments in action.

According to Weddle and Hollan (2010) the imagery and metaphors used during students' training in dentistry suggest that, to participants, the boundary between body and tool is blurred. This observation resonates with a sociocultural account of learning where the notion of appropriation has been used to describe a process where the relevant tools[2] used in performing a particular action are increasingly mastered by, while gradually also becoming transparent to, the learner. Artefacts can be incorprated in action to the extent that they function as extensions of the body (see Bateson's example of a blind man's stick 1972:458–459). For a silversmith, for instance, loupes[3] extend vision beyond the naked eye, the engraving ball provides stability and the burin affords sharpness, force and precision when making an engraving by hand on a silver plate. When the coordination of body and tool is smooth, mind and means seem to merge in interaction with the environment. The reverse, however, is also possible. Our dependence on artefacts also involves processes that 'abolish and make unnecessary several natural processes, whose work is accomplished by the tool' (Vygotsky 1981:139). While the latter might seem to suggest a view that entirely separates body from tool, this is not the case. Understood as a form of division of labour (or, in the parlance of actor network theory, as a form of delegation) this kind of relation between body and tool is instead characterized by other forms of interdependencies that allow some distancing from ongoing work. In both cases, the tools are co-constitutive of human activity as it unfolds in practice. Just *how* they are entangled in situated action is an empirical question that has implications for what it means to know and learn something within a specific professional domain. Taking these premises as a point of departure makes it relevant to explore learning and development of expertise within the field of dentistry at times when important shifts in technologies take place, since they challenge established professional conduct. From being competently attuned to one set of tools in professional action, one has to act smoothly with a set of new tools. Such *re*-mediation[4] of work implies that learning in the sense of appropriation is required among dentists, and that what constitutes professional expertise may need to be reconsidered and reformulated to some extent.

Drawing on a sociocultural and dialogical perspective this chapter will illuminate how a technology shift challenged professional dentists. The particular shift that provides the focus for our analysis is the introduction of the surgical microscope into endodontic practice.[5] A focus group discussion among professional dentists is analysed to explore the technology shift as an embodied experience of working. We examine how such experience takes shape through discourse when professionals share their individual accounts with each other.

Visual technologies in endodontic practice

The interior of a patients' tooth and in particular the preparation and treatment of the root canals used to be quite hard not only to visually share, but also to see. The dentist engaged in endodontic therapies still has to largely rely on tactile experience, even though guided by a set of tools. From using visual aids in the form of two-dimensional dental radiography, bright light, mirror and loupes, an important shift took place in the 1990s as the surgical microscope was introduced in this field.[6] As a tool for optical magnification, it mediates vision by increasing the size of an image on the retina offering a stereoscopic three-dimensional enlarged image (see Machtou 2010). In other areas of medicine, this visual technology is known to have created an entirely new work environment in which to pursue surgical procedures (Kim and Baek 2004).

In the field of endodontics the microscope has been claimed to increase the possibilities of 'identifying fracture lines, locating minuscule canal orifices, and confidently determining anatomic variations in teeth and supporting structures' (Bahcall 2008:876). In professional practice, such visible details are initially mapped and carefully considered, as they indicate what treatment is relevant to a particular case and how one can proceed. The mapping accordingly constitutes an indispensable part of the relevant contextual ecology for professional judgement and accountability along with other material-semiotic resources (such as x-rays and medical records). The technologies used, however, are also intertwined with the second part of endodontic treatment, in an intricate manner, since not only professional vision but also the coordination of hand and gaze are dependent on how the tool mediates particular affordances and constraints for action. Expertise accordingly needs to be understood in terms of how dentists' earlier experiences merge or coalesce with the particular material-semiotic means and constraints available when pursuing a procedure. As Bahcall (2008:870) for instance notes: 'the hand can perform remarkably intricate micromanipulations as long as the eye can see a magnified field and it can be interpreted by the mind'. The question to explore further is how the concrete shift to using the microscope challenges established conduct, and what this implies in terms of learning among already skilled professional dentists engaged in endodontic practice.

Technology shifts and professional learning

From a sociocultural and dialogical perspective, professional knowing and learning are conceptualized as emergent properties of engaging in social activity (Säljö 2009). Learning is conceived as emerging in situations where there is a gap between action and expectation that require alternative routes of proceeding with ongoing work (Mäkitalo 2012). When established professional ways of pursuing work are challenged *in situ*, gaps-bridging, meaning making and coordination of actions and perspectives are necessary to be able to 'go on' in ways that sufficiently maintain the integrity and quality of work. Professional vision in dentistry has, it is claimed, changed dramatically with the advent of the microscope. However, the embodied experience, the dexterity and precision needed when undertaking a procedure, and the delicacy of decision-making during the process have still not been articulated and systematically shared among professionals. In this study, the following questions were addressed with regard to this technology shift and the appropriation of the new tool:

1. How was the shift made sense of and established discursively among professional dentists?
2. How was the shift articulated as a challenge to embodied professional expertise?
3. How was professional conduct accounted for in the re-mediated work context?

Re-actualizing the advent of the surgical microscope: an empirical case

This explorative study analyses a locally arranged focus-group discussion[7] with six specialist dentists led by a professor at their university clinic. The dentists at this clinic are responsible for endodontic treatment of patients as well as for providing specialist education in their professional domain. The focus-group discussion was arranged to share the professionals' experiences of the shift, and how long they had used the microscope varied within the group. This kind of professional knowledge sharing had not been arranged earlier and it was regarded as important in order to be able to communicate what kind of challenges this technology implies in this professional field. The discussion was accordingly arranged so as to grasp the significance of the technology shift to achieve a more advanced and articulated development of competences in this field. The purpose at the special clinic was to articulate, discuss and document how their professional expertise was challenged and what new competences and skills they needed to develop as a consequence of the introduction of the technology. To harness such experiences was considered important in order to establish and articulate relevant and professionally grounded knowledge in their field.

The focus-group discussion was video recorded and the first author was given access and opportunity to analyse the material in more detail. As a communicative activity this focus-group discussion can be characterized as a rather 'informal, though topically focused, multiparty conversation' (Marková *et al.* 2007). This means that the moderator who acted as discussion facilitator did not intervene much in the discussion. He invited the group to discuss some questions and sometimes passed the initiative to the next speaker by using their first name or just through a pointing gesture. Such interventions were especially salient in the video material when the discussion seemed to have to come to a temporary standstill. The facilitator accordingly occupied a fairly withdrawn position and was careful when and how to moderate the discussion.

From the analytical perspective taken in this study, discussions like these are not understood as an arena for participants to simply display or express earlier experiences. Rather, such narration 'repackages experiential content into a form digestible not only to the experiencer, but also to an audience to whom the narrative is told and with whom, in the telling, new experiences are shared' (Murphy 2011:244). Such discussions are accordingly understood as opportunities for the participants to temporarily revisit the past, to remind themselves and each other of the technology shift by re-actualizing, noticing and verbalizing particular features of past events. Through such processes individual contributions in the form of narrated experiences, are interactionally and discursively co-constructed. This means that there is a potential to develop, establish and refine what may be considered as shared professional accounts. A dialogically informed analysis of such data has to consider the ways in which discourse is co-constructed through talk by the way questions are initiated and responses are delivered, how topics are established and how formulations are recycled and modified (Marková *et al.* 2007). Various discursive devices maybe used in the collective meaning-making process such as analogies, metaphors and metonymies. Also rhetorical discursive work (Billig 1996), such as constrasting, comparing and categorizing experiences, is often salient, and in such work the use of prototypical or deviant examples are drawn on to suggest or modify characterizations of earlier actions and experiences (Edwards 1997; Middleton and Brown 2005).

In the following sections, the results of the analysis will be presented. The first part will be more elaborate in terms of displaying how the discussion was initiated and how some of the recurrent themes were established through participants' co-construction. By presenting a longer excerpt it also provides some insight into the dynamics of this particular discourse event and how it was moderated. The second two parts of the result section will be presented without displaying utterances in their immediate dialogical context. As Markovà *et al.* (2007:205) note, topics are 'not arranged in a linear progression but emerge from past themes and project themselves into future ones'. So to convey some of the richness of the material, despite limits of space, excerpts that recycle initial themes and also contribute to the co-construction of shared experience by highlighting, articulating and specifying some aspect, will be presented.

Sharing first impressions

The very first question, initiated by the moderator (Eric), has some rhetorically interesting features. It seems to be crafted to reframe the discussion and recast the situation that the dentists are currently engaged in. By discursively putting the respondents in a particular embodied position, the question formulation allows and invites them to revisit an earlier event and reactualize their first impressions of gazing through the microscope.

Excerpt I. Initial meaning potentials of the shift

1 *Eric*	if you think about the first impression you got when using it yourself for the very first time (.) how did you experience it uh shortly (.) we can start with paul when you looked down with your eyes there that first time what was your impression?
2 *Paul*	It was the *light* especially as it was uh (.) you discovered pretty soon that it was difficult to work in high magnification (Eric: mm) but uh just that you got the light to where you wanted it was – it was so concentrated at the small area you were interested to see so that was it first and foremost
3 *Eric*	Mmm what does Roy say?
4 *Roy*	Yeah it was a *revelation* ((others giggle)) it was much easier to see while I was surprised how it actually looked in there (.) so definitely a step forward (Eric: mm)
5 *Eric*	((Pointing gesture to Lauren))
6 *Lauren*	Uh I may well latch on there it was in a way *an entirely new world* that opened up cause earlier, you had more like felt what you did and then you looked to see if what I had done was what I thought I had done (.) ehm but that you could look *precisely* down there (.) I thought was very special (.) and then you didn't quite work in the same way as you do *now* since it took a while to get these frames of reference (.) and what we got in ((mentions a small town)) was only

how to set up the microscope so we had no guidance of what to see (.) so there you in a way had to come up with your own picture of the reality you *then* thought was correct

7 *Eric*   Mm mm then Amy

8 *Amy*   Ee I started using the microscope here about a year ago and it was (.) first, it was very nerve-racking, I thought it would be *great fun* but (Eric: mm) I actually thought it was very (.) *hard* to *see* anything in the beginning to get some sharpness and you get a little dizzy in the beginning as well so the expectations were probably a bit higher than what I got out of it but after a period, it was, as you say it was a very nice revelation

((A few lines omitted))

9 *Eric*   Mm good (.) Annie

10 *Annie*   I'll have to agree with this it was like a new world (.) and before when I worked with loupes one thought one had good vision but after starting with a microscope I almost never use loupes or – you end up being like dependent (.) it's difficult to be without it, I sort of use the microscope when putting on the rubber dam now ((laughs)) I use it *all* the time almost (.) no but you end up using it more and more and so I think you feel as if you see much worse without it now than you did before (.) then you thought that you had pretty good vision without a microscope, but you don't think that any no longer (.) at least I don't

11 *Eric*   Mm Brian what about you?

12 *Brian*   As I remember it I probably thought it was quite difficult in the beginning to be honest and so I agree that you saw things you hadn't seen before and you realized the clear benefits if you were looking for canals and things we're often doing here

The responses to Eric's invitation are guided by metaphors and analogies which are rich in terms of meaning potentials and, as such, easily shared with others. Through Paul's first response 'it was the light' (2), which has several meaning potentials in this context of narrating experiences, the uptakes of other partici-pants in the group in the form of the associated metaphor of 'a revelation' (4) and the analogy to 'an entirely new world' (6 and 10) are quickly established. As the response from Roy (4) is delivered with a hint of self-distance and humour, the joint giggle which immediately follows seem to be a significant marker of some at least partially shared professional experience. As we shall see in the following, the metaphors and analogies established in the very beginning of the discussion are very rich in meaning potentials. They serve as productive discursive means by inviting the introduction of a set of relevant themes which are later explored and specified during the discussion. So, even though 'the light' might have been understood by Paul simply in terms of a technical feature of the microscope that enables enhanced vision, the connotations which are immediately recognized by the others when responding to it as a metaphor eventually seem to say something more substantial about what the technology shift means to these professionals.

While there seems to be a strong shared sense of enhanced vision provided by the light and the magnification as specific features of the technology, appropriation is also described in terms of how work is now pursued from new premises. On the one hand the dependence on the new tool is brought to the fore as well as a noticeable shift in one's own standard of what is considered 'good vision' (10). However, there are also first experiences formulated in terms of hardly being able to see anything (8) which are also established at this early stage in the discussion. These accounts relate to difficulties of knowing how to adjust the technology and how to attune to it, to optimize visual acuity.

Another interesting chain of association brought about from the very first response in this discussion is 'the light' as something which could be manoeuvred 'to get it to where you wanted it' (2). This response is also productive in teasing out professional experiences of discovering what is considered a new environment or work context. By sharing the experience of being 'surprised how it actually looked in there' (4) a chain of associations are made possible and here in the beginning of the discussion it is picked up through the analogy of 'an entirely new world' (6) in which 'you saw things you had never seen before' (12). Having articulated this through discourse it becomes publicly noted and shared in the sense that it can be picked up and returned to later in their discussion. The technology shift is here also made sense of as a challenge of orientating oneself in the new environment, since what you saw required new 'frames of reference' (6). Such references were accordingly not described as readily available but had to be established. As Lauren explains, you had to come up with 'your own picture of the reality you then thought was correct' (6).

In the following excerpts, we will further explore these themes by attending to instances when they reappear as part of professionals' accounts later in the discussion. In these excerpts, the themes are recycled and some are further specified through individual accounts of the experiences of the shift. We will focus on how the professionals describe their experience of working with the microscope, and the gaps that emerged that seemed to significantly challenge their professional conduct.

Making sense of the shift through contrasting experiences

A prominent discursive feature of the discussions among the professionals was the use of contrasts when sharing experiences of the shift. Such contrasting work makes salient distinctions that are important in rendering experiences comprehensible (Edwards 1997; Middleton and Brown 2005). The contrasts were most prominently established by means of distinctions of time, before and after the technology shift, highlighting the importance of that particular shift in their respective accounts of earlier events. Excerpt 2a–c illustrates some ways in which this distinction was productive.

Excerpt 2. From tactile to visual guidance

2a *Lauren*   Earlier, you had more like felt what you did and then you looked to see that what I had done was what I thought I had done

2b *Brian*   I remember that before it was pretty much a guessing game (.) then you had that experience but it was very much more to feel and try /.../ the difference is that now now you can see what to try and feel, that was not the case before (.) then you sort of tried to feel like everywhere until you found something to go on

2c *Lauren*   I don't really have that sensibility today /.../ maybe when you feel with the probe but then what you see is still the guiding principle 'cause I don't sit and feel my way about (.) I rely very much on visual impression

The distinction between time before and after the technology shift is frequently used in the narrations of personal experiences to highlight and formulate relevant changes retrospectively. Through participants' contributions, patterns of common experiences are established as a result of being in dialogue with the others, in responding to and acknowledging others' experience and by recycling earlier formulations. The above excerpts illustrate that the professionals understand the shift as a change in sense modality and approach: from having 'to feel' in order to orient oneself in the root canals of the patient, to relying upon one's vision as the prime orienting device. It is interesting to note that professional action in the form of searching for root canal orifices is described retrospectively in terms of fumbling, feeling and trying your way about. After the shift, professional conduct in terms of feeling and trying are still highlighted as being at the core of professional action, but now such action is guided by vision. The visual support provided by the artifact seem to also bring additional experiences of the shift to the forefront of the discussion, such as that of diminished feelings of insecurity as well as increased dependence on the microscope when performing endodontic treatments (as was initially noted by Annie in Excerpt 1, 10).

Challenges to professional conduct and the attunement of re-mediated action

As constrasting experiences like these are elaborated among the professionals, the gaps and challenges to professional conduct that emerged when working with the microscope are also brought forward in their discussion. When looking through the discussion, there seem to be several gaps to bridge before attunement with the technology can be achieved. In the following, the challenge to professional conduct initially, formulated as 'difficulties to see', were salient as three related topical trajectories. While all the following examples (Excerpts 3–5) are oriented to gaps that are articulated as emerging when they started using the specific technology in action, in this set of excerpts the professionals further specify what can analytically be distinguished as emerging gaps: a) in perceptual orientation, b) in physical coordination and c) in managing technical features when interacting with the microscope.

Excerpt 3. Perceptual re-orientation in the visual field

3a *Paul*   You discovered pretty soon that it was difficult to work in high magnification

3b *Brian*   To like get what was mesial and distal and palatal and buccal (.) in what direction you were looking (.) I thought that was quite difficult in the beginning as I remember it

3c *Paul*   You lose you lose the big picture (.) you have to have to see the whole crown when searching for canals for example

3d *Lauren* You couldn't work quite in the same way as you do now eh it took quite a while before you got these frames of reference

In relation to the professionals' articulated first impressions, the experiences accounted for at this stage in their discussion, were clearly not described simply in terms of enhanced vision. When accounting for the concrete experience of actually working with the microscope, the details provided make salient some distinctive features and premises of *achieving* enhanced vision. Such vision is, in the professionals' accounts, heavily dependent upon how they succeed in interpreting a visual field that is magnified and in which they are to operate. This difficulty seems to be one of perceptual re-orientation in what is conceived as an entirely different environment. The appropriation of the tool as a visual mediating means, however, is not described as confined to this kind of perceptual re-orientation. Rather, the way such challenges 'go beyond the skin' are also made salient in their accounts.

Excerpt 4. Physical coordination of hand with vision

4a *Lauren* It's a bit difficult to know how to do this before the brain learns to flip the images (.) you want to go to the right, but whatever I do the arm goes in the other direction (.) I can still get this at times if I start thinking about it then it's chaos and you might just as well quit and start from scratch and try to just disconnect from how to do it and to switch on automation

4b *Brian*   It's a bit tricky, 'cause your movements are a little big / ... / before you learn as I did that you can start in low magnification and then, if you need a little more, go up so you don't start too big too large 'cause then it's very easy to see something just waving in front of you without having a clue of what's happening

4c *Lauren* But on the other hand you dare, once you get the left and right in order when you're working, you dare to go on a little faster

The experiences of re-orienting perceptually is accordingly further articulated in terms of extended embodied action which includes physical coordination (in this case it is articulated as a gap in the coordination of hand and gaze). As Bahcall remarked 'the hand can perform remarkably intricate micromanipulations as long as the eye can see a magnified field and it can be interpreted by the mind' (Bahcall

2008:870). We can now begin to understand what kind of appropriation process is required when shifting to this tool. It seems to include the entire embodied realm of professional action. At the very early stage in the discussion only Amy made salient her experiences of hardship and as being still in a stage of transition when it came to the adjustment and precision work needed to achieve visual acuity. The kind of micromanipulations that are made possible through this visual technology are, according to these professionals, not only dependent on sharpness of vision. The kind of appropriation accounted for seems to be an attunement with the mediating tool that is both extensive and very specific in character:

Excerpt 5. Managing technical features when interacting with the microscope

5a	*Amy*	It was very difficult how you would manage to sit and how to set and adjust it, and I found it was- I don't even know if I'm doing it right
5b	*Paul*	It's mostly in the eight-times magnification you work then, so if you search for canals and want to look at something special down the canal you might go up a little bit then
5c	*Brian*	It was hard just like Amy says to find that which gave you a good really sharp picture (.) before you learned some tricks that you could fix with the focus a little bit and adjust it really well it was hard to get a really good picture
5d	*Roy*	I find it ((the depth of field)) very rarely to be a problem maybe when patients are moving (.) most are very alert so you position them and then you will sit and adjust the focus it's so easy to just move it up and down

As we have seen in this last set of excerpts not only are the body and brain described as in need of adjustment to merge with the technology in action. As already noted the microscope as a physical artefact also needs some fixing and adjusting to match with personal requirements and ways of working. Here tricks of the trade are shared such as how to adjust magnification while performing certain actions. As a mediating device the microscope, however, is also used in interaction with a patient and needs to be adjusted, not only for the sake of good vision per se, but also in relation to the patient's movements.

On new affordances and potential for knowledge development

The tricks of the trade that were shared and discussed in Excerpt 5 were related to a set of further concerns. One such concern was ergonomics – how one needs to position one's own as well as the patient's body – and what it could imply in terms of one's well-being compared to earlier modes of working. In addition, reduced possibilities of checking on how the patient is doing and being able to interact during endodontic procedures were raised as concerns. The potential of engaging the assistant nurse to be more proactive in collaboration with the dentist was briefly mentioned as a potential area of development to maintain the quality in these areas of professional conduct. Towards the end of their discussion the moderator asked the group to reflect on the advantages of the microscope and how its current impact on endodontic practice can be understood from their experience. Below only some of the quite elaborate uptakes of this question are summarized by the participants.

Excerpt 6 Summing up advantages

6a *Eric*   What are the the biggest advantages with it then (the microscope) 'cause it's obvious it has had a tremendous impact in the area of endodontic practice

6b *Annie*   Safer a safer treatment for the patient and more control of what you do

6c *Lauren* Much better precision

6d *Paul*   It's a great satisfaction to see what you are doing

6e *Lauren* It would never be possible to go back and feel that you are doing a good job when you know what you can look for (.) these extra canals and different canal forms that you cannot see unless you look down

6f *Paul*   But we also see quite many fracture lines and we don't know what that means ehh for example (.) we get information that we really don't know how to deal with

The question posed is productive as the participants start summing up some of the most prominent features of working in the re-mediated visual environment that has been elaborated throughout their discussion. While feelings of increased security, control and precision and of 'doing a good job' are very salient in the professionals' accounts, we can also note that Paul returns to one of the first impressions that were established at the beginning of their discussion – that of discovering fractures to an extent that might call for re-interpretation. This issue is carefully re-introduced and hence brought back into professional consideration without further discussion. It seems to merely function as a reminder of a concern yet to be dealt with. The experience of discovering unidentifiable things could be challenging in terms of professional judgement. These concerns about not knowing how to interpret new information provided through the use of the microscope incorporate potential for future development of medical treatments and knowledge in endodontic practice.

Conclusions

Through our analysis of the professionals' accounts we have recognized the process of appropriation as a new tool, the surgical microscope, was increasingly mastered by and gradually transparent to the learner. We have also learned something more substantial and particular about what such a process involves. At a general level we notice that the appropriation of the artefact did not establish a division of labour between tool and body that distanced the professional from the work to be performed. Instead this appropriation process seems to imply that mind and means need to merge in interaction with the new environment. The discussion among professionals made salient a context of professional action that was re-mediated and described a different coordination with the environment – perceptually, cognitively, technically and physically. The most salient experience of the shift, was not the tactile, kineasthetic or proprioceptive experiences that the professionals described, nor was it *what* they were able to see. Instead, we argue, the shift seemed to constitute a visual re-location into a new spatial environment which radically altered the experiential context. While the dentist takes the opportunity to describe how to explore and work in this re-mediated environment, pursuing the task deeper into the root canals, other important details and contexts for action seem to be backgrounded. The established practice of interacting more intimately face-to-face with a patient during a procedure, closely following cues and reactions, for instance, is mentioned only to a minor extent. The way that mind and tool merge in interaction with the environment accordingly seem to create a form of distance from the patient. With the surgical microscope the dentist is instead able to visually experience the tooth 'from within' and from this spatial position other potentials of mapping 'the terrain' and deciding on relevant treatments become salient. If visually shared among professionals, a space-related body of professional knowing may accordingly develop over time. We, however, note that their accounts of tactile expertise on the other hand risk becoming too reduced in significance. This established expertise of mapping and exploring is not only backgrounded in the professionals' accounts but even downgraded, and in some cases even described as trivial.

With technology shifts, new conditions for professional conduct emerge which will have implications for how expertise is enacted and understood. As has already been pointed out, the professional experience of setting a new standard for oneself of what counts as good vision after the technology shift potentially incorporates new considerations in terms of what counts as professional expertise and what requirements of professional conduct the future might bring. *In situ* such expertise is challenged in response to the features and affordances of the technology-in-use, but significant shifts will most likely also shape the normative expectations of what constitutes expertise within the specific domain. One aspect that is important to consider is whether professional accountability concerning patient safety, more explicit forms of decision-making and options for treatment, precision and efficiency, ergonomics and other important issues will possibly, on a longer term basis, be regulated on the basis of what is established as the expected standard among professionals.

Notes

1 This research has been funded by LinCS, a national centre of excellence for research in the area of learning, interaction and mediated communication, and by the University of

Gothenburg LETStudio in collaboration with the Department of Odontology at Sahlgrenska Academy.

2 The notion of tools and material-semiotic means are used interchangeably and refer to language or any other cultural artefacts that co-constitute human activity. A sociocultural perspective resists the common distinction between 'the material' and 'the semiotic'.

3 This refers to a small magnification device commonly used by engravers, jewellers, watchmakers and dentists.

4 In a sociocultural perspective re-mediation means a shift in the way that mediating devices regulate coordination with the environment. Such shifts imply a qualitative re-organization of action and perception in culturally established activities.

5 Endodontic means 'within the tooth' and refer to treatments of the root canals, the dental pulp and its supporting structure.

6 According to Kim and Baek (2004) it was introduced in otolaryngology around 1950, and to neurosurgery in the 1960s.

7 Unlike many other focus-group arrangements, these discussions were not arranged in order to retrieve different opinions and ideas on a particular matter from different perspectives.

References

Bahcall, J.K. (2008) 'Visual enhancement', in J.I. Ingle, L.K. Bakland and J.C. Baumgartner (eds) *Ingle's Endodontics*. Hamilton Ontario: BC Deckers Inc.

Bateson, G. (1972) *Steps to an Ecology of Mind*, New York: Ballantine Books.

Billig, M. (1996) *Arguing and Thinking: A rhetorical approach to social psychology*, 2nd edn, Cambridge: Cambridge University Press.

Edwards, D. (1997) *Discourse and Cognition*, London: Sage.

Goodwin, C. (1994) 'Professional vision', *American Anthropologist*, 96(3): 606–633.

Goodwin, C. (1997) 'The blackness of black: Color categories as situated practices', in L.B. Resnick, R. Säljö, C. Pontecorvo and B. Burge (eds) *Discourse, Tools, and Reasoning: Essays on situated cognition*. Berlin: Springer.

Kim, S. and Baek, S. (2004) 'The microscope and endodontics', *The Dental Clinics of North America*, 48: 11–18.

Machtou, P. (2010) 'The surgical microscope', in G. Bergenholtz, P. Hørstedt-Bindslev and C. Reit (eds) *Textbook of Endodontology*, 2nd edn, Oxford: Wiley-Blackwell.

Marková, I., Linell, P., Grossen, M. and Salazar Orvig, A. (2007) *Dialogue in Focus Groups: Exploring socially shared knowledge*, London: Equinox.

Middleton, D. and Brown, S. (2005) *The Social Psychology of Experience. Studies in remembering and forgetting*, London: Sage Publications.

Murphy, K. (2011) 'Building stories: The embodied narration of what might come to pass', in J. Streeck, C. Goodwin and C. LeBaron (eds) *Embodied Interaction: Language and body in the material world*, New York: Cambridge University Press.

Mäkitalo, Å. (2012) 'Professional learning and the materiality of social practice', *Journal of Education and Work*, 25(1): 59–78.

Vygotsky, L.S. (1981) 'The genesis of higher mental functions', in J.V. Wertsch (ed.) *The Concept of Activity in Soviet Psychology*, Armonk, NY: Sharpe.

Weddle, A.B. and Hollan, J.D. (2010) 'Professional perception and expert action: Scaffolding embodied practices in professional education', *Mind, Culture and Activity*, 17(2): 119–148.

Chapter 8

Engineering knowing in the digital workplace

Aligning materiality and sociality through action

Aditya Johri

Introduction

In this chapter, I argue that professional engineering knowledge, or knowing, emerges in practice by engaging in action that comprises both the material and social context of the workplace. This situated enactment comprises both 'knowing what' and 'knowing how'. Practice-based theories of learning emphasize the role of the social context but only pay minimal attention to the role of the material context which is critical for engineering knowing. I use a case study of a newcomer participating in an engineering laboratory to empirically illustrate the intertwined sociomateriality of knowing. The context of the case study is representative of engineering contexts across 21st century work sites infused with both digital and physical materiality, but increasingly with digital materiality. This proliferation of digital materiality is an outcome of the flexibility with which it can be leveraged for communication with and about others and to the actual undertaking of work, through data collection, representation and manipulation, and thereby to technical aspects of engineering work. The integration of these analytically distinct aspects of work – the social and the technical – forms a sociomaterial assemblage through which work is performed. Specifically, engineers engage in bricolage, or tinkering, with the tools available to them to create a relatively stable, though often temporary, work environment in the face of uncertainty. This ability of engineers to undertake what I have termed 'sociomaterial bricolage' is a defining feature of engineering knowing in the workplace. In the rest of the chapter I first briefly review literature on intertwining of the social and the material in the engineering workplace. This is followed by an empirical case study and finally with a discussion of the concept of 'sociomaterial bricolage'.

The intertwining of the social and the material in engineering knowing

Although engineering and engineers have often been subjects of serious study (Auyang 2004; Zussman 1985), research on professional engineering work[1] is sparse (Downey and Lucena 2004; Downey 2009; Trevelyan 2010; Vinck 2003).

An understanding of professional engineering work is important for many reasons but none is more critical than for preparing future engineers. This requires understanding how engineers conduct their work and how they learn to participate in professional practices (Stevens *et al.* 2014) in order to overcome the gap between professional work and student training. Furthermore, professional work is undergoing significant changes in recent years due to changes in organizations during late capitalism coupled with the proliferation and advances in information technology (Fenwick 2013). As a consequence, the landscape of engineering professional work has changed significantly, and more flexible, distributed and technology supported work structures are commonplace. In addition to work structure, there have been qualitative changes in the nature of work itself and 'knowledge' work requiring advanced studies and expertise is commonplace.

Recently, several authors have investigated learning and knowing in the engineering workplace directly (see Johri 2010) and studies of professional engineering work have established beyond contention the highly complex role of knowing and working in engineering organizations. Trevelyan (2010) draws on observational study of all main engineering disciplines and across settings in Australia and South Asia to argue that the foundation of engineering practice is 'distributed expertise' – the harnessing of tacit knowledge, expertise and skills, spread across people; equal and simultaneous emphasis on both the social and the technical. Gainsburg *et al.* (2010) examined how the project structure of engineering work shapes engineers' use of knowledge and found that two-thirds of the knowledge used by engineers in their work was generated in practice. This practice-based knowledge is necessarily a conglomeration of working with others and collaboration and communicating with them. Furthermore, they argue, not only is this practice-based knowledge paramount in solving engineering problems but can lead to more theoretical knowledge. In other words, engineering practice can contribute to engineering sciences.

In addition to its focus on domain expertise, engineering work is also unique as it involves design and hence tools that can support design. Bucciarelli (1988) studied 'the design process' within two engineering firms, using participant observation techniques and demonstrated that '[engineering] design is a social process' (Bucciarelli 1988:161) not in some trivial sense that it involves people working together but rather that '[design] only exists in a collective sense' (161), that it can only be seen as a process that is distributed across different sub-communities, which in turn requires social and technical coordination to bring different parts of a project's work together. Another early study of engineering design by Henderson (1991) described the 'visual culture' of engineering design, a culture in which sketching is the way that engineers think and communicate and in which sketches are objects through which organizational actions are frequently coordinated and negotiated. Engineering drawings and sketches are shown to be 'devices that socially organize the workers, the work process, and the concepts workers manipulate in engineering design' (Henderson 1991:452). In her work Henderson has brought attention to a unique aspect of engineering – the use of representational systems. Her work goes further though, and has highlighted the centrality of materiality to the use of representations – representations can be embedded in and constructed from different materials (Henderson 1998).

Finally, unlike other professions, most of which rely on materials produced for them, engineers are also involved with creating material for themselves as well as for others. Whether the use of materiality is simply to produce representations that can then be used in some way, or materiality is central to the development of an artifact, materiality is omnipresent and linked to work practice. Therefore, for engineers knowing (Orlikowski 2002) – in any way, shape or form – cannot be separated from materiality. These studies of professional engineering work shed light on a serious incongruence between knowing in the workplace and current accounts of engineering knowledge, starting from the early 20th century, that have become largely about engineering sciences and representations rather than about working with and thinking through materials (Seely 1999). This change has come about primarily because of large scale institutionalization of engineering training within higher education establishments, making apprenticeship, once the only mechanism for learning engineering, largely obsolete.[2]

In the next section, I look empirically at the ideas discussed above through a case study of a newcomer as he navigated the practices of his new place of work after receiving advanced training in electronics engineering.

Case study: newcomer participation[3]

My research study used a practice-based approach (Bourdieu 1990; Brown and Duguid 2001; Orlikowski 2002; Schatzki 2001) and was undertaken in the same vein as studies under frameworks such as cognitive apprenticeship (Brown *et al.* 1989), situated learning (Johri and Olds 2011; Lave and Wenger 1991) and community of practice (Wenger 1998). Essentially, this work argues that newcomer participation is a guided process that occurs as experts and novices interact within a specific context. As newcomers participate in a practice they move from a position of peripheral participation to full participation and the fundamental change that occurs – or learning that happens – is a transformation in their identity. These situated accounts of newcomer participation move beyond mere socialization arguments towards an emphasis on development of expertise and change in identity, accordingly, they argue that newcomers not only need to socialize but have to become a *participating* member of a community.[4] My study was designed to specifically examine the intertwining of the social and material environment and its role in newcomer participation. Overall, through this case study I test the argument that the social and the material – sociomaterial – are highly intertwined with engineering knowing and information and skills imparted as part of the engineering curriculum are insufficient for the enactment of engineering knowing in the workplace. Furthermore, I demonstrate, empirically, how then engineers enact knowing in the workplace and overcome their deficiencies by leveraging the sociomateriality of their work context.

Research setting and data collection

The setting for this case study was an industrial research and development laboratory – InfoLab – located on the west coast of the United States. At the time of
the field study InfoLab employed around 20 fulltime researchers and another 20
supporting personnel that included technical support staff, administrative staff
and contractors. The primary research focus in the lab was on interactive technologies and the development of interactive systems. The research topics ranged
from the design of a knowledge management system to a three-dimensional
browser for viewing images and videos. The majority of researchers had a doctor-
ate in Computer Engineering, Electronics and Communication Engineering,
Computer Science, or a related subject. This study was designed as an ethnographically informed qualitative case study. I spent five months in the field, from
April to September 2005, and conducted 70 formal interviews and over 80 days
of observations. All formal interviews were recorded and professionally transcribed, and copious observational field notes were taken. I collected archival
data that included publications, technical reports, technical memos, intellectual
property reports, travel information, monthly activity reports, videos and dynamic
slide presentations with audio. Digital data was pervasive around InfoLab and not
only was it central to researchers' practice but significantly shaped my field study
as well. Access to digital data allowed me to continuously monitor what was
going on in the organization through the intranet and mailing lists, and also
allowed me to archive data for subsequent analysis.

Understanding newcomer participation was a primary goal of my study and I
therefore collected extensive in-depth data on newcomers. During the five
months I spent at InfoLab five newcomers joined as fulltime research staff. Of
those five newcomers, I have selected the case of one newcomer, Alex, for the
purposes of this chapter. The participation of this newcomer was unique as he was
the only newcomer to actually conduct a demonstration in front of a large audience, an indication of full participation. Overall, the participation trajectory of all
newcomers progressed through the same initial stages. First, they started working
peripherally on an existing project with other researchers. Next, they either
carved out a piece of that project for themselves or slowly started a project that
they would lead. Finally, they presented the results of their work first in the form
of demos and subsequently as technical reports and external publications.

Alex's participation at InfoLab

Table 8.1 presents the trajectory of Alex's participation broken up into different
temporal and analytical stages. Alex successfully navigated the organizational and
social context of InfoLab and productively used the materials available to him. If
the materials he needed were not readily available, he constructed them, such as
the data for his demo. He assembled the demo from a range of artifacts – visuals,
animations, texts – that he generated or acquired from others as well as through

Table 8.1 Stages of participation and sociomateriality

Stage of participation	Aligning materiality and sociality through action	Knowing in practice
0: The job interview	This stage involved a presentation of work open to all researchers in the laboratory; it required individual meetings with most researchers in which, in addition to talk, the interviewee would often present work informally on a laptop to interviewers	Knowing how to do research presentations – specifically those targeted at getting a job (from watching others and practising); knowing what research labs do (from prior experience)
1: Entry into InfoLab and uncertainty reduction	Interacting with others in a new physical setting; figuring out the norms of use of different physical spaces; observing others presenting their work and interacting while presenting	Knowing how materiality can be availed – using social networks to get material to work; knowing organizational norms for presentations
2: Ideation	Creating new materials within the context of his research group; seeking legitimacy within his research group by showing his materialized ideas	Knowing what is considered new within the context of the lab
3: Creating infrastructure to generate data	Figuring out what materials and data were available in the lab by communicating with other researchers; making plans to procure new data in a manner where others supported him; creating and laying out the material infrastructure with help from others; generating and storing data while working with the person responsible for data permissions	Knowing infrastructuring
4: Creating a prototype using digital data	Working with others to understand the overall design and functionality of the intended end product; translating the requirements into software code and getting feedback on different iterations	Knowing how to get feedback and how much feedback others give and of what quality
5: Preparing for the demo	Communicating with others to understand the purpose of the demo and the norms of the intellectual property meeting; creating and testing a prototype that is relatively stable, attractive and able to demonstrate and convey the essential functionalities of the intended product; practising the demo by performing in front of an imaginary audience in the room in which the demo has to be given	Knowing what is a 'demo' and how to 'demo'

(Continued)

Table 8.1   (Continued)

Stage of participation	Aligning materiality and sociality through action	Knowing in practice
6: Performance of the demo	Performance in front of lab researchers; interaction with the audience to explain the approach and product	Knowing feedback
7: The sociomaterial construction of knowledge	Assimilation of feedback received during the demo and its incorporation in the next iteration of the product; intellectual property development in two different directions based on feedback	Knowing how to integrate feedback to generate new knowledge

Source: Adapted from Johri (2012)

his ingenuity, and he performed the demo successfully. The success of the demo was validated by the filing of two patents based on this work. At InfoLab, demoing was one instance of this amalgamation, a 'sociomaterial assemblage'. Text (visual and aural), images, video, pictures, animations and direct manipulation were all key components of this assemblage and were used judiciously by Alex to showcase his work. Demoing was a complex activity often serving as the primary indicator of both disciplinary and technical competency among researchers. Demos combined the technical competence required to build a working system with the social competence to understand the audience and users of the system and to present a working prototype to other researchers. Although for analytical purposes it is important to distinguish the social from the material (such as the data versus who he gets the data from or how he generates it with the help of others); in practice, and for Alex, this distinction did not exist. He enacted both the social and the material in a mutually constitutive manner. This case study sheds significant light on the process of learning within a community of practice. In addition to accepted issues of identity transformation and norms, this case study illustrates the sociomaterial nature of participation.

What did Alex learn through his participation? First, through enactment of accepted practices within the community of researchers at InfoLab he demonstrate his transition from a peripheral to a full member in the community and also showed that he had learnt how to become a member of a community of practice. The demo signaled his fuller participation in the community. Second, his movement from peripheral to fuller participation itself is a form of learning as through this process he undergoes an identity change from a newcomer to a more established member of the organization. Third, the feedback on the demo and subsequent knowledge construction, as well as working on the demo in the first place, resulted in gains in technical knowledge and contributions to the research lab. He reported that he learned a lot from his participation including how to develop and file a patent, how to apply his technical skills to a new content domain, and how to initiate and grow new areas of expertise.

Knowing in practice through action – sociomaterial bricolage

The case study presented above illustrates the nature of professional engineering work and knowing as being an example of 'sociomateriality'. According to Orlikowski and Scott (2008), the sociomaterial view is central in understanding human practices since the social and the material are constitutively entangled in everyday life (Suchman 2007). This position of 'constitutive entanglement' does not privilege either humans or technology but instead argues that the social and the material are inextricably related – there is no social that is not also material, and no material that is not also social (Orlikowski 2007). The sociomaterial perspective, which consists of a constellation of theories such as actor–network theory (Latour 2005), mangle of practice (Pickering 1995), activity theory (Engeström 1987) and distributed cognition (Hutchins 1995; Pea 1993), is a recent extension of the socio-technical approach, and dissolves the taken-for-granted boundaries between the social and the material and views them instead as a composite and shifting assemblage or a constellation of material and social (Orlikowski and Scott 2008). An assemblage is a heterogeneous configuration that preserves some concept of the structural (Marcus and Saka 2006) but differs from structures in that it consists of elements that function well together but may be quite unlike each other and coevolve with time. An assemblage is only momentarily specific. This assemblage or configuration neither presumes independent nor interdependent entities (Barad 2003). Instead, all entities (whether social or technological, human or material) are inseparable. In other words, in this approach neither the social aspects of our work nor the material aspect is privileged. Latour (2004) (discussed in Orlikowski and Scott 2008:455) paints a vibrant picture to capture the essence of sociomateriality. He asks us to imagine a battlefield with soldiers all lined up. He argues that there are no soldiers without their uniforms and arms, nor are the materials of any use without the soldiers; they co-constitute each other. Although not as dramatic as soldiers on the battlefield, a similar picture of sociomateriality can be painted for our approach. There is no knowing per se without some form of materiality involved. Therefore, at one level knowing can be approached as a process of working with and thinking through materials. This idea has several implications for our understanding of knowing. One important issue to understand is that although in scholarly practices we make an analytical distinction between the material and the social, 'Any distinction of humans and technologies is analytical only, and done with the recognition that these entities necessarily entail each other in practice' (Orlikowski and Scott 2008:456). Given that materiality and knowing are closely intertwined, any effort to design or study them must encompass both. For instance, the same object such as a computing device can serve either as an affordance or an obstruction in accomplishing a task. The computer can aid in getting information needed to teach something to a student but can also be used as a gaming device thereby interrupting with a teaching moment. The material gets it meaning from practice and this meaning changes as the activity unfolds.

Given the materiality of engineering work, the findings from the study I present here are uniquely relevant for understanding engineering practices. It is hard to imagine any engineering work being accomplished without some form of materiality in the equation. Even before the advent of information technology, work, whether through paper-based communication or filing systems, has always relied on materiality. This materiality in turn significantly shaped the work practices. But these materials, in and of themselves, fulfill no useful function. It is in their intersection with work practices that both the work and the materials for the work derive meaning, as Pries (2001: 22), explains,

> artifacts are sedimented results of social practices and incarnations of symbol systems, but at the same time restrict and guide social practices; systems of symbols could not exist without artifacts – artifacts as things made by human beings are the first symbols at all – nor without social practices. But at the same time as being a product of practices and artifacts, symbols structure and give meaning to them.

To better articulate the relationship between materiality and practices, I leverage sociomateriality and the concept of bricolage (Levi-Strauss 1967), to advance the notion of sociomaterial bricolage to capture the emergent and socially and materially intertwined nature of human practices. This conception provides a useful analytical lens to examine ad hoc knowledge practices. In particular, it focuses on the capacity of users to make use of the tools available to them in constellation of social practices. This making do with what is available on hand was termed by Levi-Strauss (1967) as bricolage. Levi-Strauss was interested in how people make do with what they have at hand rather than sticking to a planned approach which would require using pre-existing tools and practices as opposed to tools that are immediately available. Orr (1996) further argues,

> The point of bricolage is the reflective manipulation of a closed set of resources to accomplish some purpose. The set is the accumulation of previous manipulations, one's experience and knowledge, and in literal bricolage, physical objects. This manipulation is done in the context of a specific goal, which influences the process.
>
> (121, *bricolage*)

Bricolage is about the particular and the particularities, and in the case of learning technologies it helps explain the relationship between practice-as-designed and practice-as-practiced or emergent. Within the context of design, 'Bricolage can be described as "designing immediately", using ready-at-hand materials, combinations of already existing pieces of technology – hardware, software and facilities (e.g., Internet providers) – as well as additional, mostly "off-the-self" ones. It therefore also involves design as assembly' (Büscher *et al.* 2001:23). The concept of bricolage shifts focus away from technology design – as usually understood as the design of an artifact – towards emergent design of technology-in-use particularly by the users.

In the case study presented above and the one discussed in Johri (2011a), a socially heavy account would miss the role of material affordances and a material account would not be able to represent the social changes accompanying material use, thereby impacting a fair interpretation of the role of learning technologies in learning practices. Furthermore, the notion of bricolage allows us to leverage the 'making do' component of the practice thereby allowing us to account for the ever important dynamic and evolving component of any practice. Specifically, across the these cases we see a representation of three characteristics of bricolage identified by Baker and Nelson (2005). First, learners and knowledge workers made do – that is, they engaged in action and activity rather than lingering too long over how to create a workable solution. Second, they used the resources at hand to the best of their ability. They stretched the boundaries of what was possible with the resources they had at hand. Even though during the interviews most informants lamented the lack of access to other easy–to-use tools, they went on about their work without those resources. Finally, the informants were able to use existing resources for new purposes. For instance, Internet relay chat (IRC) emerged as a tool for informal communication, taking over the role often accomplished by water-cooler conversations. In this way team members developed learning practices that helped them work irrespective of the boundary they needed to span. All these instances of bricolage though were mediated by materiality and intricately involved the social world – whether it was team formation or creation of a participatory learning environment. Therefore, sociomaterial bricolage encapsulates the idea that practices emerge through the ad hoc use of available artifacts by people often in conjunction with others and while participating in situated activities.

One lesson that emerges is that, as Gainsburg *et al.* (2010) discussed earlier, show, a path from practical work towards engineering sciences might be a better model to engage and retain engineering students. Not all classroom-based engineering science knowledge is irrelevant, hardly so, but the right balance of practice and science is important to attract and retain students with long term loyalty to engineering work. The identity as practitioner should be encouraged and built upon, not shredded by engineering science and science requirement. Another common finding from these studies is that engineers act under severe constraints, they have to bring to bear diverse kinds of knowledge to the problem at hand, and they have to keep learning and reinventing themselves.

Discussion and conclusion

The work of Trevelyan (2010) and others (see Stevens *et al.* 2014:119–137 for a review) presents an account that diverges sharply from normative images of what historian Rosalind Williams calls 'the ideology of engineering' (Williams 2002). The normative image of engineers is that they have a distinct technical domain of knowledge that they can apply rationally and in a more-or-less linear manner to the solution of technical problems. In contrast, studies of engineering work have established that engineering work is complex, ambiguous and full of contradictions, and that the social and technical are almost inextricably tied up together in any engineering project, at least in any project that is successfully realized, an image that Law (1987) has termed 'heterogeneous engineering'. The critical conceptual point that undergirds the heterogeneous engineering perspective – as well as the broader perspective of actor–network theory (cf. Latour 2005) – is that the commonsense dichotomy between the technical and social is unnecessary and in fact misleading when trying to understand how projects are realized. My work further extends this idea and argues that as engineering sciences have advanced, the material aspects of engineering have slowly been relegated to the sidelines, particularly in the training of engineering.

In this chapter, I have advanced sociomateriality as a theoretical concept and sociomaterial bricolage as an analytical framework that can assist us in understanding engineers' knowing in practice. I have also argued that to leverage sociomaterial analytically, it is often necessary to separate the social and the material, although in practice – for informants – they are not distinct issues. I have focused on the ensemble but have found it necessary to distinguish between the underlying factors as only by understanding the emergence of the ensemble – and its parts – can we delve into aspects of learning practices such as the motivation for their inception and subsequent development. The usefulness of the concept of sociomaterial bricolage goes beyond illustrating the emergent nature of assemblages and also helps establish the idiosyncrasies of sociomaterial relations. It also, rightly, emphasizes the idea that particularities will be present and observable across practices, and, practices developed by and within the context of a combination of people and material will not automatically transfer to another scenario; even in slightly different contexts, variations of an assemblage will exist. Theoretically, sociomaterial bricolage builds on prior work on theories that address aspects of learning technology in practice. The concept is closely related to distributed cognition and activity theory where cognition is characterized as the property of a system and not a person. Sociomaterial bricolage imbibes the ideas expressed in these theories but further argues for an emphasis on the emergent connection between 'at the moment activities', materiality and sociality. From this standpoint, sociomaterial bricolage can be applied to study and design a broad array of learning practices where emergence is a key construct. By making materiality of learning practices salient in engineering this perspective allows those interested in engineering education to incorporate materiality as a useful focus of study without relegating other aspects of the practice to the margins. This is necessary to account fully and in-depth for the role of materiality in engineering practice, particularly in professional settings. For other practical applications, engineering educators who implement or directly use technology for learning can benefit from developing a more holistic understanding of their interactions with technology and from a heightened awareness of how the social and material are intertwined. One limitation of the sociomaterial account is its inability to forecast the nature or role of upcoming materialities. The engineering workplace is significantly changing with advances in digital technologies. Therefore, for scholars it might be prudent to develop and extend sociomateriality in ways that allow us to account for new technological developments theoretically, and to develop an understanding of the sociomaterial which is not beholden to specific devices or software.

Acknowledgements

Parts of this work was build on Johri (2012, 2011a, 2011b). This work was partially funded by the US National Science Foundation grant EEC# 0954034. I wish to thank my informants for their time and cooperation.

Notes

1 By work I am going to refer specifically to professional engineering practices; for in-depth discussion of work and workplace learning refer to Fenwick (2006).
2 It can be argued that students are being apprenticed into doing engineering research, as conceptualized within academia.
3 An expanded version of this case study is presented in Johri (2012).
4 In the case of InfoLab the ability to do a demo of a system was seen as a first step towards full participation in the laboratory. 'Demoing', which comes from demonstrations, is the practice of presenting a designed artifact to an audience in a way that allows viewers to understand the functionality of the artifact through an explicit display of how it works. Successful demoing requires the person doing the demo to marshal both social and material resources before and during the demo to convey an idea or action to the audience. The importance of demos was echoed in a refrain commonly heard around InfoLab – 'Demo or die'.

References

Auyang, S.Y. (2004) *Engineering: An Endless Frontier*, Cambridge MA: Harvard University Press.
Baker, T. and Nelson, R.E. (2005) 'Creating something from nothing: Resource construction through entrepreneurial bricolage', *Administrative Science Quarterly*, 50: 329–366.
Barad, K. (2003) 'Posthumanist performativity: Toward an understanding of how matter comes to matter', *Signs*, 28(3): 801–831.
Bourdieu, P. (1990) *The Logic of Practice*, Cambridge: Polity.

Brown, J. S., Collins, A. and Duguid, P. (1989). Situated cognition and the culture of learning. Educational Researcher, 18, 32–42.

Brown, J.S. and Duguid, P. (2001) 'Knowledge and organization: A social–practice perspective', *Organization Science*, 12(2): 198–215.

Bucciarelli, L.L. (1988) 'An ethnographic perspective on engineering design', *Design Studies*, 9(3): 159–168.

Büscher, M., Gill, S., Mogensen, P. and Shapiro, D. (2001) 'Landscapes of practice: Bricolage as a method for situated design', *Journal of Computer Supported Cooperative Work*, 10(1): 1–28.

Downey, G.L. (2009) 'What is engineering studies for? Dominant practices and scalable scholarship', *Engineering Studies*, 1(1): 55–76.

Downey, G.L. and Lucena, J.C. (2004) 'Knowledge and professional identity in engineering', *History and Technology* 20(4): 393–420.

Engeström, Y. (1987). *Learning by Expanding: An Activity-Theoretical Approach to Developmental Research*. Helsinki: Orienta-Konsultit Oy.

Fenwick, T. (2006) 'Tidying the territory: Questioning terms and purposes in work-learning research', *Journal of Workplace Learning*, 18(5): 265–278.

Fenwick, T. (2013) 'Understanding transitions in professional practice and learning: Towards new questions for research', *Journal of Workplace Learning*, 25: 6.

Gainsburg, J., Rodriguez-Lluesma, C. and Bailey, D.E. (2010) 'A 'knowledge profile' of an engineering occupation: Temporal patterns in the use of engineering knowledge', *Engineering Studies*, 2(3): 197–220.

Henderson, K. (1991) 'Flexible sketches and inflexible data bases: Visual communication, conscription devices, and boundary objects in design engineering', *Science, Technology & Human Values'*, 16(4): 448–473.

Henderson, K. (1998) 'The role of material objects in the design process: A comparison of two design cultures and how they contend with automation', *Science, Technology & Human Values'*, 23(2): 139–174.

Hutchins, E. (1995) *Cognition in the Wild*, Cambridge, MA: MIT Press.

Johri, A. (2010) 'Situated engineering in the workplace', *Engineering Studies*, 2(3): 151–152.

Johri, A. (2011a) 'Sociomaterial bricolage: The creation of location-spanning work practices by global software developers', *Information and Software Technology*, 53(9): 955–968.

Johri, A. (2011b) 'The sociomateriality of learning practices and implications for learning technology', *Research in Learning Technology*, 19(3): 207–217.

Johri, A. (2012) 'Learning to demo: The sociomateriality of newcomer participation in engineering research practices', *Engineering Studies*, 4(3): 249–269.

Johri, A. and B. Olds (2011) 'Situated engineering learning: Bridging engineering education research and the learning sciences', *Journal of Engineering Education*, 100(1): 151–185.

Latour, B. (2004). Nonhumans. In S. Harrison, S. Pile, and N. Thrift (Eds.), *Patterned ground: Entanglements of nature and culture* (pp. 224–227). London: Reaktion Books.

Latour, B. (2005) *Reassembling the Social – An introduction to actor–network-theory*, Oxford: Oxford University Press.

Lave, J. and Wenger, E. (1991) *Situated Learning: Legitimate peripheral participation*, Cambridge, UK: Cambridge University Press.

Law, J. (1987) 'Technology and heterogeneous engineering: The case of the Portuguese expansion'. In W. Bijker, T. Hughes and T. Pinch (eds), The social construction of technological systems (pp. 111–134), Cambridge, MA: MIT Press.

Levi-Strauss, C. (1967) *The Savage Mind*, Chicago: University of Chicago Press.

Marcus, G.E. and E. Saka (2006) 'Assemblage', *Theory, Culture & Society*, 23(2–3): 101–106.

Orlikowski, W. (2002) 'Knowing in practice: Enacting a collective capability in distributive organizing', *Organization Science* 13(3): 249–273.

Orlikowski, W.J. (2007) 'Sociomaterial practices: Exploring technology at work', *Organization Studies*, 28(9): 1435–1448.

Orlikowski, W.J. and Scott, S.V. (2008) 'Sociomateriality: Challenging the separation of technology, work and organization', *Annals of the Academy of Management* 2(1): 433–474.

Orr, J. (1996) *Talking about Machines: Ethnography of a modern job*, Cornell, Ithaca, NY: ILR Press.

Pea, R.D. (1993) 'Practices of distributed intelligence and designs for education', in G. Salomon (ed.) *Distributed Cognitions* (pp. 47–87), New York: Cambridge University Press.

Pickering, A. (1995) *The Mangle of Practice: Time, agency, and science*, Chicago: University of Chicago Press.

Pries, L. (ed.) (2001) *New Transnational Social Spaces*, London and New York: Routledge.

Schatzki, T.R. (2001) 'Introduction: Practice theory', in T.R. Schatzki, K.K. Cetina and E.V. Savigny (eds), *The Practice Turn in Contemporary Theory* (pp. 42–55), New York: Routledge.

Seely, B.E. (1999) 'The other re-engineering of engineering education, 1900–1965', *Journal of Engineering Education*, 88(3): 285–294.

Stevens, R., Johri, A. and O'Connor, K. (2014) 'Professional engineering work', in A. Johri and B.M. Olds (eds), *Cambridge Handbook of Engineering Education Research*, New York: Cambridge University Press.

Suchman, L.A. (2007) *Human–Machine Reconfigurations: Plans and situated actions*, Cambridge, UK: Cambridge University Press.

Trevelyan, J. (2010) 'Reconstructing engineering from practice', *Engineering Studies* 2(3): 175–196.

Vinck, D. (ed.) (2003) *Everyday Engineering: An ethnography of design and innovation*, Cambridge, MA: MIT Press.

Wenger, E. (1998) *Communities of Practice: Learning, meaning, and identity*, Cambridge, UK: Cambridge University Press.

Williams, R. (2002) *Retooling: A historian confronts technological change*, Cambridge, MA: MIT Press.

Zussman, R. (1985) *Mechanics of the Middle Class: Work and politics among american engineers*. Berkeley, CA: University of California Press.

Chapter 9

Interprofessional working and learning

A conceptualization of their relationship and its implications for education

David Guile

Introduction

A cursory look at scholarship about the professions in the last two decades, for example, Abbott (1988) and Friedson (2001), reveals that interprofessional working[1] and learning are absent or little discussed. This is a curious state of affairs since interprofessional work has been a discernible trend in the global economy since the 1990s (Midler 1995) and, as a corollary, the implications these developments posed for professional formation had been acknowledged (Engeström *et al.* 1995).

This chapter addresses this paradox in two ways. The first is to argue that the growth in interprofessional work, and by extension interprofessional learning, stems from a) new principles for the organization of work, and b) the concomitant pressure on professional communities to collaborate more closely. The chapter illustrates this claim by discussing a number of writers' complementary, but slightly different, ideas about the reasons for the reorganization of work, and then by presenting a case study to exemplify the implications of these developments. The second is to argue that it also stems from diminishing faith in the objective status of knowledge that has emerged globally (since the Second World War), that has gradually undermined professionals' authority and, as a result, has, gradually exerted pressure on professionals to consider how they 'interpret' (Bauman 1987) their expertise to one another and the public. The chapter then argues that, taken together, the reorganization of work and professionals' new role as interpreters, are generating pressure on universities to consider how programmes of professional formation can support interprofessional working and learning. The chapter explores the curricular and pedagogic implications of this new challenge for programmes of professional formation through reference to the concept of 'recontextualization' (Guile 2010). The chapter concludes with a number of suggestions as to how universities and professional institutes could work together to rethink the design of programmes offered for initial professional formation, so they can better assist learners to develop the capabilities required for interprofessional working and learning.

The reorganization of work and the growth of interprofessional working and learning

The growth of collaboration between professionals

The main impetus for the growth of interprofessional work (in their terms 'collaborative communities') has, according to Adler *et al.* (2008:361–3) been spearheaded by organizations increasingly using 'process management', rather than 'functional separation', as the principle for the organization of work in the private and public sector. This development has resulted in first: the emergence of 'managed professional businesses' (Adler *et al.* 2008:363) where the role of the professional is to provide services to clients, and where firms are concerned to develop and align professionals' skill sets to match client portfolios; and second, the establishment of knowledge management infrastructures to share knowledge intra- and inter-professionally.

The pattern of professional work is, as Adler *et al.* (2008:364) describe, increasingly operative across a broad range of 'knowledge-intensive' occupations and organizations. Nevertheless, its emergence has and continues to be an uneven process. This is because on the one hand, the ethos and structures of autonomy among many traditional liberal professions, such as medicine, has acted as a powerful counterweight to the pressure to greater collaboration between professionals. And on the other hand, the expert-for-hire professions, for example, software engineers and consultants, have embraced the principle of the collaborative community as being consistent with contract-based work.

Other writers have noted the above developments and interpreted them as undermining professionals' status and autonomy (Dent and Whitehead 2002; Evetts 2003). What is interesting about Adler and colleagues is that they view the above developments positively. From their perspective, the emergence of interprofessional work is paving the way for professionals to consider the implications of their expertise in relation to the contribution that other professionals' expertise might make to addressing pressing economic, social and political concerns, rather than engaging in a zero-sum game about whose expertise will dominate discussions. Adler and colleagues accept, however, that this is a complex issue because collaboration forces professionals to work with peers from other professions, co-workers, clients, stakeholders and regulators, and programmes of professional formation do not always address these issues.

Projectification and the growth of interprofessional working and learning

Other researchers have identified a different manifestation of process management – 'projectification' (Midler 1995), that is, the organization of production around project teams, and this has contributed significantly to the growth of interprofessional work. Two expressions of projectification can be distinguished: the emergence of projects in a range of new industries where they were previously not evident, for example, automobiles (Midler 1995); and, the use of projects as an organizing principle in industries, such as, advertising and film, with the result that work is distributed spatially, across sites and temporally, across time zones (Grabher 2004). Both are contributing significantly to the spread of interprofessional working and learning.

Using Renault (in the 1980s–1990s) as a case study, Midler (1995:263) highlights that one of the most profound effects of projectification was to bestow on the leaders of project teams the 'entrepreneurial' responsibility to oversee the successful launch of new models in the global economy. As a consequence, project managers had relative autonomy to determine the timescale and work process to launch a new model, to identify from the different professional specialisms employed within Renault's operating divisions who to invite to become a member of the project team, and to override the heads of the company's operating divisions – people who previously held the major sources of power in the company. The above developments generated, however, a new problem: 'Professionals trained for years in a compartmentalised corporate environment have not been prepared for inter-department, or even inter-company dialogue' (Midler 1995:274). Thus, Renault, in common with other companies who used projects to transform the organization of work, discovered that overlaying projects on top of their existing division of labour merely generated a new learning challenge – how to support professionals to collaborate with one another.

The other form of projectification – projects-as-organizing-principle of work – can either take the form of intra-company or inter-company/freelance teams, and both generate slightly different learning challenges for professionals. A good example of the former is provided by Grabher's (2004) case study of the advertising industry. The primary challenge in the advertising industry, according to Grabher (2004:108) is to develop a reputation for devising 'original campaigns' that reflect closely clients' preferences to secure new accounts. To do so, advertising companies deploy staff to work on the 'client' (i.e. liaison) or the 'company' (i.e. creativity) side of advertising campaigns in an attempt to create a continuous dialogue between company and client. The pattern of work has, in turn, generated a specific interprofessional learning challenge: members of advertising companies have to learn how to 'bridge' (ibid.) the different foci and concerns that exist between members of the same project team so that they can convince clients that they are responding to clients' needs. A good example of projectification in relation to freelance work is provided by Bechky's (2006) analysis of film crews working on location. Members of film crews work for micro businesses or are freelance workers and secure their employment from a 'contractor' (Briner *et al.* 1996), someone who has procured a contract from a producer of a film or television programme to assemble a crew for a specific production. Work in such project teams is, as Bechky (2006:3) observes, 'governed through networks of relationships rather than by lines of authority'. This positions the different specialists in the film crews to have to learn how to 'self-regulate' their work in relation to the overall goal of completing the film on time and within budget.

Co-configuration and the involvement of users in the working process

The continuing pressure to produce innovative products and services in advanced industrial economies has, according to Engeström (2008), resulted in the emergence of a more radical principle for the organization of work – 'co-configuration'. By this he means, the involvement of users in the design and manufacturing stages of production to ensure their ideas are explicitly incorporated into new products and/or services. Moreover, co-configuration has ushered in a new mode of expertise. Engeström (2008:22) defines this as 'knotworking', in other words, situations where producers and users come together for a relatively short period of time to discuss the design and realization of a new product and/or service. A recurring challenge associated with knotworking is that the current organization of work (i.e. division of labour), the formal and informal rules that members of the organizations involved in an activity follow, the web of professional communities involved in that activity, and the clients (i.e. groups whose needs that activity purportedly addresses) generate contradictions or tensions between the aforementioned parties that inhibit them from working together effectively (Edwards *et al.* 2009). This challenge, as Engeström acknowledges (2008), has always existed in capitalist economies; the crucial difference now is that co-configuration intensifies pressure on professionals and the client groups they serve to work collaboratively to resolve those tensions.

Case study of interprofessional working and learning in a co-configured project team

This section of the chapter presents case study evidence based on the work of Hall *et al.* (2002) of the general trends in the reorganization of work described above. They analyse the ways in which a temporary project team, consisting of architects, structural engineers, preservationists and librarians, worked together to remodel two public libraries. In doing so, they identify a number of steps the team had to work through to co-configure a solution to that problem by grasping and engaging with one another's insights and concerns. The steps the team undertook are summarized below:

- The team negotiated a working process that a) encouraged individual members to participate in a process of nominating and responding to suggestions; b) provided opportunities to discuss the extent to which the current health and safety guidelines facilitated and/or inhibited their search for a solution to the problems, and c) used visual representations, such as sketches and hand movements, as boundary objects to animate ideas about how to address the problems.
- The team allowed the tensions that existed among members to surface in order to formulate a solution to redesign and strengthen the library. Initially, this was difficult because the preservationists were reluctant to go along with

the structural engineers' suggestions to replace existing library walls with more structurally sound materials within the existing health and safety guidelines. The problem with this solution was, for the preservationists, that it ruined the architectural integrity of the building. The preservationists countered by asking the team to devise a solution that challenged the 'guidelines' (Hall *et al.* 2002:3).

- The team formed the view that they needed a slightly broader interpretation of the guidelines to agree a solution to their task-in-hand. Consequently, they collectively recognized that they would: 'have to not only tell the city that the classification system is no good, but also convince the city architects office and the public about the viability of their proposed solution by re-educating them about standards of safety' (Hall *et al.* 2002:201).
- Some members of the team recognized gradually that the team had created a cul-de-sac for itself because the chances of persuading the city council to change the legal rules for preservation work or the tender specification the team had accepted were fairly negligible. As a consequence, one of the structural architects began to think differently by problematizing his disciplinary-specific perception as regards how the 'seismic resisting elements' (i.e. stabilization mechanisms) could be added in the centre of the library. Instead of continuing to advocate the replacement of library walls with more structurally sound materials, the engineer suggested that resistors could be strapped to the ceilings in such a way as to enhance rather than detract from the design of the building.
- Other members of the team listened to the engineer as he conveyed his idea by holding the resistors in one hand whilst simultaneously tracing out existing walls or regions of the building where they would be strapped with his other hand. The manner in which he conveyed his idea enabled the other team members, who were not structural engineers, to grasp the implications of his professional perception, judgement and proposed course of action in relation to their concerns. These detailed, embodied renderings, which were depicted on paper and in the air, constituted, according to Hall *et al.* (2002:204), a 'boundary object' that other members of the team used to collectively visualize the implications of the solution and, in the process, develop a sense of another professionals' insights and suggestions. Hence, the interplay between the process of visualization and the engineer's explanation helped to convince the team of his proposal's validity.

Based on their case study evidence, Hall *et al.* claim that the learning challenge for interprofessional teams, which are characterized by different professional specialisms and interests, is to create the conditions for professionals to understand one another. This entails professionals making representational devices (i.e. diagrams and gestures) that other professionals who are members of interprofessional project teams can then use to orientate them to respond to orally articulated or visibly communicated ideas and suggestions.

This process of creating representational devices assists professionals to grasp others' insights and suggestions, according to Hall *et al.* because they are able to develop a way to appreciate orally articulated or visibly communicated ideas and suggestions. Stated another way, members of the team learn to use others' oral and visual communication to overcome the boundaries, for example, epistemological, jurisdictional and emotional, which exist between them. These forms of communication provide a symbolic and practical frame of reference (representational infrastructure) that enables coordinated action between communities with different interests, needs and accountabilities. The outcome, according to Hall and colleagues, is that professionals gradually develop 'hybrid and selective forms of perception and action' (Hall *et al.* 2002:207), which provides them with a working sense of the value of the artifacts and explanations in relation to the task-in-hand. However, the context must, as their case study reveals, be conducive to this happening.

The explicit message from this case study is that interprofessional learning is inextricably bound up with interprofessional working. Consequently, the purpose and composition of a project team exercises a considerable influence on the way in which the team members address challenges. Concomitantly, the implicit message appears to be that interprofessional working and learning strategies are always situated accomplishments. This raises a new challenge for programmes of professional education: how to prepare professionals for interprofessional working and learning? Before addressing that question, we need to understand the principles that have historically underpinned the design of programmes of professional education.

Knowledge and the professions

The classic assumption: professionals as 'legislators'

The classic assumption in the literature on the professions is that the study of disciplinary knowledge in universities is crucial to the formation of professional expertise and identity. A modern account of the origins of this assumption lies, as Beck and Young (2005:187) quoting Bernstein (2000) observe, in: 'the pedagogic sequencing, in which inwardness and commitment shaped the terms of practical engagement in the outer world, that "*we can find the origins of the professions*" (Bernstein 2000:85)'.

The basis of this constitutive role of disciplines is, according to Beck and Young (2005:185), their dual role of facilitating 'inwardness' (immersion in a disciplinary tradition) and 'inner dedication' (form of identity associated with a disciplinary tradition) in programmes of professional formation. Beck and Young (2005:187) acknowledge however that these processes vary depending on whether someone is studying for a degree based on 'singulars' (traditional disciplines, such as, chemistry), 'regions' (interdisciplines, such as, business economics) or 'generics' (management). Their argument can be summarized as follows. Degrees based on singulars have deeper and more extensive knowledge bases and academic traditions. As a consequence, they result in the formation of stronger commitments to disciplinary specialisms and disciplinary identities compared with regions and generics. Beck and Young (2005:190) use this argument to make a parallel argument about the relation between disciplines and professional knowledge and identity. In a nutshell, they maintain that programmes of professional formation that are based on singulars, for example, physics and physicists, enable learners to develop stronger professional commitments to knowledge and professional identities than programmes of professional formation based on regions, for example, information technology and software engineers, and that the study of singulars and regions enables people to develop stronger professional commitments to knowledge and professional identities than programmes of professional formation based on generics, for example, management science and managers.

This assumption about the constitutive relation between disciplinary knowledge and the professions has underpinned the idea that the role of professionals is, to borrow Bauman's phrase, to 'legislate' for individuals and the community on matters pertaining to their domain of expertise. Bauman coined this term in his book *Legislators and Interpreters* (1987) where he analysed the changing status of public intellectuals in relation to the diminishing faith in advanced industrial societies as regards to the objectivity of scientific knowledge. The notion of 'legislate' and its companion 'interpret' can however be modified to offer insights into the challenges associated with the changing status of knowledge in society that the professions have faced since that time.

The typical view of the modern world that gave rise to the conception of intellectuals as legislators is, according to Bauman (1987:3), one of: 'an essentially ordered totality'; the presence of a pattern of uneven distribution of possibilities allows a sort of explanation of the events which – if correct – is simultaneously a tool of prediction (and, if required, resources are available) of control. From this perspective, the legitimacy of control depends on the adequacy of knowledge about the 'natural order' and such knowledge is, in principle, 'attainable from the laboratory experiment or societal practice' (ibid.). The role of the latter is to supply criteria to classify potential courses of social action as superior or inferior to one another, and this is possible because the objectivity of the judgement is publicly testable and demonstrable.

Indeed, the above argument has provided the basis for the rationale accepted by governments since the medieval period, namely that certain occupations had an epistemological basis to their work, and they therefore could be classified as professions, and, the classic position about the constitutive role of disciplinary knowledge to professional formation as articulated by Beck and Young. This led to a consensus that the role of the professional was to legislate because they were able to:

> make authoritative statements which arbitrate in controversies of opinions and which select those opinions which, having been selected become correct and binding. The authority to arbitrate is in this case legitimised by superior

(objective) knowledge to which intellectuals [DG: and by extension, professionals] have better access than the non-institutional part of society

(Bauman 1987:4).

The basis of the authoritative statements referred to above are the procedural rules which professionals have acquired through their study of disciplines in a university and the professional translation of those disciplines through apprenticeship in a field of practice. These rules allow a professional the right and duty to not only validate some beliefs and courses of action over others, but also to become a member of an extra-territorial community that is bound together by the epistemological basis of their profession. Returning to Bauman's notion of legislation, what this meant was that professionals' views were accepted as objective statements about the matters they were called to pronounce on.

The challenge to the old assumption: professionals as 'interpreters'

Doubts began to arise in Western societies after the Second World War about the idea of objective universal criteria of truth, including the idea that membership in extra-territorial professional fields automatically guaranteed the applicability of professional judgements. These doubts escalated over the next 30 years and resulted, according to Bauman (1987:117–22), in a profound change in the status and role of intellectuals and professionals. Instead of continuing to be seen as legislators, their new evolved role vis-à-vis the public became to act as an 'interpreter' who translates: 'statements, made within one community-based tradition, so that they can be understood within the system of knowledge-based on the other tradition' to facilitating communication between autonomous participants.

In crafting this argument, Bauman (1987) makes it clear that he is not advocating that a post-modern conception of professional knowledge has literally replaced a modernist conception. Instead, he advances a more nuanced argument, where the former does not eliminate the latter because it cannot be conceived without it. It does, however, entail the abandonment of the universalistic ambitions of professions to provide unchallengeable objective knowledge, but this, in turn, does not entail an abandonment of professionals' universalistic ambitions towards their own tradition. They still retain their meta-professional authority in this context. The professions face, according to Bauman (ibid.), a two-fold dilemma. They need to learn: how to operate within the boundaries of their community in accordance with its legislative practices; and how to translate their disciplinary-based insights to other professionals and/or their clients so they can grasp the meaning of those insights and infer how to respond to them.

The new role of the professional to translate disciplinary-based insights to professionals in the same and other fields of professional practice as well as lay communities is, arguably however, rather under-developed in Bauman's work. This is primarily because as a social theorist he is more concerned to highlight the implications of changes in the debates about the status of knowledge for professional work, than to articulate the implications of that change for professional formation. The notion of translation appears therefore to be either a 'black box' (i.e. indicates what should be done but not how to do it) or a 'decontextualized' term (i.e. implies that it is relatively straightforward for professionals to explain their insights to others): translation thus highlights, rather than offers a way to address, the learning challenge of interprofessional work.

Interprofessional working and learning and programmes of professional formation

Professional formation: the starting point

The purpose, content and process of professional curricula have been widely debated in advanced industrial societies since Schön's famous critique that universities tended to teach knowledge as axioms (i.e. rules stipulating what is the case) which practitioners were then supposed to somehow apply to practice. Over the past few years, many writers from a wide range of disciplinary/professional backgrounds have used Schön's (1987:1) ideas about the 'reflective practicum' as a way to overcome the problem of the gap between theory and practice (see *inter alia* Boud and Solomon 2001; Payne 2002; Taylor and White 2000; Winter and Maisch 1996). These writers have argued, generally speaking, that aspiring professionals should be encouraged by professional educators to engage in a process of reflection in educational contexts about whether the concepts and ideas made available to them through their professional curricula could constitute a resource to help them to address the dilemmas they confronted in practice.

One problem with the work of writers who have formulated, what has been referred to as the 'pedagogies of reflection' (Guile 2010), is that they have followed Schön and assumed that: (i) professional practice is individual and profession-specific; and (ii) theoretical and practical reasoning are separate and different from one another and are best related through some reflective process. This variety of approaches subsumed within the term pedagogies of reflection struggle to support aspiring professionals to understand the relation between theoretical and practical reasoning within a profession, let alone, between professions. This is because these pedagogies are inwardly directed, in other words, they invite aspiring professionals to see whether they can make connections between their own experience and the theoretical concepts that they have encountered in their professional curricula. This results in a 'reflective struggle' to relate different types of reasoning (i.e. theoretical and practical) in their own field of practice, and to use the outcome of this struggle as a resource to work in their professional settings.

More recently, there has been acknowledgement of the limitations of the ways in which the concept of reflection has become institutionalized as described above in programmes of professional formation in higher education (Bradbury *et al.* 2009). There has also been acknowledgement that programmes of professional formation have tended to require students to only reflect on their professional practice in higher education and have, in the process, overlooked the importance of reflection as a process to facilitate professionals' workplace learning (Boud *et al.* 2006). Although these are significant and important developments, they do not address the central concern of this chapter: how to support professionals to interpret their forms of knowing and the insights that flow from them to other professionals or to the public.

A possible solution to the above issue is, however, offered in *The Learning Challenge of the Knowledge Economy* (Guile 2010). The argument contained in the book about the concept of 'recontextualization' is not explicitly framed in relation to Bauman's ideas about the change in the role of professionals from legislators to interpreters. It does nevertheless address the way that changes in the organization of work have been responsible for the growth of interprofessional working and the ensuing learning challenge for professionals. For this reason, it is possible to use the concept of recontextualization to make explicit what is implicit in Bauman's notion of translation.

From 'translation' to 'recontextualization'

The core ideas underpinning the concept of recontextualization (Guile 2010) are first, all forms of knowledge are contextual (i.e. they are part of disciplines, professional traditions, work practices, etc.) but this does not necessarily mean they are context-bound. Second, the purpose of an activity – design of curriculum or form of professional practice – influences the way in which forms of knowledge are deployed in different contexts. Third, people grasp the meaning of new concepts and practices as they learn how to 'infer' what follows from the relation between concepts and practices (Guile 2010:108). These seemingly straightforward ideas allow us to ask, as we are about to see, searching questions about how we design and deliver professional formation. This is because the concept of recontextualization can be used to provide a holistic, albeit differentiated, perspective on the multi-faceted and multi-directional ways in which knowledge is used in (a) programmes of professional formation, (b) professional practice and (c) the mediated relation between them.

Recontextualization is, as mentioned above, underpinned by a number of principles; however, and these principles play out in different ways in different contexts. Guile (2010:154–60) highlights the implications of this for professional formation by distinguishing between the following – *content, pedagogic, workplace* and *learner* – as expressions of recontextualization. The first refers to the way in which the parties, for example, universities, professional associations, involved in curriculum planning, formulate criteria to determine which aspects of the forms of knowledge, for example, disciplinary, professional/legal, work-based, should be included and sequenced in a programme of professional formation. The second refers to the decisions that lecturers take about how to teach the diverse range of concepts in a professional curriculum so that aspiring professionals can develop the capability to reason theoretically and practically in the contexts of both education and work. The third refers to both the way in which professionals working in organizations have already embedded and continue to embed the above forms of knowledge in workplace routines and artifacts as well as to aspiring professionals' engagement with those forms of knowledge. The fourth refers to the different ways in which aspiring professionals embody the form of knowledge they encounter in their curriculum or in the workplaces where they undertake work placements, and when required to call upon those diverse forms of knowledge to facilitate their theoretical and/or practical reasoning.

The argument presented here is that the concept of recontextualization can be used to explain the mediated relation between different phases of the formation of profession-specific modes of thinking, reasoning and acting, which the pedagogies of reflection are designed to relate to one another, and that ideas about 'integrating' experiences from education and work (Billett *et al.* 2012) continue to assume are separate from one another. This claim is based, as Guile (forthcoming a and b) explains, on an assumption that although professionals learn theoretical concepts in educational contexts where they are underpinned by a disciplinary 'space of reasons' (McDowell 1996) (as a resource to help them to understand the constitution of practice in their professional field and to address problems that arise in that field of practice), when they do so in the field of practice, professionals are operating in a profession-based space of reasons. This space is created, as Guile (ibid.) further explains, as professionals learn to commingle their theoretical understanding and workplace experience, that is, use both as resources to infer how to address the task-in-hand. Professionals are therefore engaged in a process of workplace recontextualization where they are making situated judgements, rather than applying or translating knowledge so it fits another situation. From this perspective, the challenge for interprofessional teams is to work together to commingle their different profession-specific modes of perceiving, knowing and reasoning into a common space of reasons, where members of project teams can duly assess the courses of action their colleagues are recommending.

The implications of the above rather general and abstract argument can be clarified by returning to the case study. The architect, structural engineer and preservationist all perceived the nature of the problem of remodelling the library to withstand an earthquake and all suggested different possible solutions to that problem. This is because their profession-specific modes of perceiving, knowing and reasoning undoubtedly influenced the different stances they adopted and the courses of action they recommended to remodel the library. It was the conjoined approach to working and learning that the team generated, which was based on listening to and assessing the ideas of different members of the team to solve the problem-in-hand, while trying to appreciate the reasons that lay behind the suggestions, that enabled them to resolve the problem they had been constituted to address. This space of reasons emerged as the team members gradually: first appreciated that they had different reasons for participating in the project and different areas of expertise to contribute to the resolution of the problem; and second realized that they were more likely to find a solution if they explained the reasons that underpinned their professional observations and insights, rather than insist on imposing their preferred solution on the others.

This process of professionals' making their implicit reasoning explicit provided other team members with a resource they could use to infer, that is, develop a provisional grasp of another professionals' suggestion(s), and work out the implication of that suggestion(s) in relation to their own ideas. By engaging in this process of inference, members of the team were gradually able to use the representational devices, such as, diagrams and demonstrations, their colleagues had produced, to appreciate the practical implications of suggestions in relation to their own professional concerns and the task-in-hand. These processes of individual and collective recontextualization provided a perspective on understanding that enabled the team to reach a position where they could agree and implement a course of action that addressed their aesthetic and technical concerns and legal responsibilities.

Rethinking initial professional formation for interprofessional work

The concept of recontextualization allows us to appreciate, as the return to the case study above demonstrated, the mediated relationship between: (a) the forms of knowledge aspiring professionals are introduced to in educational institutions and how this facilitates the first stage of profession-specific modes of thinking, reasoning and acting; and (b) the forms of experience they encounter in their profession and how this develops the second stage of profession-specific modes of thinking, reasoning and acting. The outcome of this mediated relationship is the emergence of a capacity to make conceptually structured professional judgements in situation-specific circumstances. This is a very different conception of professional formation compared with the classic argument that educational programmes develop 'know that' knowledge and professional experience develops 'know how' knowledge. This argument affirms the separation of theory and practice. Moreover, it also underpinned Schön's critique of programmes of professional formation that they perpetuated the separation of theory from practice, and his advocacy of reflection as a strategy to overcome that divide. In contrast, the concept of recontextualization, as the different expressions of the concept highlight, respects the difference and relation between the forms of knowledge aspiring professionals are introduced to in educational contexts, and the forms of knowledge they employ in practice to address professional problems or dilemmas. Another way of stating this point is to say that 'know that' and 'know how' knowledge presuppose one another, but the way in which they do varies contextually.

The argument presented in this chapter is that the challenge for interprofessional teams is to work together to commingle their different profession-specific modes of perceiving, knowing and reasoning into a common space of reasons, where members of project teams can duly assess the courses of action their colleagues are recommending. The chapter ends therefore with some questions and issues that all parties involved with programmes of professional formation could use to revise those programmes to prepare learners more effectively to work in interprofessional contexts. Parties could use the notions of:

(a) *Content recontextualization* to identify whether aspiring professionals are provided with sufficient opportunities to:

- encounter the types of interprofessional practice their profession is currently involved with in the form of, for example, case studies or work placement, and in the process help them to appreciate the difference and relation between the forms of expertise developed in their own and in other professions.

(b) *Pedagogic recontextualization* to identify whether aspiring professionals are assisted to:

- infer intra-professionally the relation between different concepts and practice to pave the way for them to learn how to infer interprofessionally when they are working in the field of practice.

(c) *Workplace recontextualization* to identify whether aspiring professionals are provided with opportunities to:

- work with professionals from other fields of practice to infer how to commingle their respective expertise to resolve problems they are jointly working on;

(d) *Learner recontextualization* to help aspiring professionals to recognize that in order to develop the capabilities required for interprofessional working and learning they need opportunities in:

- educational contexts to commingle their theoretical and practical reasoning to devise solutions to workplace problems orally and in written form;
- work contexts to make explicit to members of other professions what is implicit in the course of action they are recommending.

Conclusion

This chapter has made a number of inter-related arguments. First, changes in the organization of work – process management, projectification and co-configuration – in the private and public sector worldwide have paved the way for the emergence of a notion of interprofessional working and learning. Second, the concept of recontextualization offers a way to both analyse the way in which interprofessional project teams learn to commingle their theoretical and practical reasoning to resolve practice-based problems, and for all parties involved with professional formation to rethink the design and delivery of programmes that facilitate initial and continuing professional formation. The powerful idea that underpins this process of rethinking is that parties involved with the design and delivery of the educational and workplace contributions for programmes of initial or continuing professional formation should ask how the four expressions of recontextualization can be deployed to enhance such programmes rather than redesign them around the four expressions.

Acknowledgement

A first version of this chapter was published with the title 'Inter-professional working and learning: "recontextualising" lessons from "project work" for programmes of initial professional formation', *Journal of Education and Work*, 25(1):79–99.

Note

1   Interprofessional in the context of this chapter refers to the way in which people from different occupational specialisms come together to work on common projects and, in the process, learn how to make the implications of their insights and judgements explicit to other members of the team of people they are working with.

References

Abbott, A. (1988) *The System of the Professions: An Essay on the Divisions of Expert Labour*, Chicago: University of Chicago Press.
Adler, P. , Kwon, S. and Heckscher, C. (2008) 'Professional work: the emergence of colloborative community', *Organization Science*, 19(2): 359–376.
Bauman, Z. (1987) *Legislators and Interpreters*, London: Polity.
Beck, J. and Young, M.F.D. (2005) 'The assault on the professions and the restructuring of academic and professional identities: a Bernsteinian analysis', *British Journal of the Sociology of Education*, 26(2): 183–197.
Bechky, B. (2006) 'Gaffers, gofers, and grips: Role-based coordination in temporary organizations', *Organization Science*, 17(1): 3–21.
Bernstein, B. (2000) *Pedagogy, Symbolic Control and Identity: Theory, Research and Critique* (rev. edn), Lanham: Rowman and Littlefield.
Billett, S., Johnson, G., Thomas, S., Sim, C., Hay, S. and Ryan, J. (eds) (2012) *Experiences of School Transitions: Policies, Practice and Participants*, Dordrecht: Springer.
Boud, D. and Solomon, N. (eds) (2001) *Work-based Learning: A New Higher Education?*, Buckingham: SRHE/Open University.
Boud, D., Cressey, P. and Doherty, P. (2006) *Productive Reflection at Work: Learning for Changing Organizations*, London: Routledge.
Bradbury, H., Frost, N., Kilminster, S. and Zukas, M. (2009) *Beyond Reflective Practice: New Approaches to Professional Lifelong Learning*, London: Routledge.
Briner, W., Hastings, C. and Geddes, M. (1996) *ProjectLleadership*, Aldershot: Gower.
Dent, M. and Whitehead, S. (2002) *Managing Professional Identities: Knowledge, Performativity and the 'New' Professional*, London: Routledge.

Edwards, A., Daniels, H., Gallagher, T., Leadbetter, J. and Warmington, P. (2009) *Improving Inter-professional Collaborations: Multi-agency Working for Children's Wellbeing*, London: Routledge.

Engeström, Y. (2008) *From Teams to Knots: Activity-theoretical Studies of Collaboration and Learning at Work*, Cambridge: Cambridge University Press.

Engeström, Y., Engeström, R. and Kärkkäinen, M. (1995) 'Polycontextuality and boundary crossing in expert cognition: Learning and problem solving in complex work activities', *Learning and Instruction*, 1(5): 319–336.

Evetts, J. (2003) 'The sociological analysis of professionalism. Occupational change in the modern world', *International Sociology*, 18(2): 395–415.

Freidson, E. (2001) *Professionalism: The Third Logic*, Cambridge: Polity Press.

Grabher, G. (2002) 'Cool projects, boring institutions temporary collaboration in social context', *Regional Studies*, 36(3): 205–214.

Grabher, G. (2004) 'Learning in projects, remembering in networks?: Commonality, sociality, and connectivity in project ecologies', *European Journal of Regional Studies*, 11(1): 103–120.

Guile, D. (2010) *The Learning Challenge of the Knowledge Economy*, Rotterdam: Sense.

Guile, D. (forthcoming a) *Theory and Practice in Professional and Vocational Learning: from Participation to Recontextualisation*.

Guile, D. (forthcoming b) 'Professional knowledge and professional practice as continuous recontextualisation: a social practice perspective', in Muller, J. and Young, M. (eds), *Professional Knowledge and Professional Practice as Continuous Recontextualisation*, London: Routledge.

Hall, R., Stevens, R. and Torralba, T. (2002) 'Disrupting representational infrastructure in conversations across disciplines', *Mind, Culture and Activity*, 9(2): 179–210.

McDowell, J. (1996) *Mind and World* (2nd edn), Harvard: Harvard University Press.

Midler, C. (1995) '"Projectification" of the firm: the Renault case', *Scandinavian Journal of Management*, 11(4): 263–275.

Payne, M. (2002) *Social Work Theories and Reflective Practice*, London: Palgrave.

Schön, D. (1987) *Educating the Reflective Practitioner*, San Francisco: Jossey Bass.

Taylor, C. and White, S. (2000) *Practising Reflexivity in Health and Welfare*, Buckingham: Open University Press.

Winter, R. and Maisch, M. (1996) *Professional Competence and Higher Education: The ASSET Programme*, London: Falmer Press.

Chapter 10

Arrangements of co-production in healthcare

Partnership modes of interprofessional practice

Roger Dunston

Preface

Writing this chapter has been a challenge. As author, I wanted to acknowledge that much of what I have written is the outcome of years of conversations and shared research with my close colleague and friend, Professor Alison Lee. Alison died of cancer in September 2012. Alison and I had agreed to write this chapter together. However, due to Alison's illness this was not possible.

Alison had a breadth and depth of knowledge that was exceptional. Study, fearless exploration, conversation and writing were her tools of trade. In the context of the work and framing of this chapter – with its focus on strong co-production – Alison's way of being as a person, an academic and researcher was also strongly and passionately co-productive. She was always excited when we returned to the focus on and possibilities of co-production. The work and relationship we shared over seven years, as colleagues at the University of Technology Sydney (UTS), have been without doubt the most rewarding years of my professional career. I greatly appreciated Alison's preparedness to join me and others in applying her capabilities in the area of health research. She contributed a great deal.

To represent our shared work, I have used the subjective personal pronouns 'I' and 'we'. For the most part I have used 'I' to refer to my authorship in the chapter. However, when I felt sure that this was how Alison and I together would have written, I used the term 'we'.

I would also like to acknowledge several colleagues who participated in and contributed to the work that Alison and I were committed to. At UTS, Professor Cathrine Fowler, Dr Nick Hopwood, Ms Chris Rossiter, Ms Marie Manidis and Professor Nicky Solomon. External to UTS, and of particular importance in the development of Alison's scholarship, is Bill Green, Professor of Education at Charles Sturt University.

Introduction

This chapter engages with the rise of interest in co-production as an arrangement of professional practice, and the importance of exploring issues of learning and knowing for considering the meanings and implications of co-production for professional practice, professional and consumer identity and for professional education and workplace learning.

The chapter considers these issues through an account of the intellectual work that developed as an outcome of the conversations, shared research and writing of a small team of researchers located in the Centre for Research in Learning and Change at the University of Technology Sydney, Australia. This account takes up the above issues through a research focus on 'strong forms of co-production'. By strong forms of co-production within health, I mean practices that are purposefully, 'strongly' and expansively focused on incorporating the service user/service users[1] as competent and knowledgeable partners across all areas of health service design, development, delivery and evaluation.

Within the chapter, I distinguish between 'strong' and 'weak' forms of co-production. Whilst conceptually clumsy, this distinction was a way for Alison and myself to signal what had become for us a major problem in how the concept of co-production was often presented, that is, as categorically different from other forms of practice, in particular 'expert-based practice'. Our view is that all practice is in different ways co-productive.

I also distinguish between the potentially positive implications of strong forms of co-production in terms of (proposed) increased health system sustainability and greater participation and control for service users; and the challenging implications for professional identity, the privileging of professional knowledge over lay knowledge, and the design and conduct of health professional education and workplace learning.

The initial section of the chapter provides an overview of our engagement with the concept and discourse of co-production and how this discourse has been taken up as a central element of the health reform agenda globally. It identifies a series of issues, questions and problems that became the investigative focus for a number of small qualitative and ethnographically based research projects, primarily in the areas of child and family health service provision. I go on to provide details of each study and describe what we have learned from them. Finally, I explore the implications of strong forms of co-production for professional education, learning and sustainability and the need for more adequate ways of theorizing professional practice, education, learning and change.

Co-production – a rich but unspecified point of departure

Alison and I began our work together with a focus on health (my work context for many years) and 'co-production'. The concept of 'co-production' – its argued promise and possibilities – interested us both. Alison had become aware of the concept through her engagement with the work of Anna Yeatman (Yeatman 1994, 1998) on the development of disability services in Australia. My engagement focused on health service reform, primarily in the UK during and just after the years of the Blair New Labour government.[2]

Our point of departure was a review of the provenance of the concept of co-production and how this had been taken up in policy directions, health service reform discourse, and practice redesign initiatives from the 1970s until the present day. There is a growing literature that outlines these developments. I will only refer to selective elements of these developments (for a more elaborated account see Ostrom 1996; Alford 1998; Davies *et al.* 2006; Morris *et al.* 2007; Needham 2008; Dunston *et al.* 2009a).

We were acutely aware that the contemporary policy and practice focus on co-production as a central element of the health reform agenda was but one small part of far broader and longer-term debates. During the 1990s and into the early 2000s, the concept of co-production enjoyed a considerable resurgence in the UK, Europe and the USA. We considered how this discourse was being taken up to drive and redesign public sector service provision, and more broadly, to reconceptualize and reshape the relationships between civil society, the economy and government, within the UK (Newman 2001) and the European Union.

Within these contexts, co-production had been adopted as a discourse and practice charting new and 'desirable' forms of governance, active citizenship, public and private sector service provision and, in particular, health service development and sustainability. Within public sector service provision, co-production was claimed to be more user responsive, more effective, more efficient and more sustainable. Alison and I frequently discussed these developments in terms of a 'new relational orientation' and new 'relational configurations' in which the roles, rules and relationships that governed the way in which 'practitioners'[3] and 'service users' interacted were profoundly reshaped. Such possibilities were frequently described in highly aspirational language. The transformative promise of co-production was argued as applicable across many areas of political, social and economic life, from re-energizing participatory democracy, to reviving a sense of local community, to creating more participatory forms of product design, to delivering new and more satisfactory forms of value in the relationship of health systems and citizens (Cahn and Gray 2004; Bovaird 2007; Needham 2008). Some of the most innovative and radical elaborations on the concept and practice of co-production have been developed in the work of the UK think tanks DEMOS (www.demos.co.uk) and NEF (www.new-economics.org) and in the work of NGO organizations such as Governance International (www.govint.org).

Such ambitious 'reimagining' makes reference to core elements of co-production discourse. Firstly, service users are competent, knowledgeable – they possess lay knowledge – and always contribute. They are assets not problems. This view challenges the sharp distinction frequently drawn between the health professional as knower and provider, and the service user as passive recipient. Second, creating services and practices that recognize, legitimate, work with and build on the capabilities and knowledge of service users opens up the prospect of new relational and outcome possibilities.

Developing our investigative focus

As we engaged with the aspirational discourse of co-production we identified issues, questions and problems that became the investigative foci in a number of small exploratory studies (see below).

Much promise but little fine-grained conceptualization, description and analysis

One of the many challenges involved in translating policy into practice is the difficulty for individuals engaged with change management and professional practice in understanding what high-level generalized concepts such as co-production, partnership, participation, team work, joined-up practice, etc., mean when developed as part of day-to-day practice within diverse practice settings (Dunston *et al.* 2009; Fenwick 2012). Such terms are polyvalent and frequently lack situational specificity. Co-production is clearly such a term. For example, within the formal health service context, we wondered, what does co-production look like when practised in settings as diverse as an emergency department, an intensive care unit, a general practice consultation, a mental health service, a health education programme, a residential centre for mothers experiencing parenting difficulties, or a remote health care setting? Tony Bovaird's (2007) study of co-production was one of the first attempts to describe and categorize different forms of co-production based on his empirical studies. This work has been continued via the activities of Governance International. However, mostly there was little to guide those involved in service redesign and continuing professional development as to what strong co-productive practices should look like in different settings and, critically, what educational and organizational investment is required to establish such practices.[4]

Co-production and 'traditional' health care practice – the problem of the binary

We were also struck by what for us is a highly problematic presentation of co-production as if it were some form of unitary object, practice or approach, frequently categorized as patient-focused, respectful, empathic and holistic, as well as the sense that it could easily be distinguished from other forms of practice that were not co-productive. This dichotomy of 'it is/it is not' co-productive is inevitably conjured up when co-production is contrasted with expert-based practice. Expert practice, again presented as a unitary object, is frequently cast as not co-productive and therefore as problematic in terms of the health reform agenda. We drew this distinction ourselves, but never found it useful or accurate in categorizing something that is far more complex and nuanced. We also had difficult conversations with practitioners who felt sidelined and dismissed when we contrasted the two. To avoid this problem, we found ourselves making the distinction between 'strong' and 'weak' forms of co-production, that is, of replacing one problematic binary with another!

The strong and weak distinction developed from our long-standing view that all forms of professional practice in health are, in some ways, co-productive. This view was reinforced by what we observed and were told. However, we found that it was possible to distinguish conceptually and empirically how discrete practices or practice elements are woven together and deployed in particular ways. For example, we found Bernstein's (1971) concepts of 'classification' (how and with what strength boundaries between categories are distinguished) and 'framing' (how and with what strength the locus of control over particular practices is maintained) useful in thinking about these issues.

The relational and the site of the interface – a site of great opportunity but ...

One defining characteristic of the co-production literature is its focus on the relational, and its focus on the site in which the health professional and the service user meet, what DEMOS refers to as 'the interface' (Parker and Heapy 2006). The space in which professional and lay knowledge and agency intersect, and the choreography by all participants, especially practitioners, constitutes a site of immense importance for engaging service users differently. However, we felt uneasy about what was expected to occur in this space, particularly the expectation that relational practices would be routinely reconfigured with potentially transformative outcomes. While the promise of relational reconfiguration was promoted, relatively little attention was given to two issues that, in our view, powerfully influence and shape the potential for change at the interface. First, little attention was given to the significant implications of radical change for the status and experience of all parties, for practitioner identity, for the relationship between professional and lay knowledge, for the division of labour between participants, for professional and legal accountability, and for professional and service user education. The difficulties associated with these issues, largely about classification and framing (Bernstein 1971), have been consistently discussed in our work around the implementation of expansive approaches to co-production and around curriculum redesign in interprofessional education, learning and practice (Dunston et al. 2009b; Matthews et al. 2011). Second, relatively little attention has been given to the recognition that our relational practices, be they social, economic, political or professional, are shaped by the deeply embedded stabilities of our political, economic and social arrangements and histories. Such stabilities do not give way easily.[5]

Learning and sustainability

Our final group of questions, of particular importance in our research on health reform, professional practice change and professional learning, focused on how significant practice change is learned, stabilized and sustained. Reviewing the health reform literature, we were struck by the incommensurability between the scale of the change anticipated and/or required – learning, relearning and 'unlearning' (a term Alison used frequently), and the reliance on front-end, time-limited and cognitivist-based training approaches. Additionally, whilst stabilizing and sustaining new practices were identified in the reform literature as major organizational tasks, there was relatively little consideration of how this could be done or what would be required.

What have we learned?

This next section summarizes what we have learned across the studies referred to in this chapter. Prior to doing this, I identify details of each study – title, focus and publications. This group of studies has been selected as they represent a series of ethnographically framed research engagements, each different in terms of setting and focus, but similar in their commitment to strong forms of co-production and their use of a well conceptualized and described approach to working with service users, the Family Partnership Model.

Our initial study, the *Birra-Li Project: Learning & Development for Sustainable Health Futures*, investigated the learning dimensions of a partnership between health services, health professionals and health consumers in Birra-li, a birthing service for indigenous families in regional Australia (Dunston *et al.* 2009; Lee and Dunston 2010). A second study, *The Family Partnership Project Model*:[6] *Sustaining Practice Innovation in Child and Family Health*, examined the experiences of practice innovation in child and family health services in Australia and New Zealand (Rossiter *et al.* 2011a, b; Fowler, *et al.* 2012a; Rossiter *et al.* 2011b; Hopwood *et al.* 2013). The third study, *Seeing is Believing*, was a small study focused on building co-productive capacity in citizens, health professionals and health services. The service focus was a home visiting programme of Tresillian Family Care Centres in New South Wales, Australia (Lee *et al.* 2012; Fowler *et al.* 2012a, b).

Whilst our point of departure in this section is a focus on the service user and reconceptualizing the service user, I do not want to minimize the way in which material and other factors shape practice. Alison and I frequently discussed the importance of this matter. However, regardless of policy imperatives and other material factors operating in and around practice change, the importance of participants taking on a very different view of the service user seemed to be a critical and, perhaps, necessary first move in the development of significant practice change

Reconceptualizing the service user

Within these studies, one of the most strongly presented and elaborated themes was the way in which many participants had taken on (often enthusiastically) a very different view of the service user, shifting away from the 'deficit' view associated with traditional forms of health practice. The service user was presented in very positive terms, as competent, as knowledgeable, as an active participant, as a locus of knowing and decision-making and, critically for shaping what could then occur, as a 'partner'. The implications of this reconceptualization are, it seemed to both Alison and myself, immense. We came to refer to this as 'move 1' in the development of strong forms of co-production.

Repositioning the practitioner and practice

Arising from this shift, participants regularly commented about the work of creating an approach to practice that was aligned to and congruent with this different view of the service user. We discussed this in terms of a process of 'repositioning' and referred to it as 'move 2'. Move 3 was the utilization of practices that were seen as congruent with a new understanding of the service user. Framing this new approach as 'strengths based' seemed to us less than adequate to portray the radical nature of what we were hearing and seeing. Rather than adding one positive attribute to the traditional concept of the service user – something that was in the mix together with deficits and passivity – there was a quite profound ontological shift in understanding the nature of the other (the service user).

Learning as the central dynamic shaping practice

Alison and I increasingly talked about learning or more particularly, shared, reciprocal or dialogic learning as a way of representing and understanding what we were hearing about and observing. We also found ourselves borrowing from our work in the area of interprofessional education (IPE) and learning (Dunston *et al.* 2009b), and using the most frequently cited definition of IPE to make sense of our data – 'when two or more professions learn with, from and about each other' (CAIPE 2002). The three elements or dimensions of learning seemed to represent well what we saw participants attempting to do: *learning with* – a focus on the immediacy of the moment and a learning partnership with the other; *learning about* – a practice orientation toward the service user to identify problems and solutions – a way of going forward; and *learning from* – a recognition that practitioners can, do and need to learn from service users.

The place of expert knowledge

One of the most confusing and discussed issues for many participants was the place and status of 'expert' knowledge. A number of participants queried whether professional knowledge had any place or whether it was inimical to the process of service-user-led work. Many struggled with their understanding that they should not let their expert knowledge interfere with the service user's understanding and preferences. However, as many participants noted, referencing solely the service user could pose problems, for example, if the practitioner identified a situation of a child at risk, should they confront, should they notify? Other participants commented that adopting a partnership approach was not an alternative to being the expert; rather, their view was that it required new kinds of knowledge and capability, thus extending the repertoire of their practice skills. Some felt they were still learning how to blend partnership and more interventionist approaches, particularly in cases when the health professional perceived a situation of risk. These participants seemed more comfortable with such issues, seeing expert knowledge and experience as valuable resources that were at times needed, useful and required, but for the most part remaining nested within an overarching partnership approach.

Is it or is it not co-production?

It is important that understandings of practice and co-production are not forced into the binary juxtaposition of 'is it' or 'is it not' co-productive practice? With Ostrom (1996), we think this is not only unhelpful and dismissive, but also inaccurate. As we talked with and observed participants, it became clear that practice for each of them was somewhat different and unique. This should not be surprising. Some participants noted that what they learned though participating in a programme focused on strong co-production was simply a set of terms that they could use to name pre-existing practice. For others, much had changed and was changing. Many noted that they had always attempted to be led by service users but that the understanding of what this meant had changed, to varying degrees. For many participants, as noted above, there were complex accommodations to be made about when a more service-user-centred approach needed to become a practitioner-led approach. We were observing, we felt, practitioners remaking existing patterns of co-productive practice.

Strong co-production: what kind of practice?
A summation

It is possible to make some tentative statements about what strong forms of co-production looked like and how we understood them being developed across the study sites. In terms of practice patterning, we identified and began to discuss 'three moves' in orientation, positioning and practice, that we saw as associated with making a shift toward strong forms of co-production. Move 1, involves conceptualizing the service user as capable and knowledgeable, and as able to participate in a reciprocal partnership. Our studies demonstrated that this re-conceptualization is not a superficial matter of grafting one or more positive elements onto a view of the service user that remains predominantly defined by deficits and passivity. Rather, it involves something far more substantial, what we have termed an ontological shift in understanding. Move two, involves the practitioner repositioning how they practice in relation to the service user and within the space of the partnership. Again, it seemed to us that this repositioning was a substantial move in the practitioner's way of being and practising. When carried out with purpose and a preparedness to learn, this repositioning opened the space of the partnership to new possibilities. This involved a renegotiation around the traditional boundaries of classification and framing. We noted two areas of expansion in the partnership: a distributed approach to what constitutes legitimate and useful knowledge with the inclusion of lay knowledge; and reference to the service user as an important locus of knowing, decision-making and evaluation. Move 3, involves the adoption and development over time of practices that align with this re-conceptualization and repositioning. What we have seen and been told suggests that such practices can be usefully and generically described in terms of shared, reciprocal or dialogic learning. A pedagogy informed by concepts of strong co-production.

Our reflections highlighted additional related points: strong forms of co-production aim to connect with, build on and resource existing service user knowledge and capability; practitioners take responsibility for creating the conditions for shared learning and deploying a user-centred learning methodology; disciplinary knowledge and professional experience are redefined and relocated as important resources to be used as and when required. Such moves in their aggregate, it seems to us, require well-developed relational and learning facilitation capabilities that can be directed at creating the conditions for and facilitation of shared learning.

Learnings and implications

This final section speculates about the implications of what we have learned from the reported studies. I develop this speculation around four interconnected issues central to the success of the reform agenda: learning and sustainability, theorizing practice, learning and change and, the need for more practice-focused research in the area of strong co-production.

Learning and sustainability

The studies referred to in this chapter demonstrate the extent to which strong forms of co-production require a radical reconceptualization and remaking of deeply embedded socio-cultural patterns of professional practice in health, what we might refer to as the disciplinary contours of classification and framing. It also seemed to us that the 'disturbing' implications and realizable possibilities of strong forms of co-production are as yet not well understood in a conceptual and empirical sense, nor are they well described or theorized.

The change initiatives we studied were generally characterized by interested and motivated staff; an investment in front-end change activities, particularly training; little follow-up; and the expectation that staff or teams would develop and maintain new practices. Practice located within this framework seemed conceived as a 'product' rather than a 'process', as static rather than dynamic and adaptive, and as something that once grasped and performed, was maintained. This static view of practice and what is required to keep practice developing, was not a view shared by many of the practitioner participants involved in the three studies being reported on.

Many practitioner participants discussed constant frustration with the gap between what their understanding of what was required to enable and support ongoing learning and the focus on front-end training. They also frequently discussed the ad hoc and, at times, non-existent supervisory arrangements referenced to a strong co-productive framework. We were frequently struck by the disjunction between the importance, scale and difficulty of what was being asked of participating organizations and practitioners, and the limited educational opportunities, methods and capacity being committed to this work. We considered how several participants in the *Sustaining Practice Innovation* study viewed practice.

> They presented practice as something that is dynamic, relational – developed between the participants involved – and continually evolving. Participants consistently talked about the challenge of developing their practice in response to the particular circumstances of an individual family and, importantly, in a process of learning with and from the family. That is, working in partnership.
>
> The implications and possibilities of seeing practice in this way are, we think, profound. They pose new challenges for how we think about effective practice, practice capability, learning and change; and, in terms of where most learning takes place, require far more attention on the possibilities for learning and development in the workplace.
>
> (Rossiter *et al.* 2011a:30).

It is important to contextualize these comments. Managers were not unsympathetic to requests for more educational opportunities. At a pragmatic level, supervisory and managerial staff talked openly about the immense difficulty created when even a small number of staff were not available for operational duties. The capacity to release staff for longer periods or the possibility of establishing ongoing workplace learning initiatives seemed almost unthinkable. After the initial training process, which was generally viewed very positively, the other important place of learning seemed to be when highly motivated staff made time with peers who were practising in a similar way.

Within the higher education sector, one can observe considerable but still small-scale progress. For instance, the need to re-conceptualize and open up pre- and post-registration health professional curricula to the idea of interprofessional practice and education as core elements is now well recognized, although little implemented (Dunston *et al.* 2009b). Also noticeable from the perspective of national higher education curriculum development is the great divide between professional education occurring in pre-registration professional education, and professional education occurring in the workplace. Working closely with other colleagues, we have spent considerable time promoting the case for a far greater educational focus on the transition years and beyond (The Interprofessional Curriculum Renewal Consortium, Australia 2013).

It is hard not to develop concern about the capacity of the health and higher education sectors to build a strongly co-productive health system and workforce in, for example, the next two decades. It seems clear that many health service organizations simply do not possess the human resource capacity or education and learning capabilities to generate the type and scale of learning required. Whilst globally there is momentum in the areas of service user participation and interprofessional education and learning, these developments remain small-scale, provisional and, we think, fragile.

How we better realize the opportunities and possibilities of practice-based and workplace-based education and learning requires, we believe, urgent and substantial attention. The focus on short front-end didactic training is clearly misaligned with the nature of professional practice, the exercise of professional judgement, the requirement for ongoing learning, and the development and refining of new approaches to practice.

Conclusions – theorizing professional learning in practice

As a consequence of our research and thinking about what is required to progress a strongly co-productive learning and practice agenda, we found ourselves working closely with colleagues, to argue the need for different and, from our point of view, more adequate ways of conceptualizing and theorizing professional practice, professional learning and practice change. Like many others writing in this space, we distinguish two very different ways of conceptualizing health professional education. First, a way of thinking about practice and change that focuses predominantly on the human person (privileging human agency), the individual, the cognitive, and with the demonstration and assessment of behavioural competencies and learning occurring, for the most part, outside the setting of practice. Second, a way of thinking about practice and change that aligns far more with what we have observed and been told.

In our joint publication on retheorizing professional education (Lee and Dunston 2011), we summarize our view as follows.

> All of these deliberations lead of necessity, we suggest, to a reconceptualization of what has become known as 'practice-based education'. This reconceptualization engages with practice theory to work with the mediating conditions and 'preconditions' (Kemmis 2009) of practice: the local, specific, embodied, materially mediated, routinized, relational nature of practice. Learning that is directly engaged with the doing of practice is learning that is

situated, dialogic, collective, shared, participatory, as exemplified by the Birra-li case study [see above]. There is, perhaps, a need to conceptualize an 'in-between' or translational space between professional practice as it unfolds, particularly in the case of new and emergent forms of practice, and the codifying of knowledge about practice within research and formal education.

(Lee and Dunston 2011:492)

We never wished to be prescriptive in arguing this matter. Our view was about the need for far more critical discussion and exploration as to the nature of practice, learning and change. Whilst we have taken a particular interest in the work of Schatzki (2002) and, more broadly, practice theories, the far broader category of socio-material theorizations seems highly relevant to the critical tasks of understanding and guiding the development of professional practice, education, learning and change (see Fenwick *et al.* 2011).

As we extended our research focus on strong forms of co-production between practitioners and service users, to include work in the areas of interprofessional education, learning and practice, it seemed to us that what was required was a different understanding of and theoretical approach to practice and learning. Such an approach would recognize practice and learning as a co-produced and co-constructed achievement; something that was social and collective, involving processes of distributed knowledge, knowing and decision making. Adopting such a way of thinking would, we thought, add significantly to what uni-professional disciplinary education currently provides, and would prepare students for the complex relational and learning work of co-designing, co-producing and co-evaluating services, interventions and outcomes with colleagues and service users. For many participants in the studies we undertook, these were the areas in which they felt least capable and confident.

This final point returns me to where Alison and I started our engagement with co-production. We began with great interest. With a sense of considerable potential and significant challenge. However, also with major deficits in the area of practice focused research, close description and socio-material analysis. It seemed to us then, and seems to me now, that to support those involved in policy, practice development and professional education and learning, a coherent and well-coordinated programme of research, description and analysis remains an urgent requirement.

Notes

1 Choosing a term for the 'service user' is always problematic. Within the co-production literature a variety of terms are used, from citizen to patient. I have chosen to use the term service user.
2 1997–2010.
3 I have used the term 'practitioner' instead of the longer term 'health professional'.
4 I have used the term 'practice' to refer to a larger unit, an approach, a model, etc. I have used 'practices' to refer to elements or components of the larger practice unit. I trust this distinction is understandable in the context of what is being discussed.

5 For both Alison and I, naming and working with such issues is a critical and not-well-addressed task.
6 The Family Partnership Model was developed by the Centre for Parent and Child Support (National and Specialist Child and Adolescent Mental Health Directorate of the South London and Maudsley NHS Foundation Trust, UK). We have worked closely with the Centre and its director Dr Crispin Day. We regard this approach as being an exemplar of strong co-production.

References

Alford, J. (1998) 'A public management road less travelled: Clients as co-producers of public services', *Australian Journal of Public Administration*, 57(4): 128–137.

Ball, S. (2007) *Education PLC: Private Sector Participation in Public Sector Education*, London: Routledge.

Bernstein, B. (1971) *Class, Codes and Control*, London: Routledge & Kegan Paul.

Bovaird, T. (2007) 'Beyond engagement and participation: User and community coproduction of public services', *Public Administration Review*, 67(5): 846–860.

Cahn, E. and Gray, C. (2004) *Reciprocal Co-Production*, Bloomington, IN: The Working Colloquium Series.

CAIPE (Centre for the Advancement of Interprofessional Education) (2002) http://www.caipe.org.uk/about-us/defining-ipe/ (accessed 13 March 2013).

Centre for Research in Learning & Change, University of Technology Sydney (2009) Birra-li Birthing Service: a case study of co-productive practice, Centre for Research in Learning & Change, UTS. http://www.rilc.uts.edu.au/pdfs/birra_li_birthingcasestudy.pdf.

Davies, C., Wetherell, M. and Barnett, E. (2006) *Citizens at the Centre*, Bristol: Policy Press.

Dunston, R., Lee, A., Boud, D.J., Brodie, P. and Chiarella, M. (2009a) 'Co-production and health system reform – from re-imagining to re-making', *Australian Journal of Public Administration*, 68 (1): 39–52.

Dunston, R., Lee, A., Lee, A., Matthews, L., Nisbet, G., Pockett, R., Thistlethwaite, J. and White, J. (2009b) *Interprofessional Health Education in Australia: The Way Forward*, University of Technology Sydney and The University of Sydney, Sydney.

Fenwick, T. (2012) 'Co-production in professional practice: a sociomaterial perspective', *Professions & Professionalism*, 2(2): 1–16.

Fenwick, T., Edwards, R. and Sawchuk, P. (2011) *Emerging Approaches to Educational Research: Tracing the Socio-material*, London: Routledge.

Fowler, C.M., Rossiter, C.L., Bigsby, M., Hopwood, N., Lee, A. and Dunston, R. (2012a) 'Working in partnership with parents: The experience and challenge of practice innovation in child and family health nursing', *Journal of Clinical Nursing*, 21: 3306–3314.

Fowler, C.M., Dunston, R., Lee, A., Rossiter, C.L. and McKenzie, J.A. (2012b) 'Reciprocal learning in partnership practice: An exploratory study of a home visiting program for mothers with depression', *Studies in Continuing Education*, 34(2): 99–112.

Fowler, C., Lee, A., Dunston, R., Chiarella, M. and Rossiter, C. (2012) 'Co-producing parenting practice: Learning how to do child and family health nursing differently', *Australian Journal of Child and Family Health Nursing*, 9(1): 7–11.

Giddens, A. (2003) 'Introduction: neoprogressivism: A new agenda for social democracy', in A. Giddens (ed.) *The Progressive Manifesto: New Ideas for the Centre-Left*, Cambridge: Polity Press.

Hopwood, N., Fowler, C., Lee, A., Rossiter, C. and Bigsby, M. (2013) 'Understanding partnership practice in child and family nursing through the concept of practice architectures', *Nursing Inquiry*, DOI: 10.1111/nin.12019.

Kemmis, S. (2009) 'Understanding professional practice: A synoptic framework', in B. Green (ed.) *Understanding and Researching Professional Practice* (pp. 19–39), Rotterdam: Sense Publishers.

Lee, A. and Dunston, R. (2010) '"Working in the spaces between": Co-production and changing professional practice in health', in J. Higgs, D. Fish, I. Goulter, S. Loftus, J. Reid and F. Trede (eds) *Education for Future Practice* (pp. 61–74), Rotterdam: Sense Publishers.

Lee, A. and Dunston, R. (2011) 'Practice, learning and change: Towards a re-theorisation of professional education', *Teaching in Higher Education*, 16(5): 483–494.

Lee, A., Dunston, R. and Fowler, C. (2012) '*Seeing is Believing*: An embodied pedagogy of "doing partnership" in child and family health', in P. Hager, A. Lee and A. Reich (eds), *Practice, Learning and Change: Practice–Theory Perspectives on Professional Learning* (pp. 267–276), Dordrecht: Springer.

Matthews, L., Pockett, R., Nisbet, G., Thistlethwaite, J., Dunston, R., Lee, A. and White, J. (2011) 'Building capacity in Australian interprofessional health education: Perspectives from key health and higher education stakeholders', *Australian Health Review*, 35(2): 136–140.

Morris, P. and O'Neill, F. (2006) 'Preparing for patient-centred practice: Developing the patient voice in health professional learning'. Paper presented at Professional Lifelong Learning: Beyond Reflective Practice Conference, University of Leeds.

Morris, P., O'Neill, P., Armitage, A., Lane, R., Symons, J., Dalton, E., Gaines, M., Katz, A. and Reed, J. (2007) 'Moving from tokenism to co-production: Implications of learning from patient and community voices in developing patient centred professionalism'. Paper presented at Professional Lifelong Learning: Critical Debates about Professionalism Conference, University of Leeds.

Needham, C. (2008) 'Realising the potential of co-production: Negotiating improvements in public services', *Social Policy & Society*, 7(2): 221–231.

Newman, J. (2001) *Modernising Governance: New Labour, Policy and Society*, Thousand Oaks, London, New Delhi: Sage.

Ostrom, E. (1996) 'Crossing the great divide: Coproduction, synergy, and development', *World Development*, 24(6): 1073–1087.

Parker, S. and Heapy, J. (2006) *The Journey to the Interface: How Public Service Design Can Connect Users to Reform*, London: Demos.

Rossiter, C., Hopwood, N., Dunston, R., Fowler, C., Bigsby, M. and Lee, A. (2011a) *Sustaining Practice Innovation in Child and Family Health: Report to Partners*, Centre for Research in Learning & Change, University of Technology Sydney. Available at http://www.rilc.uts.edu.au/projects/pfd-child.html

Rossiter, C.L., Fowler, C.M., Hopwood, N., Lee, A. and Dunston, R. (2011b) 'Working in partnership with vulnerable families: the experience of child and family health practitioners', *Australian Journal of Primary Health*, 17(4): 278–383.

Schatzki, T.R. (2002) *The Site of the Social: A Philosophical Account of the Constitution of Social Life and Change*, University Park, PA: Penn State University Press.

The Interprofessional Curriculum Renewal Consortium, Australia (2013) *Interprofessional Education: A National Audit. Report to Health Workforce Australia.* Centre for Research in Learning and Change, University of Technology Sydney.

Yeatman, A. (1994) 'The reform of public management: An overview', *Australian Journal of Public Administration*, 53(3): 287–296.

Yeatman, A. (1998) 'Activism and the policy process', in A. Yeatman (ed.) *Activism and the Policy Process* (pp. 16–35), Sydney: Allen and Unwin.

Section III

Reconceptualising professional responsibility

Rethinking professional responsibility

Matters of account

Tara Fenwick

Introduction

In June 2009, Air France Airbus flight 447 crashed in the Atlantic Ocean en route from Rio de Janeiro to Paris. All 216 passengers and 12 crew members were killed, making it the worst accident in the history of French aviation. The final report of the crash investigation (AF 2012) listed a number of mingled factors. Apparently ice formed inside the small 'pitot tubes' on the plane's underside, interfering with the airspeed sensors. These caused the autopilot to disconnect, and the (human) pilots assumed manual control of the aircraft. Over the next three minutes, the pilot increased and then levelled the plane's nose-up pitch in response to a series of inconsistent air speed readings and intermittent stall warnings being received. However the flight path had become 'destabilised', leading to a stall and rapid descent. In the final report, the pilot's actions were described as 'inappropriate control inputs' (AF 2012), but this was only one dimension in an interwoven assemblage of technological, material, and human forces that together resulted in a horrific crash. Nonetheless, aviation experts interviewed in an analysis of these events placed the central accountability on human error: the key problem, they stressed, was inadequate pilot competency on manual landings, and inadequate pilot training (BBC 2012).

This is not an uncommon response, particularly in linking professional responsibility with competency and with learning. Professionals are often held personally accountable for complex situations involving myriad elements that are fully entangled with – influencing as well as influenced by – human decisions and actions. Sometimes this is called scapegoating, as when a particularly visible actor attracts the full measure of societal wrath and guilt in an inexplicable situation. We see examples of this periodically in child protection services: a recent well known case in the UK was the sacking of ex-children-services-director Sharon Shoesmith in the case of Baby Peter Connolly, a child who died in 2007 with over 50 injuries despite 60 visits by social services professionals (Butler 2011). But more broadly, professionals in services ranging from social care, education, and police services to medicine and aviation are expected to mediate the increasing general anxiety of a complex society. Whether or not we agree with Beck's (1992) analysis of our 'risk culture' increasingly characterised by a 'negative logic' framing risk as danger and seeking to identify who has done the wrong thing, arguably a key expectation for professionals is to manage our societal risk and solve complex problems. Calls for professional responsibility often are based on assumptions that problems have identifiable causes, that humans can take decisions to resolve them, and that there are clear imputabilities when bad things happen.

This may be why professional responsibility has traditionally been treated as a defining site for the nature of professionalism itself, invoking an ideology of professionals' obligations to both the client's interests as well as the needs of society broadly. The existing literature on professional responsibility is characterised by much moral prescription, opinion, and concern for methods to educate professionals to perform more responsibly. These circulate amidst complaints and public concern regarding professionals' perceived irresponsible practice and failure to appropriately regulate responsibility. Professional education and training are frequently invoked as key sites for developing professional responsibility. Solbrekke (2008a:77) is among those who argue that higher education – and society in general – must explicitly educate professional responsibility, to 'ensure that we have qualified professionals with the kind of intellectual and cultural capital necessary to make wise decisions in light of the challenges of the 21st century'.

But does this emphasis on individuals and individual decisions really help to understand, account for and respond to the complex situations in which professionals must act every day? Perhaps it is more comforting to focus on human skill and imagine that this can be resolved through training and discipline, rather than attempt to consider how responsibility might be distributed among the heterogeneous entanglement of Airbus designers, autopilot practices, pitot tubes, ice, sensor readings, human adjustments and volatile airspeeds. Surely these material and technological assemblings cannot be simply banished to the background in an anthropocentric move that insists upon humans taking the central role of the story, whether it focuses on risk and danger or upon more mundane service and care. Literature on professional practice increasingly shows that its stakeholders are multiple, demanding conflicting accountabilities (Cribb 2005; Stronach *et al.* 2002). Clearly these are not simply human and social stakeholders, but material ones too.

This chapter argues that professional responsibility deserves a more sociomaterial sensibility than it frequently receives in discussions of professional learning and professional accountability. A missing or obscured element in these explorations is often the materiality of professional practice – the mixing of the social and personal with the material elements of bodies and flesh, wind and fire, objects, technologies, texts, institutions, natural forces and so forth. A 'sociomaterial' approach to understanding professional responsibility adopts what some refer to as a relational ontology: capacities for action, as well as knowledge and phenomena, are performed into existence through associations. These associations of both human and nonhuman elements, or perhaps more aptly, 'intensities' as

Bennett (2010) refers to them following Deleuze, emerge in precarious assemblages (Fenwick *et al.* 2011). When notions such as individual agency, morality and intentionality are challenged by foregrounding these sociomaterial assemblages comprising practice, the question of responsibility becomes reconfigured. The focus becomes the material enactments of conflict and compromise that appear in enactments of professional responsibility.

The chapter begins with a discussion of the changing nature of professional responsibility, and elaborates a sociomaterial perspective that draws particularly from Latour (2005) and Orlikowski (2007). Turning to examples of professional practice generated through recent studies, the discussion works with a sociomaterial sensibility to explore those mattering elements that are more-than-human. What responsibilities are enacted in these sociomaterial assemblages, and how are accountabilities framed? How do professionals negotiate the ambivalences of these complex becomings to find lines of whatever they might call 'responsible' action? What matters most to professionals in these 'mattered' enactments of responsibility?

Toward a sociomaterial conception of professional responsibility

Solbrekke (2008a:76) argues for the centrality of professional responsibility in practice defined as 'the ability to act in a professionally responsible manner in complex, unique and uncertain situations with conflicting values and ethical stance'. She goes on to explain the nature of this action amidst the frequent undecidability of practice: 'the individual professional, when encountering risk and uncertainty in his or her daily tasks, must employ his or her own capacity for critical reflection and take immediate moral and responsible decisions while at the same time linking his or her personal specialised knowledge to a collective commitment' (76). Many professionals might agree that responsibility is an individual matter of decision-making informed by particular moral commitments and knowledge expertise.

Yet, as Solbrekke also has acknowledged, there is growing research pointing to the pluralism of professionals' obligations and the conflicts in responsibility that individuals must negotiate. Professionals must balance obligations to their employing organisation and its rules of practice, to broad social needs served by their profession, to the profession itself and the standards and regulatory codes governing its practices, to individuals for whom the professional adopts a caring responsibility, and to personal allegiances influencing a sense of the 'right thing to do'. This 'web of commitments' often necessitates what May (1996) has called 'legitimate compromises'. Practitioners almost always must navigate a path of action that simultaneously balances concerns for different stakeholders without necessarily meeting the full expectations of any one of them. For example, Solbrekke (2008b) shows that while practitioners in law and psychology continually must negotiate difficult compromises, they appear overly governed by externally defined regulations.

Professionals' negotiations of these conflicting responsibilities are becoming exacerbated by particular conflicts between the claims of increased efficiency and economy and the best interests of clients, students and patients (Colley *et al.* 2007; Robinson 2009; Stronach *et al.* 2002). Stronach and his colleagues report that nurses and teachers appear to manage this particular conflict by simultaneously juggling conflicting discourses of professionalism in their everyday work: an economy of performance, and an ecology of practice. Colley *et al.*, drawing from Cribb (2005), describe this work as ethical labour: practitioners not only are tasked to difficult work in managing these ethical conflicts, but find their ethical work itself commodified. While professionals are often depicted as continually 'becoming', in practice they must often choose to act in ways 'unbecoming', such as when they feel compelled by professional responsibilities of care and compassion for an individual patient or student to work around or subvert more general regulations oriented to certain performance outcomes.

More broadly, some have signaled a demand for new forms of professionalism in these conflicts. For instance Noordegraf (2011) argues for an 'organised professionalism' that recognises the ways that changing circumstances are requiring organisationally based capacities for responsibility. He identifies three changes that are requiring a more systemic approach to professionalism and responsibility: (a) professionals are increasingly seeking organised work conditions; (b) they face new ambiguously bounded *cases* that call for well-organised multi-professional acts; and (c) these cases present new critical *risks*, that are better managed through an organised response. Collaborative multi-agency practice is becoming a more typical response to such complex and boundary-blurred cases, but raises new issues of responsibility. Different positionings of professionals invoke different ethical sensibilities as well as focus and scope for responsible practice, argues Cribb (2005). Doctors focus on curing, nurses on caring, or at least that is the myth promoted by some clinicians. But beyond the ways that practitioners position (or accuse) each other, it is clear that different groups are fundamentally enmeshed in their own epistemic communities. Particularly in synchronistic situations such as in multi-professional team work, researchers continue to show that each professional group's knowledge and sense of what is most important or what is the right thing to do is oriented around a distinct history of practice that is tightly woven to particular instruments and tools, language and commitments. Edwards (2007:2) has shown that what is called for in such situations is 'relational agency', which involves distributed expertise and mutual responsibility, as well as mutual attunement and adjustment to others' worlds of practice: 'a capacity to align one's thoughts and actions with those of others to interpret aspects of one's world and to act on and respond to those interpretations'. Working from activity theory, Edwards stresses that artefacts as well as people and activity are critical in mediating practice, knowing and responsibility.

All of this speaks to a more systemic, relational and material approach to understanding professionalism and 'professional responsibility'. Yet like professional learning, professional responsibility has long been understood as a personal, and sometimes social, phenomenon. As Solbrekke and Sugrue (2010) show, professional responsibility is mostly treated as a matter of individual ethical decision-making, informed by professional knowing of particular values and commitments that can be inculcated through education and ethical codes. A sociomaterial approach offers a different configuration for rethinking professional responsibility, where the material and the social are viewed as mutually implicated in bringing forth the world. As the introduction to this volume argues, professional practice weaves together knowing with action, conversation, affect, and materials in purposeful and regularised orderings of human activity. Material forces – flesh and blood, forms and checklists, diagnostic machines and databases, furniture and passcodes, snowstorms and dead cell zones – are integral in shaping professional practice both as a repertoire of routines as well in particular moments of response and decision. Yet materiality is often dismissed or ignored in analyses of professional responsibility.

The central premise of sociomateriality adopted in this argument is, as Orlikowski (2007:1435) puts it, 'the constitutive entanglement of the social and material in everyday life'. All things – human and non-human, hybrids and parts, knowledge and systems – are understood to be *effects* of connections and activity. They are performed into existence in webs of relations. There are no received categories. The point is that material things are performative and not inert; they are matter and they matter. They act together with other types of things and forces to exclude, invite, and regulate particular forms of participation in enactments, some of which we term knowing. The move here is what Jensen (2010:7) characterises as 'from epistemology and representation to practical ontology and performativity'. The question of producing knowledge and learning shifts from a representational idiom, mapping and understanding a world that is out there, to a view that the world is doing things, full of agency. When we accept such a configuration, processes such as acting, learning and responding are understood to be sociomaterial enactments. A focus on the sociomaterial therefore helps us to untangle the heterogeneous relationships holding together these larger categories, tracing their durability as well as their weaknesses. From this approach, no anterior distinctions, such as human beings or social structures, are presupposed. Everything is performed into existence: 'the agents, their dimensions and what they are and do, all depend on the morphology of the relations in which they are involved' (Callon 1991).

Particularly for purposes of examining professional responsibility, one key contribution of sociomaterial analysis is to de-couple knowing and action from a strictly human-centred sociocultural ontology, and to liberate agency and responsibility from its conceptual confines as a human-generated force. Instead, agency is understood to be *enacted* in the emergence and interactions – as well as the exclusionings – occurring in the smallest encounters. Bennett (2010:1) describes this as the 'force of things', 'the agency of assemblages' and 'the vitality of materiality', drawing from Deleuzian discussions of vital materialism of energies coursing through matter. Her argument focuses on why materiality is critical to reformulating a politics and responsibility that moves beyond oppositions, blame and self interest. She shows how public life is dramatically acted upon by matter, such as food and fat, stem cells, metal and electricity. The North American electricity blackout of 2003 that affected 50 million people, for example, was enacted through a heterogeneous assemblage including electricity, power plants (with overprotective mechanisms and understaffed), transmission wires (with limits on their heat capacity), a regulatory commission and policy act (that privatised electricity and separated transmission of electricity from distribution), energy-trading corporations (profiting from the grid at the expense of maintaining infrastructure), consumers (with growing demand for electricity), and a bush fire in Ohio. The point is not that individual objects have agency, but that force is exercised through these sociomaterial assemblages. Non-human materiality, Bennett argues, is interpenetrated with human intensities in these assemblages in ways that must be treated symmetrically. Human responsibility, then, is the effect of particular distributions and accumulations enacted through such assemblages. This view

> multiplies the potentially relevant actors and force attention on their differences and relations. The aspiration is to thereby facilitate more nuanced analyses of how humans and things (broadly construed) together create, stabilize and change worlds. Analyses, in other words, that are sensitive to human and nonhuman activities as *practical ontology*: efforts to concretely shape and interrelate the components that make up the worlds they inhabit.
> (Jensen, 2010:5)

Capacity for action is relational, and distributed among the elements of these entangled assemblages. All things are continually acting with one another, not as separate entities but as overlapping waves that are *intra*-active (rather than *inter*-acting, which implies separate things that come together). Barad (2003:817) argues that the sociomaterial real becomes performed into existence through specific intra-actions that she calls 'agential cuts' in 'the ongoing open process of mattering'. Through these agential cuts, matter becomes separated into distinct entities, allowing us to see boundaries and relationships among knower, known and knowledge. Agency is not confined to humans or human-associated desires and energies. Instead, agency emerges through the dynamic openness of each intra-action, which enable iterative changes. Thus for Barad (2003:823), 'matter comes to matter through the iterative intra-activity of the world in its becoming'. Following a similar line of analysis, educational philosopher Bai (2001:26) writes, 'changes are the result of our interpenetrating the world', more than of human conscious intentional action to do something.

These notions of 'intra-active' assemblages of human and non-human, 'vital materialities' and human action as 'interpenetration' in the living matter and technologically mediated worlds of everyday professional practice hold profound transformative potential for many social sciences and humanities. As Braidotti

(2013) argues passionately, they open an expanded, radical relational conception of subjectivity, a transversal and ecological posthumanism. While this conception has profound ethical and political commitments, following Braidotti's arguments (as well as Barad's, where an ethical feminist project is central) it provoke serious challenges to classical notions of individual agency, morality and intentionality that are usually central to thinking about professional responsibility. Difficult questions arise, particularly in considering professional responsibility – the tip at which public trust, societal anxiety and regulatory scrutiny converge. Who and what is responsible in difficult encounters when capacities for action are distributed, when action and subjectivities are emergent? Where are the points of accountability? How can professionals negotiate these ambivalent encounters?

Dilemmas of professional responsibility: the politics of materials and practice

To begin to explore these questions, let us turn to some specific examples of dilemmas in professional practice, and try a sociomaterial reading of problematics of responsibility that arise. In this short chapter little more can be done than to offer a brief taste of what a more-than-human perspective might offer when considering professionals' everyday practices. Two small scenarios will be shared, drawn from different studies of professionals at work. The first study focused on inter-professional practice in emergency mental health care. The second examined issues of co-production (community involvement in generating solutions and developing needed services) in rural policing.

Inter-professional practice, as was described earlier, often involves a collision of different practices, terminology, instruments and forms of knowledge. Emergency mental health care is one example. An emergency call for care can range from attempted self-harm to psychotic or aggressive episodes related to a mental health disorder. It typically involves paramedics, police and hospital-based health professionals. As was found in recent studies that interviewed these different personnel, emergency mental health care often presents ambivalent situations across a vast range of diverse conditions (Aberton and Slade 2012; Essington 2011). There are no standardised procedures or specified 'care pathways' for these emergencies, and little training. Yet there are clear duties of responsibility for each of the professions involved, although these do not map easily onto the situations that emerge or mesh together smoothly. For instance, while the police duty of care is to promote security and safety of all persons involved in an incident, for Scottish ambulance practitioners their duty of responsibility is to care for and deliver the patient to a safe place (with minor variations depending on job classification). This concept of 'safety', a core principle for both groups, can be enacted very differently in their own worlds of practice. In one case recounted in our study, where a man was threatening to jump off a bridge onto a motorway, the police explained that 'we grabbed him by the shoulder ... [and he] was put in handcuffs for his own safety ... and put in the back of the police vehicle … until he calmed down', and 'it took three of us to kind of hold him down … just trying to calm him down'. Grabbing, handcuffing, and holding down constitute a particular enactment of safety and response to a distressed man, which cannot be separated from the intermeshed actions of all present.

The apparatus of each group also clearly distinguishes two different material worlds of practice, organised around different purposes and practices: the ambulance outfitted with medical equipment, assessment devices and cots for emergency clinical diagnosis and care, and the police van that may be equipped with emergency shields, handcuffs and possibly firearms. Ambulance practitioners are not able to restrain a patient, but police have the power to exercise involuntary detention of a mental health patient in an emergency. Meanwhile hospital staff, who typically refer to paramedics' work as 'pre-hospital care', tend to view the hospital activity as the site where the most reliable and robust treatment occurs. Everything else, from this perspective, ought inevitably to flow to the hospital. To 'join up' the different worlds of practice involved in a single emergency call, practitioners must rely on professional judgement, improvisation, close attunement to the others involved and their traditions and limits of practice, and a personal sense of the 'responsible' thing to do.

Another example from Aberton and Slade (2012) illustrates the different material worlds at play, as well as the ways that transitions among them must be achieved. A patient, reportedly in a schizophrenic condition, was balancing on a window ledge two floors up. Paramedic Kaitlyn was called to the scene:

[She] hadn't been taking medication and stuff for a matter of weeks, and was basically balancing on a window ledge, and it was her heels that were kinda more or less holding her on. But she was hallucinating at the same time, and she could hear people in the garden telling her to come, come to her, come, come to them, to basically jump. And obviously there was me and a policewoman … If you engaged enough with her then she would keep speaking to you, but I think as soon as somebody was not speaking or she wasn't, didn't want to speak to you anymore then it was obviously the hallucination or the voices that she was hearing. And there was a few occasions that I thought she was gonna go … but we managed to get her back in (with a cigarette because we learned from the other people in the house that she was a smoker), and the policewoman was saying to her that she could go in the ambulance and that. But due to the circumstances of the actual job, the ambulance has a side door and the two back doors, and obviously … in the back of the ambulance, you've got different things … And the way that she, that she was I, I didn't feel it was safe for the patient to be in the back of an ambulance

(from interview transcript: Kaitlyn: lines 16–17).

An assemblage of heterogeneous elements interact in the emergency. The patient's heels, voices, hallucinations, window ledge, the mental state of the patient, broken glass door, absence of usual medication, paramedics, a policewoman, a cigarette, trust, ambulance doors and equipment in the back and police van. The job of the paramedics and police is to relocate the patient to 'a place of safety'. On closer examination of the data the movement between different related entities can be identified for the sake of description as four enactments which merge and emerge. First, 'If you engaged enough with the patient she would keep speaking to you'. The voice of the paramedic effected temporary disengagement from the seductive voices in the garden. The patient's attention could be diverted from the seductive voices below which were inviting her to jump. Second, the urge to smoke and the enticement of a cigarette precipitated this transition from the window ledge to 'safety' inside the house. Third was the transition to hospital in a police car, which was deemed 'safer' than the ambulance with its doors and equipment, but risked a new transition in patient behavior after the promise of an ambulance.

(adapted from Aberton and Slade 2012:3–4)

This scenario illustrates how enactments of professional responsibilities for care and safety are the effect of relations between assemblages of heterogeneous elements. Responsibility is distributed – not just across different professionals each making or deferring decisions, but also across and through the different materials engaged the various events. Elements and humans are not distinct and separate, but act on each other, respond to and overlap with each other. Responsibility lies more in individuals' attunement to these different relations, and their intra-engagement with the networks of action that produce difficult encounters, than with any one professional's choice of action.

Co-production is another area that illustrates the difficulty of drawing tight lines of professional responsibility in providing public services. Fast becoming a dominant policy discourse in the UK, Australia and North America, 'co-production' can be defined as professional services and products that are co-developed with clients or service users. In public sector services such as health, policing and social care, co-production increasingly calls for active community participation whereby service users are centrally involved in planning and designing as well as delivering services. Boyle and Harris (2009:12) explain that it goes well beyond the idea of 'citizen engagement' or 'service user involvement' to foster the principle of 'equal partnership'. But critical questions about co-production touch issues of responsibility. To what extent, in various cases, are users and families even interested in such 'partnerships'? How are they trained and compensated for taking on these responsibilities? And where does accountability fall when things go wrong?

These questions are related to processes of negotiating decision-making, authority and expectations in co-produced public service. In a recent study of co-production in policing, we examined these everyday negotiations (Fenwick 2012). The context was a large rural area policed by one constabulary, where practice often had to be conducted from single-officer stations responsible for covering dozens of square miles characterised by significant geographical challenges (mountains, a lengthy coastline and many islands). Experienced officers learned a variety of work-arounds to stretch resources and to 'play the long game' in everyday moments, as one sergeant put it. Rather than leaping to action by following prescribed protocol strictly, they often negotiate to sustain a longer trusting relationship. This negotiation has practical material ends as well as social ones, for much investigative police work in the community relies on information that one's neighbours are willing to share freely.

> It's a minor road traffic infringement and you can use your discretion and say 'OK Mike, next time put your seatbelt on or get that light fixed' rather than booking him or giving him a ticket, because tomorrow that person could be a key witness in something more serious and if you've got their backs up they're no[t] going to come to you with the information.
>
> (constable, town in northern Scotland)

The importance of materiality continually emerges in these narratives of negotiations. In one incident, a constable was called to a hit-and-run scene, where a lorry allegedly had backed into a shopkeeper's wall. Recognising some metallic blue paint shavings left on this wall, the officer scraped them into an envelope and drove round to see the fellow he believed they belonged to. After some conversation seeking the man's assistance, the paint shavings were produced, inducing his sudden recollection of 'oh, *that* wall!', and his promise to pop round and fix the wall that afternoon. According to the officer, even the shop owner was satisfied because his wall got fixed so quickly. The entire incident was contained as an issue of some material damage needing repair, inflicted by a truck. It was neither personalised as an escalated case of injury and defence, nor labelled, disciplined and recorded as a crime. The community members involved worked with the police officer to co-produce this construction of the incident, stepping away from the conflict script of defensive perpetrator/outraged victim and taking up positions of cooperation.

The situation becomes complicated where lives are at risk. One man, now an inspector and instructor, told stories of his first postings in communities on the long undefended coastline of northwest Scotland. Here as a single officer, he and colleagues typically improvised a range of material and social resources to manage issues ranging from attempted drug smuggling to air-sea emergency rescues. In one story, he tells of being called to a scene of alleged assault. Arriving to confront a very large and physically aggressive intoxicated man, the lone officer engaged a nearby fisherman to help wrestle him to the ground, using the fisherman's ropes to secure him. Naturally, the interviewee noted, this wasn't recognised standard procedure, but safety for all sometimes requires improvisation. Another described being a single officer called to a major motorway vehicular crash. To secure the scene for investigation, obtain emergency help for the injured, and ensure the safety of oncoming traffic, he needed to mobilise any tools to hand and anyone who stopped to help – while managing his own emotions and those of all involved.

Overall, these instances indicate a little of the intensive dialogue, negotiation and consultation that Needham (2007) emphasises to be critical elements in co-production. They show, however, that responsibility is a complex activity that transcends conversation and social relations – it is also embodied, and invokes materiality in ways that skilled practitioners can leverage. Many opportune moments for negotiating responsibility were not planned, but seemed to emerge *within* encounters involving a range of sociomaterial entanglements. Resourceful officers found ways to work effectively within and through these assemblages to interrupt, reframe and avert problem situations in moments that may be best characterised as knowing-in-practice. 'Responsible' action emerges in the sociomaterial mix, in being attuned to possibilities available in this mix at any moment, and in being sufficiently resourceful to improvise with these possibilities.

Conclusion

In situations calling for responsible decision-making, professionals must balance competing versions of the 'good' in highly uncertain encounters. They are called to act in what Caputo (1993) describes as 'disasters' where response 'can occur only as a leap into an abyss, a plunge into the density and impenetrability of the event, the novelty and the surprise of singularity' (1993:92, 97). Professionals' action in this leap rarely reflects a considered rational application of moral principles to a problem. Instead, decisions emerge through enactments in which a range of material as well as sociocultural phenomena and knowledge resources are entangled with practitioners.

Following Barad's (2003) conception of sociomaterial intra-activity, the issue in considering professional responsibility may be approached as understanding how professionals delineate their intra-actions within these sociomaterial assemblages. They do not act morally on an already existing real, but come into existence themselves within activity that materialises the moral. That is, professionals select actions – they perform agential cuts that help shape and redirect the real – but this process can only be enacted through particular material possibilities, forces and other capacities producing assemblages of practice. In the examples here of police and paramedic practices, we can see how professionals learn how to work with and through these entangled vitalities where human and material elements are almost inseparable in their continual overlapping and intra-acting, constituting the professionals' world of practices as well as the immediate encounter demanding action. They leverage the forces that they can, while holding open the tensions of competing goods. This sociomaterial juggling suggests a conception of professional responsibility that decentres the individual and materialises the moral, but without flattening or erasing the importance of human choice and ethical commitments in professional action.

Two questions were posed at the beginning of this chapter: Who and what is responsible in difficult encounters when capacities for action are distributed, when action and subjectivities are emergent? Where are the points of accountability? This sociomaterial view begins by making visible the capillaries of action, the networks of Latour's conception (2005), through which the multifarious associations comprising professional practice and its various responsibilities are produced. Paraphrasing Latour (2005:44) we can state that any practice, encounter or decision is a knot or conglomerate of many material and human forces. These associations are 'knotted' and sustained through coordinations of human and non-human mediators such as plans and contracts, assessment sheets and report forms, handcuffs and paint scrapings. Such an analysis focuses attention not on *who* is responsible, but *how* responsibility is enacted – and often enacted differently – at different points among these associations. Further, it examines how particular accounts of responsibility are produced. How, for instance, are particular locations for professional responsibility in any given encounter achieved and stabilised? How do human beings and their competency become the centre of an accountable order, and how is this reproduced and disciplined? How does a particular person become the lightning rod for accountability, as in scapegoating of professional individuals, in complex cases that clearly are composed of myriad contributing factors? A sociomaterial analysis not only can help to unpick the assembling processes and the continuing work that produces practice and responsibility in particular ways, it can also make visible the ways in which we account for (ir)responsibility.

The third question raised at the chapter's beginning was: How can professionals negotiate these ambivalent encounters? The argument suggests that the way forward lies in an extraordinary attunement to all aspects of a case, not just the human or social elements that are most readily identifiable. There is a mindfulness required here, an ethical consideration extended to things. This is about an appreciation not only of the multiple human stakeholders in any case, but also of the complex associations of materials and people, equipment and emotions, technologies and desires.

This is a view that moves far beyond a focus on individual professionals' ethical decision-making to an appreciation of how these decisions are entangled in networks of things that each have their own trajectory. Rather than attempting to dismiss or ignore these entanglements, or to control them through protocols of practice and ethical codes, a sociomaterial view recognises the vital intensities produced within this emergence, and opens new ways to think about professional practice and responsibility. Because in this view, as Barad (2003) argues, (unknown) radical future possibilities are available at every encounter.

References

Aberton, H. and Slade, B. (2011) 'Material enactments of care: Paramedics, police and mental health-related emergency calls', Paper presented to the ProPEL International Conference, 8–10 May, 2012.

AF (2012) 'Final report on the accident on 1 June 2009 to the Airbus A330-203 registered F-GZCP operated by Air France flight AF 447. BEA'. Online. Available at: www.bea.aero/docspa/2009/f-cp090601.en/pdf/f-cp090601.ed.pdf (accessed 6 June 2012).

Bai, H. (2001) 'Beyond the educated mind: Towards a pedagogy of mindfulness, body and mind', in B. Hocking, A. Haskell and W. Linds (eds), *Body and Mind: Exploring possibility through education*, (pp. 86–99), Vermont, NH: Foundation for Educational Renewal.

Barad, K. (2003) 'Posthumanist performativity: Toward an understanding of how matter comes to matter', *Signs*, 28(3): 801–831.

BBC (2012) 'Fatal flight 447: Chaos in the cockpit', Channel 4, BBC, 16 September 2012.

Bennett, J. (2010) *Vibrant Matter: A political ecology of things*, Durham NC: Duke University Press.

Boyle, D. and Harris, M. (2009) *The Challenge of Co-production*, London: New Economics Foundation.

Braidotti, R. (2013) *The Posthuman*, Cambridge: Polity Press.

Butler, P. (2011) 'Sharon Shoesmith wins appeal against sacking over Baby P tragedy', *The Guardian*, Friday 27 May 2011. Online. Available at: www.guardian.co.uk/society/2011/may/27/sharon-shoesmith-baby-p-tragedy (accessed 2 September 2012).

Callon, M. (1991) 'Techno-economic network and irreversibility', in J. Law (ed.), *A Sociology of Monster: Essays on Power, Technology and Domination* (pp. 132–165), London: Routledge.

Caputo, J. (1993) *Against Ethics*, Bloomington and Indianapolis: Indiana University Press.

Colley, H., James, D. and Diment, K. (2007) 'Unbecoming teachers: Towards a more dynamic notion of professional participation', *Journal of Education Policy*, 22(2): 173–193

Cribb, A. (2005) *Health and the Good Society: Setting healthcare ethics in social context*, Oxford: Oxford University Press.

Edwards, A. (2007) 'Relational agency in professional practice: A CHAT analysis', *Actio: An International Journal of Human Activity Theory*, 1: 1–17.

Essington, T. (2011) 'Preliminary summary of findings: Multi-professional responses to mental health calls: Knowledge, practice, and decision-making', Working Paper. Online. Available at www.propel.stir.ac.uk (accessed 11 November 2012).

Fenwick, T. (2012) Co-production in professional practice: a sociomaterial perspective. *Professions and PrProfessionalism*, 2 (2): 1–16.

Fenwick, T., Edwards, R. and Sawchuk, P. (2011) *Emerging Approaches to Educational Research: Tracing the socio-material*, London: Routledge.

Jensen, C.B. (2010) *Ontologies for Developing Things: Making health care futures through technology*, Rotterdam: Sense Publishers.

Latour, B. (2005) *Reassembling the Social: An introduction to actor–network-theory*, Oxford and New York: Oxford University Press.

May, L. (1996) *The Socially Responsive Self: Social theory and professional ethics*, Chicago: University of Chicago Press.

Needham, C. (2007) 'Realising the potential of co-production: Negotiating improvements in public services', *Social Policy and Society*, 7: 221–231.

Orlikowski, W.J. (2007) 'Sociomaterial practices: Exploring technology at work', *Organization Studies*, 28: 1435–1448.

Robinson, S. (2009) 'The nature of responsibility in a professional setting', *Journal of Business Ethics*, 88: 11–19.

Solbrekke, T.D. (2008a) 'Educating for professional responsibility: A normative dimension of higher education', *Utbildning & Demokrati*, 17(2): 73–96.

Solbrekke, T.D. (2008b) 'Professional responsibility as legitimate compromises – from communities of education to communities of work', *Studies in Higher Education*, 33(4): 485–500.

Solbrekke, T.D. and Sugrue, C. (2010) 'Professional responsibility: Retrospect and prospect', in T.D. Solbrekke and C. Sugrue (eds) *Professional Responsiblity: New horizons of praxis?*, London: Routledge.

Stronach, I., Corbin, B., McNamara, O., Stark, S. and Warne, T. (2002) 'Towards an uncertain politics of professionalism: Teachers and nurse identities in flux', *Journal of Educational Policy*, 17(1): 109–138.

Chapter 12

Developing professional responsibility in medicine

A sociomaterial curriculum

Nick Hopwood, Madeleine Abrandt Dahlgren and Karin Siwe

Introduction

In this chapter we present the notion of a sociomaterial curriculum, drawing on Schatzki to theorize learning and pedagogy as bundles of practices and material arrangements. A sociomaterial curriculum refers to the ways in which practice-arrangement bundles facilitate learning and organize its structure and content. It invokes established ideas of the curriculum as enacted, rather than as articulated in static texts, and draws new attention to the role of things in practice and learning. We argue that this new concept is useful in connecting developments in sociomaterial theories of practice with questions of learning and pedagogy. This casts professional knowledge and responsibility in a radically different light. While traditionally seen predominantly as cognitive and ethical phenomena, we portray their learning and enactment as a tight weaving between bodily actions and things.

The context is a learning programme for medical students focused on the pelvic examination, in which professional patients play a role as instructors alongside a university teacher.

Most women will have a pelvic examination at some time in their lives. It serves an important diagnostic function for several gynaecological conditions (such as ovarian tumours, myoma, cervical abnormalities), and is also performed by midwives with healthy women in relation to pregnancy and contraception. However, the procedure may often be experienced negatively by women who feel their bodies and selves have been treated invasively and without due sensitivity (Wijma *et al.* 1998). The pelvic examination thus has direct and particular connections with issues of professional knowledge and responsibility.

The pelvic examination involves two main procedures. The first stage involves a visual inspection of the uterus, beginning with a brief external assessment, and then looking into the body, facilitated by the use of metal instruments that widen the vagina. The second stage is a bimanual palpation. The doctor inserts two fingers into the pelvis, and uses them to locate and assess the surface shape and texture of the uterus and ovaries (this is termed palpation). The doctor's other hand rests externally on the lower abdomen. Learning how to insert and use the instruments without causing discomfort, and locate and palpate organs constitute particular difficulties for students.

The intimate character of the pelvic examination presents challenges for medical educators. Several of the pedagogic approaches in use, including plastic models, sedated bodies and hi-tech simulators are limited in their potential to help students work with a patient (Siwe 2007).

An alternative approach to learning the pelvic examination, involving professional patients, was introduced in Sweden at the Faculty of Health Sciences, Linköping in 1982. Since 1992, this has been co-ordinated by one of the authors (Karin Siwe). Professional patient pedagogy for teaching the pelvic examination was developed by Kretzschmar in the USA in the 1960s. Kretzschmar noted that working with 'real' patients produced significant anxiety for both student and patient, given the complex, intimate and emotionally charged nature of the procedure. A focus on technical skills hindered communication and interpersonal skills. Furthermore, there was no way for the instructor or the students to confirm they were palpating the correct organs (Kretzchmar 1972).

Professional patients are now used in several medical schools around the world (Frye and Weisberg 1994; Kamemoto *et al.* 2003; Wanggren 2005). In Linkoping, professional patients are healthy women who volunteer to assist students learning the interpersonal and technical skills needed to perform a pelvic examination. Preparatory education is provided for professional patients to help them develop knowledge of their anatomy and the procedures of the pelvic examination. They then make their bodies available for students to practise the examination, while also enacting a teaching role at the same time. The aim is to create a safe learning environment, where the patient is confident as a pedagogic guide for the student. The presence of a body as both patient and pedagogic figure offers different opportunities for students to navigate the complex relationships between sex, professional power and medical knowledge (Siwe 2007). This approach aims to build confidence in students and to foster different power relationships in future clinical practices. Professional responsibility is not simply for a patient-as-body, but doctors take up a responsibility to facilitate a collaborative interaction, in which patients can make a transition from a subordinate position to one of partner during a consultation.

Theoretical background

A sociomaterial perspective and site ontology

Within the diverse range of sociomaterial approaches to understanding professional learning and practice (Fenwick *et al.* 2012), we focus on the work of Theodore Schatzki (1996, 2002, 2010). Schatzki's (2003) ontology proposes that the site of all social life comprises a nexus or bundle of practices and material arrangements. He argues against the theorization of social phenomena as if materiality did not matter (2010).

Schatzki (2003, 2010) adopts an ontology that can be distinguished from other sociomaterial approaches: social life (including professional education and practice) transpires inherently as part of bundles of practices and material arrangements. In contrast to actor–network theory (ANT), or other 'posthumanist' approaches, Schatzki rejects symmetry or equality of agency between human and non-human. He maintains that there are differences between the two, but articulates a strong role for materiality. It is strong in the sense that materiality is not seen as interwoven with social life, inevitably and ubiquitously linked, but rather a dimension of social life (2010).

Key concepts in Schatzki's framework

Schatzki (2001) defines practices as embodied, materially mediated arrays of human activity (doings and sayings), organized around shared understandings. Practices are organized by *practical understandings* (bodily know-how, the ability to carry out actions, for example, the physical knowledge involved in listening through a stethoscope), *rules, teleoaffective structures* (what motivates practices and what ends they serve), and *general understandings*. We interpret the latter to include disciplinary knowledge such as anatomy, medical ethics and wider knowledge about what it means to be a doctor. Professional knowledge reflects a combination of practical and general understandings, and is not only a basis for practice, but organizes it. We focus on general and practical understandings as means to link practices to the notion of a sociomaterial curriculum, though this is not to suggest that rules and teleoaffective structures are not also at play.

In using the term materiality, Schatzki refers to people (i.e. human bodies), organisms (non-human living things), artefacts (things that have been shaped by human activity) and things (or things of nature) (2002, 2003, 2010). *Material arrangements* refer to any group of things that are connected in some way. There are four ways in which material arrangements and practices are bundled together. The first is through *causal relations.* Here, Schatzki means X leads to Y rather than X brings about Y, and the relationship can go in both directions: human actions can alter, create or rearrange material entities, but people also react to material entities or changes among them. The second form of bundling is termed *prefiguration*, referring to the way in which materiality shapes the future. This is not strongly determinative, nor neutral (as the notion of affordance might be). Rather materiality qualifies or suggests possible actions as, for example, easier or harder, more or less obvious. A well-trodden path through a field suggests walking in a particular direction makes it easier. It does not force walkers, but it is not neutral because it does not just make walking through the field possible, it guides and invites movement in a particular direction.

Practices and arrangements also *co-constitute* each other. Some objects are essential, without which practices could not be carried out – a pelvic examination requires a pelvis to be examined. Others are pervasive and come to shape how practices are done – gynaecological chairs have become characteristic of the practice without which the examination would assume a different form. Finally, Schatzki refers to *intelligibility*. Material entities that make up arrangements are intelligible to humans who carry out practices amid them. The practical function of an object is not inherent or stable, but results from the way it is bundled with doings and sayings. A door handle is intelligible as a handle when it is used as a lever and pulling device, but can also be intelligible as a hook when it is used to hang a coat. A piece of human tissue can become intelligible as a specific part of anatomy when it is pointed to and named as such. Thus the way materiality provides a setting for activity is not a fixed property, but one that depends on how things have a bearing on, are brought into relation to, practice.

In summary, the material world forms a setting for activity (what Schatzki refers to as spatiality), while actions are performed amid, with and attuned to material entities. People react to material events or states of affairs, must negotiate the physicality of the material world, yet can produce and alter objects or relationships between them.

The listing of human bodies as one of four kinds of materiality does not imply its conceptual reduction to physical substance. But it does represent a deliberate strategy to avoid the erasure of bodies as a material presence that has characterized other social theories. In Schatzki (1996), the body is not a biological body of the kind invoked in medical discourse. The body feels, speaks and acts. It is both a material being and a social one, subject to the world and playing an active role in constituting it through practices and their bundling with (other) material arrangements. These ideas form an important thread in our analysis of the dual role played by the professional patient as both examined body and a body that acts and speaks back.

Our analysis also draws on the notion of body geometries. This has been discussed elsewhere (Hopwood 2013) and builds on a Schatzkian perspectives. It emphasizes fluid spatial arrangements of bodies, and bodies and other things, raising questions of position, distance, lines of sight, reach and posture. It is used below as a means to highlight aspects of materiality and embodiment that might otherwise be overlooked, but which nonetheless play a crucial role in enacting a sociomaterial curriculum.

Conceptualizing curriculum

We link sociomaterial theories of practice with concepts of knowledge, learning and pedagogy, proposing the idea of a sociomaterial curriculum. Curriculum is often taken to refer to articulations of intent regarding the structure, content and outcome of learning. Our notion is quite different, and builds on widely used alternative views of curriculum as dynamic and enacted.

In Hopwood *et al.* (2010), Lee describes curriculum as a motivated selection from relevant aspects of a culture, including disciplinary knowledge and professional practice, and a vision of a future for that culture. Curriculum intersects with issues of professional responsibility. The idea of curriculum thus leads us to question how the encounter with professional patients selects relevant aspects of disciplinary knowledge and practice, and nurtures future practices that foster professional responsibility.

Views of curriculum as something that is enacted shift attention away from what is required or planned, to what is done in practice and the experience this constitutes for learners. Curriculum is understood in dynamic terms as a property of relationships between knowing and doing (Barnett and Coate 2005). Ideas of the enacted curriculum thus bring us directly to questions of practice as learning unfolds and is emergent. Such curriculum theorizing has been fundamental in enabling researchers to better understand the pedagogic qualities of many experiences and practices, including non-educational settings such as workplaces. We draw on curricular concepts in order to link practice theory to questions of learning and pedagogy. Simultaneously, we offer a more material notion of curriculum.

Empirical approach

We draw on field notes made during joint observation of one evening class. Madeleine and Nick were invited by Karin to observe teaching involving professional patients, and this presented an opportunity to explore some of the questions that come out of an engagement with sociomaterial theory. Our approach followed the ethnographic tradition in paying close attention to objects and their use – producing accounts which were rich in sociomaterial terms. The presence of observers was at the invitation of the instructor (Karin), and with explicit consent of the professional patients and students.

The observations took place on a Monday evening and lasted three hours. The students were in their final semester, and this was the first time they had performed a complete pelvic examination (they had worked with professional patients and practised only bimanual palpation earlier in their degree). The episode began when four students arrived in a waiting area and were introduced by Karin to two professional patients. After some discussion the group moved to a clinical room. The students donned medical gowns and one patient changed into a robe, ready for the demonstration of the pelvic examination by Karin. The students watched this, and then split to work in pairs with each professional patient. Karin moved between the pairs, but observations remained focused on how two students worked with one patient. After each student had performed the examination, the group returned to the waiting room and their ordinary clothes for a concluding discussion. The whole session was conducted in Swedish, which led Nick (who does not speak Swedish) to focus particularly on doings and objects, while Madeleine's notes were infused with more references to sayings. Excerpts presented below reflect a merging of both accounts.

How is a sociomaterial curriculum being enacted?

We address this question in three sections. The first concerns how students learn to *collaborate with a patient as a person* rather than examining a biological body. The second explores the *performance of the visual inspection* as a set of bodily doings and sayings that require close and responsive attunement between bodies and things. The third explores practices that *make the body see-through*, helping both students and the teacher become aware of things they cannot see (organs, movements, etc.), particularly during the manual part of the process. We interpret these in Schatzkian terms, using his ideas of general and practical understandings to make links between practices and learning.

We explore professional responsibility in terms of managing sensitivity, treating patients with respect as human beings, and fulfilling professional obligations in the conduct of the examination. We show how the curriculum incorporates these crucial elements of professional learning, and in doing so cast the legal and ethical obligation of responsibility as something that is practised and material. We call attention to the professional patient as a living body that speaks back, contributing doings and sayings of her own as part of a socially and materially enacted curriculum. This highlights what is special about professional patient pedagogy.

Collaborating with the patient as a person, not as a biological body

The medical constitution of human bodies as biological entities, complexes of organs and tissue, foregrounds the materiality of medical work, but problematically neglects the person. As discussed above, pedagogies of the pelvic examination based on an exclusively biophysical notion of the body fail to provide contexts for students to develop the interpersonal responsibilities that are a crucial feature of this practice. The curriculum that we observed being enacted attended to the professional patient as a material presence (the position, size, shape and texture of bodily organs), and a living, social presence. This is key to helping students develop professional responsibility vis à vis their relationships with patients. Consistent with a Schatzkian perspective, the point here is not to suggest two separate bodies, but to offer an analytic distillation of features that are inherently part of the bodily whole. The dual material-and-social presence of the professional patient underpins her pedagogic function as a body that speaks back into practice, using speech to feed back sensations of touch she feels within her body. Many doings and sayings (including those of the patient, teacher and students), and the managed use of things (curtains, instruments) come together and are choreographed in this enactment.

We begin our engagement with field notes by exploring how the pelvic examination is established as a practice-arrangement bundle that involves working with the patient as a person, as a social as well as a material body.

As the students are waiting for the patient to get ready, Karin says, 'I know some places where they put a poster in the ceiling to distract the patient during the examination. You would never see that in my clinic'. The patient emerges from behind the curtain, dressed in a blue robe and long white socks, and walks towards the gynaecological chair. 'Remember, that the most vulnerable moment is when the patient sits up in the chair and spreads her legs', says Karin, 'you should respect that and step to the side, while the patient does so, and wait for the cue that she is ready'. The students are standing on the right hand side, turning their bodies, as the patient makes herself ready. She nods to Karin, giving the cue that she is now ready for the examination to start. The students move around to get a better view of Karin as she demonstrates. She moves to stand facing the patient, sits down on the stool. She changes the height of her stool, and the angle of the gynaecological chair, raising the patient's head. 'It is important that you adjust the height of the chair to allow eye-contact between the doctor and the patient.'

Karin's talk makes connections to instances of practices where 'normal' doctor–patient roles are enacted, as she discusses walking from the waiting room with the patient. These sayings expand the curriculum by making available selections of professional knowledge (general understandings) that are not part of the immediate actions and material arrangements. Karin explains how that brief transition is crucial in establishing respectful and collaborative relationships with patients. Her talk also draws attention to material absences – the lack of a picture on the ceiling. Links are made to fostering interactions between doctor and patient, and this saying speaks directly to the importance of things (including their managed absence) in the pelvic examination.

This bundling of doings, sayings and things in the enactment of professional responsibility is seen again in the movements of bodies (prompted by Karin's sayings, and then by the nod from the patient to Karin) as the patient takes her position in the chair. The adjustment of the stool and chair to establish eye-contact points again to how performing the pelvic examination with a person rather than on a body, is a sociomaterial accomplishment. Karin's commentary links these doings with sayings, making them explicit. The specific instance of adjusting stool height leads us to the next section, in which we explore the first part of the examination, a visual inspection, in terms of relational geometries between bodies and things.

Body geometries of performing the visual inspection

As well as helping students understand how to work collaboratively with patients, the pedagogic practices we observed also enacted a curriculum that gives students opportunities to develop practical understandings – the bodily know-how and physical skills required to conduct a pelvic examination proficiently and without causing the patient discomfort. We use the notion of body geometries to highlight learning how to use of instruments to provide a line of vision into the patient's body. While our focus here is on the actions of the examiner, the practice is understood as a joint accomplishment, including actions of the patient whose posture and drawing of breath play an active role in making the visual inspection possible, and whose holding of a model of the uterus (to normal scale) adds a crucial pedagogic dimension.

> The students move closer to Karin and the patient, the female students standing closest to the patient, the male students remaining towards the back. Karin reaches to the trolley nearby and picks up a speculum, a smooth-edged, metal instrument comprising a ring with two protruding strands on hinges, and a level used to adjust the angle between them. She demonstrates how to hold it and how to insert the instrument into the patient's vagina. Karin explains how the shape of the speculum is attuned to the female anatomy, 'Look at this, the angle of the instrument, the speculum, is the same as the angle of the vagina … the speculum is an extension of my arm'. She inserts the speculum, fluidly, with confidence and ease. The patient holds a model of the uterus over her pelvis to help the students visualize the anatomical space into which the speculum is inserted. Karin moves her head to look through the line of sight created by the speculum: 'Now, can you see the cervix? Tell the patient that it looks normal, not fine or OK'. The student standing closest to Karin sighs and says 'It looks so simple'.

What does this extract help us say about a sociomaterial curriculum? We notice the arrangement of bodies – Karin and the patient close together, and the students spread in two rows behind. These can be understood as bodily and material geometric relations. At the end of the previous extract we saw how Karin is positioned in three-dimensional space (adjusting the placement and height of the stool), and adopts a posture that provides an appropriate line of sight into the pelvis. Now we see a larger arrangement, offering multiple lines of sight for students. These lines of sight are not those of performing the visual inspection, but rather those of a learner, observing Karin, and, at times, bending down or leaning over to share in what she sees.

What things are made of, their shape and size, has a bearing on arrangements and practices, making things possible, easier, harder (Schatzki 2010). Karin's arm length and joints enable her to reach the trolley, and grab instruments from it. But this action also requires the trolley to be positioned within a certain range of angle and distance. The students' bodies can stand, lean forward, and turn. Their eyes have a field of vision that reflects their location in this body, and how body postures and positions locate the eyes in physical space. As Karin manipulates the speculum, and commentates on her actions, these doings and sayings cause (lead to) changes in the bodily material arrangement of the students. The combination of these prefigured arrangements and their emergent, fluid attunement (through vision and hearing) to what is going on, makes crucial features of the examination available. In this way, embodied relational geometries constitute a sociomaterial curriculum by making learning possible.

The speculum has physical properties that are designed to complement those of the pelvis in terms of shape and size. Karin's narration highlights the geometric alignment between the patient's body and the instrument as she inserts it. These connected doings and sayings foreground general understandings about anatomy and the use of clinical tools, and practical understandings of how to manipulate the instruments. We return to our field notes as Karin completes her demonstration (including that of the bimanual palpation), and hands over to the students.

> 'Now, who wants to go first?' A moment of hesitation before one of the female students steps forward, 'I'll start'. She sits down on the stool, Karin adjusts the light, moving the trolley closer, kicking away the bin that is in the way, changing the height of the stool to make sure that student and patient can have eye-contact. She helps the student select correctly sized gloves.
>
> Karin stands behind and to the right of the student, leans in so her chin is almost on the student's right shoulder, and reaches her left arm behind the student. She gives the student a short cotton bud to use as a pointer, so that the student can identify what she is naming. The student is slow, tentative and hesitant as she inserts the speculum. Karin squats down next to the student's right thigh, and places her right hand on the student's right hand, which is in turn gripping the second instrument the speculum (tf).
>
> Karin guides the student's hand movements in order to adjust the movements of the speculum inside the patient's body. 'Your hand needs to go down, down towards the floor, this will make the tip of the instrument go up'. The students who are watching shadow these movements with their empty hands in mid air.

Karin performs a number of adjustments to the material arrangements amid which the student performs the visual inspection. The movement of the light, bin, stool and trolley all produce geometric relations that assist the student. In undertaking these doings herself Karin is enacting curricular selections, enabling the student to focus on other things.

As the student inserts the speculum, Karin's physical actions, her bodily movements, along with her verbal guidance, enact a curriculum that shares practical understandings in a sociomaterial way. Different bodily and material geometries are evident here, prefigured by the physical composition of the material arrangements, and made intelligible through the doings and sayings with which they are bundled. As Karin squats behind the student, reaches around, and holds her arm, there are intimate geometries as the bodies perform the doings together. Karin's practical understandings are shared bodily and materially. The cotton bud is made intelligible as a pointer, through gestures of pointing. These things, doings and sayings constitute the sociomaterial curriculum. They render the patient's pelvis practically intelligible in new ways that include general understandings of anatomical size, shape and angles, and practical understandings of how to use the speculum to make these available for visual inspection. Meanwhile the other three students perform shadow movements in rehearsal and anticipation.

Making the body see-through

A key pedagogic challenge presented by the pelvic examination is that much of the practice involves doings that cannot be seen, because they take place inside the patient's body. The second phase of the pelvic examination, which involves bimanual palpation of the uterus and ovaries, requires very specific, fine motor movements and contact between the examiner's hand and the organs of the pelvis. This is focused on touch and interpretation of what is felt. In order to monitor and guide students as they practise, the inside of the body must be rendered visible, the body must become 'see-through'. This is done through doings and sayings bundled with material arrangements of the pelvis, hands, fingertips, and a model of the uterus. We join the first student again as she begins this second stage.

> The pelvic examination now shifts into a new phase, where the professional patient takes over the teaching of the student in a very close dialogue. Up until now, the patient has said little, adding minor comments and responses to Karin through the demonstration, and as the student performed the visual inspection. The student stands up, preparing to start the bimanual examination. The patient holds the model of the uterus and ovaries over her stomach to indicate where the anatomical structures are located inside her body. She makes eye contact with the student and comments on what she feels inside: 'OK, how are you now holding your fingers? Spread them a little bit more, just like that ... and try and lift'. She presses her hand to her stomach, to help the student feel the uterus. 'Imagine that you are to grab a little ball. Well, well,' she smiles to the student, 'what do you have there? A uterus!!'.
>
> The professional patient continues, offering detailed guidance to the student. 'Continue with that grip, just move around. Here you can come around, it's more difficult on the other side. Can you feel that? That's because I have myoma there. Excellent grip you have there, you can go deeper than that. Can you feel the structure?' The student has a big smile on her face, confirming that she feels the uterus. She continues the palpation as the patient demonstrates on the uterus model, 'Look, this is what you are palpating now, you have to lift first, take that grip one more time'. 'Yes,' says the student triumphantly as she has another go, 'now I can really feel it! Thank you so much'. The patient responds, 'Now you should palpate the ovaries'. She demonstrates with her own hand on her stomach. 'Before you stop now, take that grip of the uterus again. That is excellent, I am very satisfied with you, well done!'

Here dual roles of doctor–student and patient–educator are being enacted through doings and sayings bundled with things. The professional patient gives commentaries on what is happening inside her body. Her pelvis provides the material focus for the student's actions, but also comprises feeling organs and tissue. Her sensations and sayings enact a sociomaterial curriculum by making her body see-through, helping students link their own sensations of touch to their general understandings of anatomy. The patient's sayings provide further action guidance by pointing to and demonstrating on the model of the uterus to help the student. The material form of the model helps link general understandings to physical doings and thus scaffolds the development of practical understandings. The professional patient also plays a role in helping students 'see' through touch, offering textural, material and bodily metaphors, as in the description of grabbing a little ball.

The learning of precise physical procedures involves a sociomaterial combination of modelling, technical explanations, including explanatory metaphors and analogies, punctuated by traditional pedagogic devices such as praise. The analysis of these doings and sayings, amid things, shows the complex choreography of seeing, talking, listening, touching and the enacting of a sociomaterial curriculum.

Conclusion

Schatzki is one of a number of theorists seeking to address the neglect of materiality in accounts of social phenomena. We have used his framework to explore professional learning and its connections to practice, knowledge and responsibility. Our account has foregrounded a wide range of things, including bodies, understood as more than a physical setting for activity, more than things that are used in practice or learning. Rather we have shown how they become intelligible (functional and significant) through the practices with which they are bundled: doings and sayings come together with things in ways that demonstrate attunement in terms of purposeful and careful use, but also relational geometric alignment.

Schatzki offers a philosophy of social life, not a theory of learning. We have shown how his ideas can be brought into meaningful connection with learning through the concept of a sociomaterial curriculum. Practices, bundled with things, can constitute a curriculum by selecting elements of professional knowledge, and making them available to students. These bundles also organize educational experiences, as in the demonstration that preceded the students undertaking the examination themselves. The sociomaterial curriculum has been described as a fluid enactment, as Karin layered sayings onto actions, here foregrounding materiality, there bracketing elements off in order to facilitate a focus on something else. This concept offers researchers and professional educators a sophisticated means to understand the role of materiality in learning, offering a perspective that treats things not as curricular resources but as part of the curriculum itself.

Our third author (Karin) read the initial observation notes, and offered reflections from her position as a clinical educator. We use these as a basis to capture what we feel the chapter might offer people in similar roles.

> I realized how much this account helps understand what it means to work in clinical education. I cannot teach other people something, but I can facilitate their learning. This chapter helps understand how this facilitation is as much material as it is conceptual, and requires much more than setting up a good learning environment. Rather than being limited to thinking about what I do as a teacher, or even what the professional patient does in her educative role, I think about what it takes for students to learn: this is what the socio-material curriculum captures for me. When I first read the observation notes, many of my own actions were drawn to my attention – some that I didn't realize I was doing, others that I was more aware of, but without understanding their educational significance. I also realized how much my pedagogic approach is based on my bodily movements, and I recalled my earlier days when I would be much more static. These kind of accounts can be useful as holding up mirrors, reflecting what we do all the time in practice, but highlighting aspects, and providing concepts and a language to grasp and reflect on what is pedagogically important.

What has our analysis told us about professional knowledge and responsibility and how these are learned? A sociomaterial approach helps us to better understand professional patient curriculum and pedagogy in contrast to other approaches. Textbooks, plastic models, three-dimensional digital images and sedated bodies offer a materially focused curriculum. These foreground the patient as a biological body and not as a social one and in doing so make curricular selections that focus on anatomy. We have seen that the professional patients bring that body to life, as a social and biological body. The combination of doings, sayings and things can make the body see-through, and help manage the complex, intimate relational geometries that the pelvic examination involves. This enhances students' ability to connect general understandings of anatomy with practical know-how in terms of how to visually inspect and manually examine it. Professional patient pedagogy can do more than this, as this social body also becomes an actor in a different kind of relationship where professional responsibility is recast collaboratively: working with a person rather than on a body.

Acknowledgements

The authors would like to thank the professional patients and students for permission for the evening class to be observed. We also acknowledge the special contribution of Alison Lee. She read the two sets of field notes, and helped us see that there was something important we could learn from them. Her death is a truly great loss.

An earlier draft of this chapter was presented at the 9th International Conference on Researching Work and Learning (University of Stirling, 19–22 June 2013), in Hopwood, N. and Abrandt Dahlgren, M., 'The sociomaterial curriculum: how professional learning and pedagogy are enacted through relations between practices and things'.

References

Barnett, R. and Coate, K. (2005) *Engaging the Curriculum in Higher Education*, Maidenhead: Open University Press and the Society for Research into Higher Education.

Fenwick, T., Nerland, M. and Jensen, K. (2012) 'Sociomaterial approaches to conceptualising professional learning and practice', *Journal of Education and Work*, 25: 1–13. doi: 10.1080/13639080.2012.644901

Frye, C.A. and Weisberg, R.B. (1994) 'Increasing the incidence of routine pelvic examinations: behavioral medicine's contribution', *Women Health*, 21: 33–55.

Hopwood, N. (2013) 'Ethnographic fieldwork as embodied material practice: reflections from theory and the field', in N.K. Denzin (ed.), *Studies in Symbolic Interaction*, Volume 40, Bingley: Emerald Press.

Hopwood, N., Boud, D., Lee, A., Abrandt Dahlgren, M. and Kiley, M. (2010) 'A different kind of doctoral education: a discussion panel for rethinking the doctoral curriculum'. Paper presented at the *9th Quality in Postgraduate Research Conference*, Adelaide, 13–15 April.

Kamemoto, L.E., Kane, K.O. and Frattarelli, L.C. (2003) 'Pelvic examination teaching: linking medical student professionalism and clinical competence', *Hawaiian Medical Journal*, 62: 171–172.

Kretzschmar, R.M. (1978) 'Evolution of the gynecology teaching associate: an education specialist', *American Journal of Obstetrics and Gynecology*, 131: 367–373.

Schatzki, T.R. (1996) *Social Practices: A Wittgensteinian Approach to Human Activity and the Social*, Cambridge: Cambridge University Press.

Schatzki, T.R. (2001) 'Introduction: practice theory', in T. R. Schatzki, K. Knorr Cetina and E. von Savigny (eds), *The Practice Turn in Contemporary Theory*, London: Routledge.

Schatzki, T.R. (2002) *The Site of the Social: A Philosophical Account of the Constitution of Social Life and Change*, University Park, PA: Pennsylvania State University Press.

Schatzki, T.R. (2003) 'A new societist social ontology', *Philosophy of the Social Sciences*, 33: 174–202.

Schatzki, T.R. (2010) *The Timespace of Human Activity: On Performance, Society, and History as Indeterminate Teleological Events*, Lanham, MD: Lexington.

Siwe, K. (2007) *Learning the Pelvic Examination*. Published Ph.D. thesis, Linköping: Linköping University Medical Dissertations, 1031.

Wanggren, K. (2005) 'Teaching medical students gynaecological examination using professional patients – evaluation of students' skills and feelings', *Medical Teacher*, 27: 130–135.

Wijma, B., Gullberg, M. and Kjessler, B. (1998) 'Attitudes towards pelvic examination in a random sample of Swedish women', *Acta Obstetrica Gynecologica Scandinavica*, 77: 422–428.

Chapter 13

Dilemmas of responsibility for nurses in independent practice

Knowledge, learning and innovation

Sarah Wall

Introduction

For professional nurses, extensive efficiency-focused organizational and health system restructuring, based on ideologies of individualism and free enterprise, has had direct consequences. Significant job change and work stress have compounded nurses' longstanding professional marginalization. In the profoundly changed yet persistently traditional context of nursing practice, some nurses have turned to self-employment to bolster their sense of professionalism. This chapter explores the forms of responsibilities that emerge from this very unique practice arrangement, and the ways in which these are negotiated and interpreted by self-employed nurses.

The work of self-employed nurses occurs in a dynamic political and economic climate. Over the last two decades, Canada's ideals of collectivity have shifted toward market-oriented values, based on self-reliance and competition, and social responsibilities have been transferred from the state to individuals as participants in the free market (Bakker 1996; Brodie and Trimble 2003; Ilcan, Oliver and O'Connor 2007; Maxwell 2001). In this context, the significant public financial commitment to healthcare attracted the attention of Canadian politicians and policymakers, resulting in efficiency-focused organizational restructuring in healthcare. Structural changes had a 'profound impact on the social organisation of work' (Allen and Pilnick 2005:683). Nurses experienced increased workloads, job uncertainty, restricted professional autonomy, and disrupted professional relationships, all of which led to significant work-related stress (Aiken, Clarke, Sloane and Sochalski 2001; Daiski 2004; Laschinger, Sabiston, Finegan and Shamian 2001; Shannon and French 2005; Wynne 2003). In spite of unprecedented organizational change, many traditional ideas about nursing as women's work, including nursing's professional status and the value of nursing knowledge, have gone unchallenged (Armstrong and Armstrong 2003; Canam 2008). Nursing work continues to take place within a system that displays an inflated regard for medical technology and high visibility, physician-based services (Campbell 2000). In the current healthcare delivery system, privilege is increasingly given to economics-based decision-making, while scientific evidence and the medical model of care continue to enjoy dominance.

Despite a loss of permanent nursing positions and a casualization of the nursing workforce (Armstrong and Armstrong 2003; Grinspun 2003; Laschinger *et al.* 2001), most nurses still work as front-line employees, mainly in hospitals (Canadian Institute for Health Information 2010). Nurses who turn to self-employment as a career option are especially fascinating because they represent the few who have opted for a dramatic departure from nurses' traditional organizational circumstances in an effort to enhance their professional potential. Self-employed nurses work in diverse settings, clinically, geographically, and interpersonally, dramatically altering the nature of nursing practice. Yet, there has been virtually no academic investigation into this form and field of nursing work. This ethnographic study explored nursing self-employment to illuminate the emerging issues in non-traditional nursing practice. Taking a practice-based perspective and considering the sociomaterial aspects of nursing entrepreneurship, this chapter delves into the unique working conditions and demands placed upon self-employed nurses, and addresses the following questions: What knowledge and ethics do these nurses draw upon in the enactment of their non-traditional practices? What conflicts do they face between notions of 'care' and 'market'? What are the tensions between conservative regulatory standards and dynamic professional knowledge that allows for innovation and creativity in professional practice? What possibilities flow from these nurses' innovative professional activities? Ultimately, the ways in which the nurses in this study negotiated these issues offers an example of how shifts in professional knowledge, responsibilities, and learning can be turbulent but also how they can present important possibilities when reconsidered.

A practice-based sociomaterial perspective

The concept of 'practice' has become increasingly popular in studies of work and organizations (Gherardi 2009). Practices are 'embodied arrays of activities organized around a shared practical understanding or 'way of doing'' (Gherardi 2009:146). The 'practice lens' offers an approach to considering new, innovative, intersubjective, material, and emergent aspects of work within a dynamic organizational world (Bjorkeng, Clegg and Pitsis 2009; Feldman and Orlikowski 2011). A practice perspective focuses on the dynamics of everyday activity and the continuous, emergent nature of people's recurrent actions in their social contexts (Hager, Lee and Reich 2012; Johri 2011) and provides a platform for unique explorations of knowledge, learning, and change in professional work.

Seen through a practice lens, knowledge is much more than something that can be held and transmitted. Rather it can be thought of as a collective, situated, and ongoing process of knowing-in-practice, of linking knowing with working (Hager *et al.* 2012). Citing Schon, Orlikowski (2002) explains that professional practice does not involve the application of *a priori* knowledge to a specific decision but is instead typified by knowing that is inherent in practice. Knowledge understood as practice-based is 'something that people do together ... in every mundane activity,' which allows them to 'participate with the requisite competence in the complex web of relationships' within a field of practice (Gherardi 2009:118). From a nursing perspective, Doane and Varcoe (2008) argue against common understandings of knowledge as being about what nurses know and how they apply it. Instead they conceptualize knowledge use as being about 'the kind of person [a nurse] wish[es] to be' (290) and the relational, meaning-making process through which multiple forms of knowledge are interpreted and enacted in 'particular moments of practice' (292) to inform that way of being. Learning, then, can be similarly viewed as located in the enactment of practice. It is an 'ongoing, temporally changing process' that 'emerges from contexts and practices in unanticipated and unpredictable ways' (Hager *et al.* 2012:6) as practitioners work 'with and in relation to each other ... in order to accomplish their goals' (Johri 2011:210).

In today's dynamic economic and organizational climate, the notion of change has been given considerable scholarly attention. However, it is usually seen as a linear, manageable process, whereas theories of practice propose 'messier, more complex' ideas about change (Hager *et al.* 2012:9). Orlikowski (2000) notes that 'a practice lens assumes that people are purposive, knowledgeable, adaptive, and inventive agents' who work toward 'various and dynamic ends,' flexibly choosing to 'reinforce, ignore, enhance, undermine, change, work around, or replace' certain aspects of their work (423, 424). Some practices are 'transgressive practices' that imagine new possibilities, disrupt the status quo, and gain force, allowing people 'to reconfigure problematic practices' (Fenwick 2012:67, 68).

The practice-based perspective lends itself well to the consideration of the sociomaterial dimensions of professional practice and learning. Most inquiry into professional practice and learning 'tend[s] to focus more upon the sociocultural and sociopolitical aspects of practice activity than on the actual materiality of practice' (Fenwick 2012:67). Yet, human social processes are fully intertwined with the material dimension. Materiality plays a role in every aspect of practice, from the more obvious materials including bodies, clothing, furniture, buildings, and technology to the less evident materials such as texts, documents, discourses, and spaces (Bjorkeng *et al.* 2009; Fenwick 2012; Orlikowski 2007). The relationship between the social and the material is constructed in particular moments of practice, as meaning is assigned to material artefacts (Johri 2011). Practitioners can interact with materiality to promote change and implement new ways of working (Orlikowski 2000).

For self-employed nurses, practice-based knowledge, learning, and change are fundamental as they strive for innovation, change, and new meaning in their work. The study findings presented in this chapter about their work experiences and professional values demonstrate how these dimensions of practice interact in a fluid, organic way, revealing the connections among what they know, how their knowledge evolves, and how they negotiate change while continuing to value the essence of nursing practice.

A study of self-employed nurses

Seen from the inside, with a respect for the primacy of members' accounts, it is possible to view the subjective meanings, motives, connections, and negotiations that take place in the daily actions associated with practice (Gherardi 2009; Bjorkeng *et al.* 2009). Thus, focused ethnography, as used in this research, is the perfect approach to research that seeks to uncover 'the ordinary members' sense of what they are doing' and to ground the research in 'everyday knowledge and action' (Bjorkeng *et al.* 2009:146). In addition, ethnographic research lends itself well to exploring the as yet under-theorized sociomaterial dimensions of emerging professional practice (Fenwick 2012).

This study of nursing entrepreneurship was set in western Canada. At the time of the study, there were 241 self-employed nurses (also referred to as nurses in independent or private practice) registered with the provincial regulatory association (J. Machtemes, personal communication, November 2, 2007). Internationally, the numbers of self-employed nurses are rising (Canadian Nurses' Association 1996; International Council of Nurses 2004), yet this is a virtually unstudied area of nursing practice. This study, then, offers unique and rich insights into how this new work arrangement and the realities of private practice promote particular forms of learning and professionalism and generate change regarding nursing's role in and contribution to healthcare.

Recruitment to the study was undertaken through the provincial association of registered nurses in private practice. Nurses that had been self-employed for at least 18 months were invited, via mass e-mail and through snowball sampling, to participate. Twenty nurses (nineteen female and one male) participated. All were experienced nurses who worked in a diverse range of clinical and administrative practices such as wound and foot care, health education, counseling, alternative and complementary therapy, laser hair removal, management consulting, project management, and complaint investigations.

Data were collected mainly through interviews. Opportunities for observation were limited due to the isolated and sensitive nature of the work, although I was able to attend several meetings of the private practice nurses' association. Relevant provincial legislation and nursing documents were reviewed. The analysis followed an iterative process of coding, categorizing, and abstracting to identify themes in the data and develop explanations about the nature of this unique, emerging form of professional practice (Mayan 2009; Morse and Richards 2002). Specifically, themes pertaining to professional identity, knowledge and its evolution, practice settings and activities, and social contribution were identified.

Ethics approval was obtained from my university research ethics board. Participant names used herein are pseudonyms.

Tensions, responsibilities, and emerging possibilities in nursing entrepreneurship

The findings of this study show how the unique social, spatial, and material aspects of nursing self-employment interacted to both shape and constrain this form of nursing work, and the potential for change that was inherent in these emerging nursing practices.

Opening new spaces for practice: moving out of the hospital

All of the self-employed nurses in this study had been hospital-based employees prior to becoming entrepreneurs. These nurses described their prior hospital work environments as dysfunctional, abusive, demeaning, and disrespectful toward nursing. They used spatial metaphors to portray the ways in which nursing knowledge and practice were undervalued in the contemporary health system ethos. Lindsay explained how innovative services, such as health promotion, were being 'dropped' and Carla lamented that care and compassion were 'falling off the table.' Steve commented that 'you could tell where occupational health fit because we were right next to the morgue in the basement.' Nancy observed how lean operations and a focus on the traditional medical model of care meant that 'only a person's physical needs are attended to, not the whole person ... families need sit-in, hold-your-hand support but nurses are just doing clinical tasks and can't do supportive care.' For her, it was a loss to see nurses constrained in their ability to be present for their patients in a way that brought the body and emotions together.

Although these nurses worked in diverse settings, their movement out of the hospital structured their practices in a spatially non-traditional way. Without this spatial shift, the innovative sociopolitical dimensions of their practices would not have been possible. Carla explained that, through self-employment, she moved 'over on this other side,' away from 'caring through the chemicals and the procedures' toward a focus on caring through the mind/body connection and other non-traditional approaches to health and healing, which is the 'spirit of nursing.' She said:

> Everything I believe I am – innovative, professional, problem-solver, empowered – all those things that I could not use, in my opinion, in the hospital. Those skills are not needed there. So here, I can still be a nurse, with all these unique attributes.

Through the observation of many of their work spaces, it was possible to see that these nurses' material environments were entirely entangled with the social meanings and purposes that they attached to their practices. For example, Lindsay had an energy healing practice in a small clinic. Her clinic, however, unlike the traditional clinic, smelled of incense, had a burbling fountain in the corner, and was decorated with earthy colours and exotic hanging tapestries. The purpose of her work was to promote physical healing and emotional well-being by balancing the body's physical energy centers. This process began as each client entered her space. Denise, a corporate wellness consultant, worked with organizations to promote staff well-being. Her workplaces were the workplaces for which she consulted but she took a similar philosophical approach in each one. Her goal was to teach people to 'learn how to care for your body ... [to have] boundaries, the balancing of life, the genuine stuff of wellness.' She did this by beautifying the physical environment, making healthy food available, and creating a culture that supported a connection between workers and their daily home life, among other health promoting strategies. Although Lindsay's and Denise's practices differed, they both emphasized and appreciated the material dimensions of their work and the power they had in the healing process. In addition, by moving away from traditional healthcare work settings such as hospitals, they conveyed materially and spatially a new social purpose for nursing.

Many of these nurses worked in their own home offices, especially those nurses who did administrative work such as project management and consulting. While many employed nurses work in management and administrative positions, working for oneself in one's own home is a rare working arrangement for nurses, one that creates entirely new patterns of interaction and sets up a new kind of independence and opportunity in nursing work. For Diana, working at home eliminated the mundane yet stressful aspects of full-time employment. She wanted to make adjustments to the timing of her daily life by eliminating the commute to a demanding and time-consuming job. She explained that 'I left because I hated driving on the freeway. It came to the basics. I hated driving in rush hour and I hated spending two hours driving home or two hours driving there in the winter.' Grace, who did project management, found that maintaining her own office gave her tremendous flexibility in her lifestyle: 'We live in a holiday trailer out [at the lake] and in the winter we've gone down to the States ... we're going to go back and forth. I just took the work down with me. It doesn't matter where I live to do project management.'

For these two nurses, and others who worked at home, their home-based physical workspaces allowed them flexibility, a closer connection to family members (such as spouses and children), and separation from negative working relationships. For example, Doris, a foot care nurse, left her position in long term care to free herself from the 'attitude of who happened to be the team leader at the time.' The downside of the physical separation from an employer was that, 'It can be really isolating. It's nice to have some social interaction. You don't have that in your everyday in the same way' (Diana, project manager). Beyond the lifestyle flexibility and the social consequences of independent working arrangements, nurses who worked on their own were able to tap into unique opportunities, to 'think outside the box, think for yourself, do something unique' (Mary-Jane, nurse practitioner). They were able to tap into their networks and accept work to which they felt connected 'rather than what an employer want[s] me to do' (Evelyn, wound care).

Reconstructing nursing professional knowledge and responsibilities

New sociomaterial work arrangements led to new modes of practice that ultimately promoted particular forms of knowledge use, learning, and professionalism in nursing practice. These were incorporated into and emerged out of the daily realities of practice, producing a shift away from conventional conceptions of nursing knowledge and its contributions.

While many of the nurses worked in practice areas that did not necessarily require them to be registered nurses, almost all of the nurses expressed a strong sense of affiliation with nursing and saw their nursing identities as significant in terms of trust, knowledge and skill, and ethics. Diana declared her 'strong value in registered nursing. I would never want to give up my registration. I'm always, first, and foremost a nurse.' Denise described how nursing was 'so important to me. I went in for the right reasons. Bedside nursing wasn't my niche because it was just too confining but I never left nursing.' She felt that, in her private practice, she was 'the biggest PR [public relations] person for nursing.' Kelly 'knew I didn't want to abandon nursing' despite her strong entrepreneurial drive.

These nurses articulated the usefulness and value of nursing knowledge across diverse, non-traditional nursing practices. Diana saw her contribution as being 'value-added by bringing nursing knowledge' to project management because 'you do see things ... your network is so much broader [than many managers] and you have your knowledge base.' Many of the nurses talked about the care, attention, and trust that their nursing experience allowed them to integrate into new sites of practice. Doris talked about the time, connection, and quality that went into her foot care practice so that her clients 'feel like they had a pedicure, although it's from a nursing point of view.' Speaking of nurse-provided foot care, Carla said, 'We know that they're not just doing foot care. They're doing a health assessment, they're talking to the elderly about their drugs, a person about their diabetes. They're examining, they're doing the whole nursing assessment.' Allison, the owner of a laser hair removal clinic, observed that 'there's a huge difference between going to an esthetician for a service and going to a nurse.' She said that her clients felt cared for and comfortable because 'that's just natural to nurses ... you are the confidante ... you use a lot of nursing communication skills.' Sylvia, who investigated complaints about care in healthcare facilities, often met family members who were stressed and concerned about the care of a loved one. She saw that 'families are immediately comfortable when they know a nurse is investigating the case.' Many times, she observed that family members would 'bring me in to interview their parents and say, 'This is Sylvia. She's a nurse.'' She understood this as meaning 'here's a person we can trust.'

Tensions and conflict in entrepreneurial nursing practice

Despite their innovative, knowledge-based practices, these nurses faced a number of issues regarding the recognition of their work. The public and other health-care professionals did not understand the nature of these nurses' work because of a limited conception of what nurses know and can do. The public can find it hard to comprehend the role of nurses outside of hospitals. Denise lamented this, noting that 'it's a very funny concept that society has of nursing. It's per-haps not as empowering as I would like.' Carla was often asked questions that reflect 'the usual perception of nursing,' such as, 'What hospital do you work at?' The public's response to nursing self-employment was further complicated by the problematic link between nursing and market-based ideologies. Carla thought some people saw private nursing practice as 'evil' because of a percep-tion of greediness. Gabby had to justify her earnings to many of her clients who did not want to pay directly for them. For Mary Jane, a nurse practitioner, the need to charge her clients directly led to questions about her ethics. While most other healthcare professionals are covered by public and/or private insurance plans, the lack of insurance coverage for nursing services reflected society's lim-ited conception of the roles and potential contributions of nurses. While they capitalized on the opportunities presented by the contemporary economic cli-mate, they wanted to see nursing brought into the established system of reim-bursement, which would make their unique healthcare services accessible to the public without financial barriers.

Furthermore, other professionals did not appreciate and were threatened by private practice nursing. Denise, who practiced initially in crisis mental health, was told once by a psychologist, 'I think you're just taking over.' In her alterna-tive therapy practice, Nancy saw 'a fear of spiritual healing being out in the open.' She found that 'some physicians are on board but there is still a lot of resistance and they feel threatened.' Steve observed that when he approached senior orga-nizational managers to promote his occupational health programs, they generally had 'a bad perception of what they think the nurse's role should be' noting that, 'if they're stuck in the 1960s where the nurse was to sit there and wait for people to get hurt and put a bandaid on then that doesn't help me.' Carla explained that understandings about what nurses can do are based on conventional ideas about knowledge and how knowledge is used in practice. She said, 'We see the activities, the science, the evidence. [But] it's not the tasks we do. It's how we inform the experience of health.' This statement reflects the possibility of an emergent per-spective on how nurses use what they know.

The nature of self-employment in nursing also sheds light on new perspectives on learning in emerging sites of professional practice. All of the nurses in this study went through formal nursing education programs and some had graduate degrees in nursing and other relevant fields. Several of them had also done addi-tional formal coursework to prepare themselves for innovative entrepreneurial practice. Yet, what was especially notable about the learning that these nurses experienced in their private practices was its informal, relational, embedded, continuous, and reflexive nature. Several of the nurses talked about working with others and learning from them and through the work they did together. Diana, for example, explained that 'you meet all kinds of really great people that bring you on to other people. You learn so much.' The importance of a having a network of likeminded people was mentioned, as well. Learning occurred not only in relationships but also through the work itself. Georgette's love of learning was satisfied because 'every project is a huge learning experience.' Sometimes that meant learning the hard way, 'learning as you go' (Georgette), through an iterative process of making mistakes and refining one's approach as a result. Some of them found their practices evolving over time, in response to client demand and emerging needs, making it necessary for them to learn new skills and acquire new knowledge on an ongoing basis. This required a certain ability to 'stand in the unknown' (Carla) and let the learning emerge.

The opportunity to grow and develop was a key aspect of independent practice for many and this was linked to professional learning. Grace said that the very reason she was self-employed was because it was possible 'to challenge yourself, to push yourself, to learn something different.' For some, this involved self-reflection and personal growth. Grace had to learn to value herself and her contribution and shift her thinking away from being a selfless caregiver. After an 'awakening' and a resulting sense of restlessness about her traditional nursing practice, Carla considered how she would make the shift into private practice. She thought, 'This is what I do now through my education from before. This is what I believe in now. How can I close this gap and still remain a nurse? Can I take it with me into this new phase of my life?' Similarly, Kelly, a home care agency owner, connected learning to 'being in control of your own destiny.' As Lindsay completed her training in energy healing, she was required to do 'lots of personal process work.' Initially, she just 'wanted to do the work, not learn a lot about myself' but the program she was in took her through a reflexive process. Learning for these self-employed nurses was personal, emergent, and connected with the daily realities of practice.

Judgements about nursing knowledge and learning for practice took on a new level of meaning when it pertained to the formal regulation of professional nursing practice. Canadian nurses are regulated by legislatively empowered professional regulatory associations. In addition to the fairly streamlined annual license renewal process that all registered nurses undertake, self-employed nurses in the province studied are required to secure additional formal regulatory approval through an arduous process in order to be able to count their self-employed working hours toward their ongoing professional registration. Almost all of the study nurses told emotional stories about their experiences with the regulatory association.

Self-employed nurses were and are required to obtain initial approval for their practices in order to have them considered as nursing practices. The bi-annual re-approval process was just as onerous and stressful as the initial one. As Gabby noted, 'I have so many people depending on me and then I get faced with filling out 15 pages of stuff. If I don't fill it out exactly right, what happens to my business? It's like waiting for the rug to get pulled!' Several nurses described the application process as 'grueling' (Paula) and likened it to 'writing a thesis because you need an evidence base to support your practice' (Nancy). Carla thought that the regulatory association was looking for explanations of independent nursing practice that fit dominant perspectives about nursing work: 'We look at nursing and say nursing isn't interested in supporting this. They don't want soulful practice. They don't want holistic nursing. They want programmed, contextually based, academically sound, evidence-based, scientific, doctor-like practice.' She believed that the application form contained 'inane and often uninformed questioning' that did not reflect the realities of independent practice. Denise, a corporate wellness consultant, was asked questions such as, 'What part of the patient do you work on? [and] Who do you check with before you make a decision?' while Steve, an occupational health nurse, was asked to list the tasks he performed in his job. Questions structured with traditional hospital practice in mind made these nurses feel, as Paula said, that they 'couldn't convey through the process how I viewed myself as a nurse and what my nursing practice was about.'

Although the application form constructed a certain perspective on nursing knowledge and skill and shaped the ways these nurses were able to speak about their practices, some of the nurses acknowledged the importance of maintaining professional standards, noting that 'we want clear concepts; we want the nurse to be able to articulate clearly what it is she or he offers the public' (Carla). To this end, they used the application form and other official professional documents to present themselves as credible professionals who were well-aligned with disciplinary thinking. The formal practice standards document for the nursing profession outlines the standards for nursing practice in the areas of professional responsibility, knowledge based practice, ethics, and public service. Carla pointed out that, while hospital-based nurses refer to policies and standards very infrequently, self-employed nurses 'write our own policies and procedures that have to align with the standards of practice. We just can't fake them and we don't.' Noting that 'only private practice nurses do this,' she 'went through every single [nursing] practice standard and asked myself this question: How does my service meet or not meet or coincide or interact with this particular standard?' Several other nurses talked about their reliance on specialty-related practice standards. Some also wrote their own mission statements and policies. In this way, they were able to use professional discourse, as codified in the standards, to their advantage by embracing them and demonstrating their creative conformity to them.

New possibilities for professional work

Despite the ways these nurses struggled against convention in the system and nursing profession, they spoke passionately about the possibilities flowing from successful nursing businesses that are oriented toward an expanded vision of health. All of the nurses in this study spoke about the satisfaction they got from being self-employed in nursing. Their job satisfaction was intimately connected to the opportunity to create a unique and meaningful role for nursing that began with them. Paula explained that she 'was in a unique position to make a difference,' a perspective echoed by Sheila who expressed her belief that 'the work that I'm doing makes a difference to people in the world.' Similarly, Evelyn was satisfied by what she could offer to others. She said, 'I get my satisfaction from seeing the results with the clients. I see how appreciative the clients are that I'm able to improve their quality of life and improve their health status.'

In contrast to the traditional illness intervention model, Lindsay recognized her clients' own needs for self-healing and described nursing as being 'very much about getting people off on their own and being well.' Many of the nurses spoke hopefully of a broad new vision for healthcare that might be accomplished through private nursing practice. Carla saw the self-employed nurse as 'the nurse that can fill a niche where the heavily controlled, institutional [hospital] care can't meet the need for the client.' Moving toward an alternate vision of health, Lindsay believed that nurses would be able to 'start to think about how we're failing from the traditional point of view [and] how we could add to it.' Nancy, who did similar work to Lindsay in alternative therapies, saw an 'important shift from the traditional perspective' on the horizon, one that utilized holistic healing and viewed patients as partners in their own care. A holistic perspective on healthcare was mentioned by several of the nurses in this study. As Paula explained, nurses 'have a capacity to see the whole picture and to understand what others are doing in this whole picture.' In this study, nurses in both clinical and administrative roles explained how a holistic focus allows nurses to infuse healthcare delivery with a new perspective.

Conclusion

The physical departure that these nurses made from traditional hospital-based practice created the social conditions they needed to re-invent nursing practice and to re-focus it around an alternative set of values and practices. The spatial dimension of materiality has not been widely studied but the findings of this study of self-employed nurses corroborate research done by Bjorkeng et al. (2009) on a construction program. Participants in the construction program felt it important to move their work and interactions out of the corporate boardroom and out into the sites of construction. They found that the change in venue represented and constructed 'the site as a 'sacred site' of/for practice' by 'giving shapes, smells, and sounds to the practices' and by being in touch with the constantly changing nature of the site (155). Likewise, for the nurses in this study, their moves away from the hospital allowed their practices to become and emerge in direct relation to the tangible, spatial, material aspect of their work spaces.

Despite the range of practice types these nurses created, they found that their material independence shaped their social independence in a way that allowed them to focus on their professional contribution in a way not often seen by employed nurses.

In starting out and identifying their practices as nursing practices, these nurses were required to work with several texts that had the potential to constrain and construct the ways in which they were able to define their work. The application form that they completed to have their practices recognized and the formal nursing practice standards for registered nurses were two examples of material texts that represented the dominant discourse in professional nursing. Although they were frustrated with the practice approval process, most of them found ways to manage and adapt the ideologies that were apparent in the documents. Fenwick (2012:68) refers to these strategies as 'workarounds and rule bending that are often engaged to make codified practices work'. These nurses worked flexibly and creatively with the expectations inherent in the texts in order to demonstrate a high level of respect for professional standards and behaviour. Although as devices of professional control these documents ensured that there were boundaries to how nursing practice could be described, these nurses were able to apply them in an enhanced way and use them to substantially alter their existing way of doing things (Orlikowski 2000).

The notion of knowing-in-practice was uniquely evident among these independent practices. The nurses conveyed a relationship to knowledge that was much less about applying prior knowledge than it was about building their knowledge based on the needs inherent in their work and on learning as a constant process. As Doane and Varcoe (2008) suggested, knowing for these nurses was about who they were as people in their practices, how they related to their clients, and the difference they were able to make. Even in practices that were more task oriented, the nurses emphasized an ethical and philosophical orientation to the use of their knowledge rather than a technical, skill-based approach. In addition, nurses have historically endeavored to demonstrate their professional status by demonstrating that they possess the requisite professional characteristics, including specialized knowledge and autonomy over nursing practice (Yam 2004). Interestingly, the nurses in this study have been able to break away from the need to prove their professional status according to these traits. To them, the key issue was not whether they were indeed professionals but, rather, finding a space for professional practice that would allow them to use their knowledge and skills fully, beyond the constraints of the traditional healthcare system.

Nursing self-employment provides an excellent example of the fluidity of practice, knowledge, learning, and change in professional work. The experiences of these nurses illustrates beautifully how 'the nature of the system as well as its elements and their practices – both human and non-human – emerges through the continuous rich and recursive improvisational interactions among these elements' (Fenwick 2012:72). By authoring new boundaries, re-negotiating new competencies, and adapting materiality in practice, these nurses have shown how 'through practicing, we may become better in ways that we might never have institutionally imagined' (Bjorkeng *et al.* 2009:157).

Acknowledgement

The findings of this study are also reported elsewhere. Articles appear in *Qualitative Health Research* (Wall 2013) and *Canadian Journal of Nursing Leadership* (Wall 2013) and may also appear in future publications that illustrate the various theoretical and practical applications of this work.

References

Aiken, L.H., Clarke, S.P., Sloane, D.M. and Sochalski, J.A. (2001) 'An international perspective on hospital nurses' work environments: The case for reform', *Policy, Politics, & Nursing Practice*, 2(4): 255–263.

Allen, D. and Pilnick, A. (2005) 'Making connections: Healthcare as a case study in the social organisation of work', *Sociology of Health & Illness*, 27(6): 683–700.

Armstrong, P. and Armstrong, H. (2003) *Wasting Away: The Undermining of Canadian Healthcare*. Oxford: Oxford University Press.

Bakker, I. (1996) 'Introduction', in I. Bakker (ed.) *Rethinking Restructuring: Gender and Change in Canada*, Toronto: University of Toronto Press.

Bjorkeng, K., Clegg, S. and Pitsis, T. (2009) 'Becoming (a) practice', *Management Learning*, 40(2): 145–159.

Brodie, J. and Trimble, L. (2003) 'Introduction: Reinventing Canada', in J. Brodie and L. Trimble (eds) *Reinventing Canada*, Toronto: Pearson Education Canada.

Campbell, M. (2000) 'Knowledge, gendered subjectivity, and the restructuring of healthcare: The case of the disappearing nurse', in S.M. Neysmith (ed.) *Restructuring Caring Labour: Discourse, State Practice, and Everyday Life*, Don Mills, ON: Oxford University Press.

Canadian Institute for Health Information (2010) *Regulated Nurses: Canadian trends, 2005–2009*. Ottawa, ON.

Canadian Nurses' Association (1996) 'On your own – the nurse entrepreneur', *Nursing Now: Issues and Trends in Canadian Nursing*, 1: 1–4.

Canam, C.J. (2008) 'The link between nursing discourses and nurses' silence: Implications for a knowledge-based discourse for nursing practice', *Advances in Nursing Science*, 31(4): 296–307.

Daiski, I. (2004) 'Restructuring: A view from the bedside', *Canadian Journal of Nursing Leadership*, October, online exclusive.

Doane, G. and Varcoe, C. (2008) 'Knowledge translation in everyday nursing: From evidence-based to inquiry-based practice', *Advances in Nursing Science*, 31(4): 283–295.

Feldman, M.S. and Orlikowski, W.J. (2011) 'Theorizing practice and practicing theory', *Organization Science*, 22(5): 1240–1253.

Fenwick, T. (2012) 'Matterings of knowing and doing: Sociomaterial approaches to understanding practice', in P. Hager, A. Lee and A. Reich (eds) *Practice, Learning and Change: Practice-Theory Perspectives on Professional Learning*. Netherlands: Springer.

Gherardi, S. (2009) 'Introduction: The critical power of the "practice lens"', *Management Learning*, 40(2): 115–128.

Grinspun, D. (2003) 'Part-time and casual nursing work: The perils of healthcare restructuring', *The International Journal of Sociology and Social Policy*, 23(8/9): 54–80.

Hager, P., Lee, A. and Reich, A. (2012) *Practice, Learning and Change: Practice-Theory Perspectives on Professional Learning*, Dordrecht: Springer.

Ilcan, S., Oliver, M. and O'Connor, D. (2007) 'Spaces of governance: Gender and public sector restructuring in Canada', *Gender, Place and Culture*, 14(1): 75–92.

International Council of Nurses (2004) *Guidelines on the Nurse Entre/intrapreneur Providing Nursing Service*, Geneva.

Johri, A. (2011) 'The socio-materiality of learning practices and implications for the field of learning technology', *Research in Learning Technology*, 19(3): 207–217.

Laschinger, H.K.S., Sabiston, J.A., Finegan, J. and Shamian, J. (2001) 'Voices from the trenches: Nurses' experiences of hospital restructuring in Ontario', *Canadian Journal of Nursing Leadership*, 14(1): 6–13.

Maxwell, J. (2001) *Toward a Common Citizenship: Canada's Social and Economic Choices*, Ottawa: Canadian Policy Research Network.

Mayan, M. (2009) *Essentials of Qualitative Inquiry*, Walnut Creek, CA: Left Coast Press.

Morse, J.M. and Richards, L. (2002) *Readme First for a User's Guide to Qualitative Methods*. Thousand Oaks, CA: Sage.

Orlikowski, W.J. (2000) 'Using technology and constituting structures: A practice lens for studying technology in organizations', *Organization Science*, 11(4): 404–428.

Orlikowski, W.J. (2002) 'Knowing in practice: Enacting a collective capability in distributed organizing', *Organization Science*, 13(3): 249–273.

Orlikowski, W.J. (2007) 'Sociomaterial practices: Exploring technology at work', *Organization Studies*, 28(9): 1435–1448.

Shannon, V. and French, S. (2005) 'The impact of the re-engineered world of health-care in Canada on nursing and patient outcomes', *Nursing Inquiry*, 12: 231–239.

Wall, S. (2013) '"We inform the experience of health": Perspectives on professionalism in nursing self-employment', *Qualitative Health Research*, 23(7): 976–988.

Wall, S. (2013) 'Nursing entrepreneurship: Motivators, strategies and possibilities for professional advancement and health system change', *Canadian Journal of Nursing Leadership*, 26(2): 29–40.

Wynne, R. (2003) 'Clinical nurses' response to an environment of healthcare reform and organizational restructuring', *Journal of Nursing Management*, 11: 98–106.

Yam, B. (2004) 'From vocation to profession: The quest for professionalization of nursing', *British Journal of Nursing*, 13(16): 978–982.

Chapter 14

Putting time to 'good' use in educational work

A question of responsibility

Helen Colley, Lea Henriksson, Beatrix Niemeyer and Terri Seddon

Introduction

The current context of global financial crisis, and the accompanying intensification of neo-liberal policies and managerialist practices, are placing educators – along with many other public service professionals – under considerable pressure. A combination of diminishing resources, inappropriate targets and growing need among students can be toxic. This raises not only the question of turbulent times, but also of how educators' time itself is put to use, by whom, and in whose interests. In this paper, we draw on three very different projects in Finland, England and Germany, to look at how this is happening, and to consider questions of ethical responsibility that arise.

We do so through a socio-material analysis of time which challenges the 'commonsense' and taken-for-granted ways of understanding time as an inescapable dimension of our lives. We begin by offering a very different way of thinking about time, drawing on Marxist and feminist theoretical perspectives and on our own transnational discussions about this theme. We then present three empirical case studies from Finland, England and Germany. Each of these illustrates particular ways in which time orders are being reconfigured – and brought into tension – in the current phase of capitalism. They reveal the political economy of time that currently prevails in educators' work and learning. Our concluding remarks focus on how we might move forwards from an analysis of this political economy towards an ethically sensitive politics of time and professional responsibility.

Understanding time differently

Time is a notoriously difficult concept. On the one hand, it can appear as an objective fact of nature, independent of human beings, defined by daylight, darkness and changing seasons, as the earth spins and revolves around the sun. On the other hand, philosophical notions of time, such as that of Kant, have often regarded it as a figment of human consciousness with no external, material reality: simply an inescapable aspect of how our minds come to know the world.

Whichever of these views are taken, time is understood largely as a contextual backdrop against which our actions take place.

A very different, socio-material perspective, drawing on the work of Karl Marx, radically challenges this view (Harvey 2006; Mészáros 2008; Postone 1993). Rather than seeing time as the background to human practice, instead it understands it as *engendered by practice*: time itself is brought about by the human doings of human beings. And rather than seeing it as just one dimension of our experience, it reveals different dimensions of time itself, a series of inter-related 'time orders'.

This framework points first to the *historical* time order, the importance of understanding different eras of society (such as feudalism, or capitalism). These eras are also usefully divisible into smaller elements; recognizable epochs, periods and moments, expressing the distinctive character of particular times (Heydebrand 2003). Today, for example, we find ourselves in the era of capitalism, in its imperialist epoch, in a period marked since the oil crisis of 1973 by repeated global recessions, at a moment dominated by neo-liberal politics and disastrous financial collapses. These are how we understand the 'turbulent times' alluded to in the introduction of this book.

Two other time orders are also important. On the one hand, *clock* time (expressed more theoretically as 'abstract time'), is essential for calculating profitability in the workplace (Postone 1993). Any reader who has been subjected to a time-and-motion study or worked for piece-rates will be familiar with this time order. Clock time is disciplinary: employers use it to measure our labour as we sell it to them, but they also use it as a regulatory force upon us. Clock time is concerned primarily with the exchange-values of our work products, obscuring their use-value – the practical, social and moral purpose. It therefore operates as a tyranny that is both degrading and alienating for workers (Heydebrand 2003; Meszáros 2008).

On the other hand, *process* time (or 'concrete time') is associated primarily with the use-values of work, and is anchored in the duration of social practices, tasks and processes (Postone 1993). Here, labour is the measure of time, rather than time the measure of labour (Ylijoki and Mäntylä 2003). It is therefore particularly visible in spaces devoted to (largely) women's work of social reproduction, where use-values rather than exchange-values are the primary concern of those involved in caring for others. In these spaces, processes take as long as they take, and cannot be hurried, whether they consist of feeding an elder or engaging a troubled youngster in learning. Davies, considering early years care and education, elaborates the concept of 'process time':

> Needs are frequently unpredictable and the relation on which care is premised often requires continuity and a form of time that is not primarily determined by a quantitative and abstract conceptual measure. Care requires process time.
>
> (Davies 1994:279)

She notes the non-linearity of this time order, as well as its association with quality in caring work and its inherently political and ethical dimension, and emphasizes its difference from simple task-orientation:

> The latter tends to stress the task per se and risks separating the activity, at least conceptually, from its context. Process time, on the other hand, emphasizes that *time is enmeshed in social relations* ... process time is on many occasions not measurable or at least hard to measure. The boundaries are fluid.
>
> (Davies 1994:280, original emphasis)

Whilst appearing very different, even contradictory, all three time orders are inextricably inter-related. In the current *historical* conjuncture of intensified neoliberal policies and increasing privatization of education and other public services, *clock* time serves to privilege economic rationality over a 'rationality of caring' (Waerness 1984), and in doing so, it permeates and dominates *process* time, creating intense pressures for practitioners.

This has implications for the ethical and political nature of educational and care work. As Postone (1993) notes, process time is intimately associated with ethics, since it is principally concerned with practice and with use-values. It can be well-spent or ill-spent, from the perspective of educators and learners. We can see this clearly in current social and economic development. As capitalism responds to global economic crises by reducing social expenditure (as we see so graphically in current austerity policies) and privatizing services to produce exchange-value, it also shifts the purpose of remaining public expenditure further towards use-values of social control rather than the use-values of care (Shaikh and Tonak 1994; Harvey 2006). This poses difficult questions about whether public service work is being put to 'good' use, about ethical tensions that may arise in frontline work, and about the responsibilities of policy-makers and managers as well as practitioners for the ethical compass of this work.

Researching time orders in educational work

These issues of time, work and learning have been further problematized through our collaborative work across national borders. Working across national boundaries, we have confronted the effects of competing time orders and the ways in which their relationship plays out differently in distinct social and geographical spaces. From an English perspective, for example, it has been a struggle to reconceptualize the character of historical time in the very different social location and welfare regime of Finland. Generalized assumptions about the oppressive nature of feminized care work as experienced within the historical context of a residualist welfare regime, such as in the UK (Esping-Andersen 1990), could not account for the post-war struggles of women in

Finland – within a Nordic model that entailed an egalitarian welfare settlement; struggles which led successfully to female-dominated healthcare work attaining relatively high status, with correspondingly high levels of education. On the other hand, discussions about the potential for counter-hegemonic practices within educational work had to take into account evidence of the brutal impact of austerity on practitioners in England. There, outcome targets driven by abstract time imperatives have drastically limited the process time available for practitioners' work, with serious consequences for their mental and physical health, and a considerable attrition rate. Yet our discussions helped identify incipient collective resistances and the possibilities of a politics of time.

Elsewhere we have described in greater detail the qualitative research projects on which we draw here (Seddon *et al.* 2010; Colley 2012; Chadderton and Colley 2012; Niemeyer 2012; Newman *et al.* 2014). In these studies of educational work from Finland, England and Germany, time has emerged as a central aspect of occupational boundaries and their negotiation. Reading our case studies transnationally across borders has extended these national cases by providing comparative insights that further enrich our analyses of competing time orders, and reveal their deeper complexities. Examining each case in turn, then, we show how different time orders are generated and interact in educational work.

Finland: competing historical periods in health and social care education

Over recent years, the Finnish government has launched a series of policies aimed at re-ordering the infrastructure of welfare in the country. This case study draws on an analysis of a governmental process (ME 2010) to reconsider the educational degree requirements for health and social care educators, along with 29 consultation responses from vocational education and training (VET) providers, welfare service employers, trade unions and professional bodies.

As noted above, the Nordic welfare system has been renowned in the past not only for its egalitarian approach, but also for its emphasis on the use-values of care work, expressed as a 'rationality of caring' (Waerness 1984) that contrasts with the economic rationality that now dominates UK or US welfare systems. The Nordic welfare state was a regional expression of a particular historical period, defined by the post-World-War-II settlement in times of upturn in the capitalist economic cycle. It also was won through the struggles of women, and in turn created space for women's professional citizenship and agency within the care sector (Henriksson *et al.* 2006). Based on a conceptualization of human service work as 'people work' praxis – the unity of consciousness and action for people (Goffman 1969; Stacey 1984) – it placed particular importance on high-standard educational opportunities and terms and conditions of employment for the predominantly female workforce, which raised the status of paid care and its societal value. However, this settlement, along with the entire Nordic welfare tradition, is being challenged in the current economic context. In this historical moment, neo-liberal policies impose a rationality of efficiency rather than caring (Wrede *et al.* 2008), reductions in public expenditure, and a renegotiation of praxis as a commodified service *to* people rather than *for* them. Practitioners have faced a worsening of working conditions and employment security, leading to a crisis in recruitment and declining attraction of the field.

The government's response to this has been contradictory. First, it has hybridized a number of previously distinct health and social care roles at the upper secondary level into a new occupational category entitled 'the practical nurse in social and health care'. In this process, the length of education required for the 'practical nurse' diploma has been upgraded (Henriksson 2008). However, the ministerial report considered here (ME 2010) proposed reducing the qualification levels for all vocational teachers, and particularly for those educating practical nurses. The 'hot spot' in the governmental process considered here (ME 2010) is nevertheless whether the qualifications for all VET teachers should have parity, or whether the criteria should be reduced, in particular for those educating practical nurses.

At the time, around 80% of health and social care teachers held a Master's degree, in addition to teaching qualifications and at least three years' work experience – a very high proportion compared with teachers in other vocational fields in Finland, reflecting the historical status of this workforce. But, echoing the discourse of neo-liberalism and local managerial practices, responses to the ministerial report by a range of employers and education providers characterized these requirements as 'old-fashioned' and 'behind the times' – generating a re-definition of the historical context. The former level of VET teacher qualification was held to be too 'extensive and expensive' – a clear appeal also to the efficiency of clock time versus the process time needed for educational processes. This was given an epistemological rationale by arguing that study for a Master's degree supposedly distanced teachers from the workplace, and that the creation of a more hands-on occupational identity was educationally more appropriate in today's context. Accordingly, it was also emphasized that organizations providing care would be better placed than education institutions to take on vocational education in the sector, reducing both time and costs. The curtailed VET proposed for practical nurses, was also endorsed by the trade union of nurses and the education providers. They advocated that either the upper-secondary school practical nurse qualification accompanied by pedagogic studies, or a Bachelor's degree, should be sufficient for a VET teacher – a significant downgrading from the established norm of a Master's degree.

Other stakeholders, however, robustly defended 'strong teacher professionalism' (Heikkinen 2002) and objected to the speed with which the reform was being pushed through. One typical argument defending the status quo was put by the National Teachers' Union. They advocated that VET in Finland was so popular, desirable and internationally high-quality that it should not be endangered. In this vein, the Board of Education and its commissions claimed that, in social and health care, teachers traditionally have high motivation to pursue continuing education and professional development, and that therefore a broad knowledge base in addition to nursing is essential for them. Based on its historical ethos and legacy, care work requires process time, and therefore VET is not only about practice-oriented capacities, they argued; it is also about guiding and supporting vocational growth more broadly. These accounts defending the process time order of use-values in VET emphasized that shortages in the workforce would be better met by ensuring high-standard employment terms and conditions than by lowering eligibility standards. On the contrary, accounts by service employers and education providers promote abstract time and exchange-values, also reinforced by European harmonization incentives and the streamlining of qualification frameworks. In Finland, this mainly refers to male-dominated VET fields like transportation and forestry, where the teacher workforce is less qualified than in female-dominated health and social care. It is notable that with the support of the employer groups – the recruiters – new employment and professional opportunities are created for a less-expensive workforce, for practical nurses. This creates a historical context in which two process time orders compete with each other: namely the use-values of the nurses and those of the practical nurses. In the current era of a competition state, however, it is the clock time and exchange values of both the work and educational preparation for it that dominate in policy reforms.

However, the pressure of the neo-liberal historical time order also came to bear upon the process time of consultation over the proposed policy changes. Although the committee working on the proposals to re-regulate VET argued for more preparatory work, the government foreclosed further discussion, and promulgated a statute in 2011 enacting the 'flexibilization' of VET teachers' qualifications by increasing the autonomy of the education provider to hire the top talent for 'the teaching task at hand' (FINLEX 2010). It is now the remit of education managers to decide whom they recruit: a teacher with a Masters degree or one with a Bachelor's degree. But this case study, like the one which follows, throws a question mark against the distinction between professions and other occupations highlighted by the editors of this book. The current interplay and competition of time orders, we suggest, not only blurs these boundaries and value orders, but also calls for human service practitioners to say 'we' (Sennett 1998) and go beyond the professional/less-professional divide (between themselves and other occupations). In this way, by jointly opposing economic rationality, with its 'just in time' recruitment labour measures that downplay educational values, work-related social rights and the dignity of care workers in the former historical period, they might collectively reclaim process time and an ethos that values the rationality of caring.

England: clock time *vs* process time in youth support work

This next case study focuses on practitioners' day-to-day experiences of increased tensions between clock time and process time in their work to support young people in school-to-work transition, particularly those not in education, employment or training (NEET). It draws on career history interviews with 26 practitioners who worked in – or had quit working in – this field in England. Unlike the Nordic model, the English welfare system is one typified by high risk of social exclusion (Esping-Andersen 1990; Niemeyer 2007), and dominated throughout New Labour's rule (1997–2010) by neo-liberal welfare-to-work policies. Policies for young people focused on measures to improve their 'employability', despite the weakness of the British youth labour market and insufficient high-quality education and training opportunities. The historical moment of banking collapse in 2008, prompting harsh austerity policies, led to rapid and severe cuts in funding for public services; more marginal areas less likely to arouse public opposition, including youth support, were hit soonest and hardest.

The principal national organization in this field, *Connexions*, had been founded in 2001, bringing together a range of youth practitioners in what was supposed to be a 'holistic' service provided by a new generic occupation of 'Personal Advisers' (PAs). Although the government prospectus for *Connexions* had promised a workforce of 15,000–20,000 PAs, only around 8,500 were actually employed. As a result, caseloads were up to four times higher than expected, creating unfeasible workloads. At the same time, the service's funding was tied to targets for reducing numbers of youth in the 'NEET' category, whatever their social problems, and despite a lack of adequate or appropriate opportunities for many of them. In this context, time orders – and the tensions between them – emerged as a central aspect of practitioners' experience, and we discuss three particular aspects of these here.

First, managing the boundaries between quantity and quality of work was a constant concern, not only because caseloads were so large, but also because PAs were expected to take on roles outside their specialism with minimal time for training. Former careers advisers, for example, found themselves required to give sexual health advice with only two days' training on this topic. At the same time, excessive caseloads left them little time for the ongoing research required to maintain their specialized knowledge of and links with the labour market and educational provision. This clock time pressure on process time for both continuing professional development and work with individual clients often led to unsustainable tensions, with some PAs deciding to quit the job (taking themselves outside the occupational boundary altogether) as a result, as both a current and a former PA recount:

> Well, it's too much really. You can't really do a proper job with all young people and you have to start prioritizing and this is not something that I'm terribly happy with.
>
> (Delia, PA)

> [I was] killing myself, spreading myself so thin that there was hardly anything left of me ... I just felt like I was being stretched too thin, doing a really poor quality of job everywhere, and actually not being particularly effective with anybody, and that was really stressful, and I thought that I'm not going to continue doing this. It's not me.
>
> (Helen, ex-PA)

Second, the size of PAs' caseloads and the unfeasible nature of service targets generated constant ethical decision-making about how many clients they could help, which clients they would help, and how they would try to help them. PAs felt under pressure to prioritize work with young people most likely to come off the 'NEET' register quickly (because they needed less support), and to avoid devoting longer time to the most vulnerable. This represented a paradoxical process of double exclusion – Connexions was supposed to prioritize the most excluded youth, but in fact its targets focused on the 'easiest-to-help' of the 'hard-to-help'. As one PA explained:

> The pressures are on increased figures. We've got targets, what seem like absolutely crazy targets for next year and so, [I'm] quite focussed on that, to be honest. That's the message that we get from above is: 'You focus on the targets and to the detriment of the people'.
>
> (Beth, PA)

Beth talked about how she struggled with this dilemma, devoting one week's work mainly to supporting a young man with devastating problems, who was highly unlikely to come off the 'NEET' register; but knowing that she was likely to get into trouble with her manager for doing so. She also noted that the young man's previous PA had become emotionally burnt out trying to help him. Others talked of coming under pressure from managers to push young people into opportunities, however vocationally inappropriate, according to abstract timescales for meeting targets: before the young person's 18th birthday; to meet monthly targets for 'NEET' reduction; and especially approaching the annual government census of 'NEET' figures. These examples show how the policy and institutional privileging of clock over process time could shift practice along the spectrum from caring and meeting needs to surveillance and control. Conflict over defending process time was often described by PAs as a regular feature in supervisory encounters with their managers. But again, refusing to cross these ethical boundaries also led some PAs out of the occupation, whether through disciplinary action by managers or their own decisions.

Third, alongside these bleaker outcomes of competing time orders, PAs also talked of 'making time' and forming collectivities to support each other. Sometimes this peer support revolved around small-scale sharing of specialist occupational knowledge, expertise and problem-solving to combat de-skilling and the erosion of occupational boundaries. PAs would cluster at the same 'hot desks', often squeezing time for this into lunch hours or at the end of the working day. For PAs working with the most disadvantaged young people, given the lack of clinical support and the managerial focus of their supervision, it was important to make time to offer and gain emotional support amongst themselves. It was in these looser collectivities that specialist occupational boundaries seemed most permeable. Nevertheless, worrying about clients and engaging in peer support were most likely to spill over into weekends and evenings, extending the abstract time of the working day. In trying to overcome the logic of the organization – which purported to be about social inclusion, but was in practice more geared to surveillance and control of young people – PAs were resisting the privileging of clock time over process time, and seeking to defend the use-value of caring against the use-value of control.

Since the end of this research, there is a postscript to add, however: one which points to the power of the state to overcome such resistance on the part of a small and marginalized group of educators. A further wave of austerity measures from April 2011 saw funding for the Connexions service entirely withdrawn, with large-scale redundancies among staff, and a loss of provision for young people in many areas of the country.

Germany: defending process time against abstract time in youth support work

We turn now to a more optimistic case from Germany, which illustrates how, in a different national and economic context, over time and in small, localized ways, the struggle to make time for educational process can achieve some success.

This case also focuses on front-line work in the field of support for youngsters outside of mainstream education, training and employment, but needs to be set first in the context of the historical time order. Within the global historical period identified above, we are also witnessing a particular historical moment in Germany, arising from the convergence of long-term, medium-term and recent trends. These trends concentrate effects on young people through the growth of youth unemployment since the late 1970s, and the collapse of the apprenticeship market in east Germany after national reunification in 1990.

More recently, the former 'youth support jungle' of relatively uncoordinated initiatives has coalesced into a more coherent school-to-work transition system with a variety of learning programmes focused on work experience (Niemeyer 2011). This reform has created a historical disjuncture with the traditional corporatist culture of German welfare and its social contract of lifelong employment security.

These changes also relate to a globalized historical acceleration and compression of the social time of learning (cf. Harvey 1990). Periods of learning are becoming shorter, and qualifications must be achieved 'just in time' and kept constantly up-to-date (Seitter 2010). In the framework of lifelong learning and social inclusion policies, the demands on individuals to 'upskill' themselves now extend over the whole life course. This results in an *extensive* time-stretching process, which at the same time *intensifies* the pressure to learn and adapt one's skills rapidly and often. This extensive intensification is most evident in the field of school-to-work transition support, where a complex mix of political strategies, technical instruments and institutional arrangements, including shortened periods of funding and budget cutbacks in education and welfare, disrupt the established time orders of the normative model of a lifelong, upwardly mobile career.

'Model programmes' for youth at risk of 'dropping out' now offer disadvantaged pupils with learning and social difficulties two to three days' work experience per week, with an accordingly reduced school timetable (Niemeyer and Frey-Huppert 2009). Other programmes provide workplace experience through long-term internships for 'disadvantaged' school leavers. These projects are funded mainly by the European Social Fund and shaped by its employment and social inclusion policies. Abstract time is foregrounded sharply: schemes are supposed to make young people employable as early and as quickly as possible – ranging from six weeks to a maximum of 11 months. However, the work practices of educators in transition programmes are determined by the concrete 'process' time needed to enable a young person to develop a career perspective and to (re-) build their motivation to learn and work. The following micro-study illustrates these conflicting time orders and shows how the command of process time is part of workplace policy and politics.

Here, we draw on one interview with a founding practitioner in an institution within this system to explore the time pressures he experiences, and the way in which he has worked against them to defend process time against clock time. Mr M. has worked in his institution for eight years, always on one- or two-year contracts. His main role is to coach and case-manage boys who are 'NEET' or at risk of becoming 'NEET'. The boundaries of his occupational role have shifted over recent years, from office-based work receiving referrals from other organizations to much more mobile multi-agency working in local VET schools and other youth services, including the youth justice system. While this has accelerated his personal work rhythm, he values the flexibility of space and time it allows him to respond to demand, and especially the importance that process time can have in his educational work.

At the moment he is counselling and accompanying unemployed youths over a period of two years, assisting them to find their way into adult life. Allowing them adequate time to make this transition is a central aspect of his work, going through problems with them, and discussing obstacles over and over again. He gives an example:

> Well, right now I am working with a guy with whom I visited a workplace where he is supposed to start an internship. This was four weeks ago, and for three meetings we have been talking about his fears. Like 'Oh, what will happen if I can't cope, what will happen to me then?', and we talk that through. And with this guy, it's so obvious that he is so surprised – that this is possible. Well, in the beginning I really made the mistake of telling him: 'Okay, next time we are going to decide on it!' I guess this was far too quick for him. And every time he really is surprised that I am going through all his fears with him again. But this simply is a large part of our work task.

Here we can see that surprise is an interruption of a continuous time flow. It stops an on-going process and enables it to start again, thereby allowing for and inviting change. The paradox of being surprised by being given time hints at a tension which runs through the whole interview. The funding regulations and expectations of awarding authorities push for rapid integration of unemployed school leavers into the labour market, thereby imposing abstract time, but Mr M. distances himself from other colleagues who measure their success according to these outcomes. He has had to learn for himself that pressure is an approach that does not work in relationship-building with young people, and that allowing time is crucial. Hence the political economy of time constitutes a part of his practice. It plays out in the way he structures his counselling practice *and* forms part of his workplace politics.

Together with his team, Mr M. successfully negotiated with their funding bodies to get a reduction of the caseload from 350 to around 220 young people per year. This was a collective effort to secure the process time they believed necessary to do their educational work in an ethical way. Becoming aware of the importance of process time in young people's career histories, as an educational as well as a personal resource, has been a crucial step in taking command of time as a part of workplace policy. Here then, we see a local and contingent success in generating (process) time as opposed to making targets. The strategy of the team was neither active resistance nor mere compliance. Rather they were consciously negotiating the boundaries of their educational work by collectively engaging in a politics of time to secure the space needed for ethically responsible education work.

Conclusion

> I am convinced that re-creating our use of time is absolutely essential to re-creating democracy.
>
> (Allman 1999:130)

These case studies, each from a very different historical welfare state tradition, make visible the class interests and practices that generate particular time orders – and tensions between them – in educational work. Dominant social groups have ruptured established historical time orders by generating and imposing a new, neo-liberal period sharpened by the current moment of global economic crisis. Far removed from the front-line of provision, their interests conflict with those of both practitioners and learners or other service users (Tronto 2010). As a result, global, regional and national policies for welfare services and educational work within them are being re-configured to prioritize clock time over process time, and thus to compress and/or simply restrict the time for learning processes. At the same time, such policies – and those who make and impose them – are responsible not only for prioritizing exchange-values over use-values, but also for shifting use-values towards those of control rather than care. These are deeply ethical and political issues, encountered on a daily basis (and often painfully) by educational practitioners.

Yet the discourse of time is also a resource for those who take up the responsibility to resist the impact of neo-liberal policies: it offers a way of challenging the dominant mantra that we must accept 'the realities of the times'. Recognizing the social, moral and political embeddedness of time offers a basis for intervening at every level of decision-making to argue that educational work requires time to be generated differently. Those who take responsibility for asserting clock time over practitioners and learners, rather than providing process time for them, can and should be held accountable.

These discussions about time are fundamental to the development of professional responsibility in initial and continuing education for practitioners. They should be integrated into their learning about ethics; and pursued vigorously by professional bodies, trade unions, and service user organizations. There is also a place for wider public debate that needs to be encouraged through media channels, one which speaks to the lived experiences most people will have of these competing time orders (whether as practitioners or service users), and discusses which groups can and should take responsibility for challenging and changing our use of time. The point is that the experience of competing time orders is widely shared and can build into a movement for change.

In any such movement, however, there is also a need for a longer-term vision of an alternative settlement, one which offers a far-reaching critique of the wider systems reproducing inequality in capitalist society, and poses the need for more radical social transformation. As Haug points out: 'The art of politics is about building connections and creating a space of orientation which can re-contextualize fragmented struggles' (2010:222). Without this approach, the problems addressed by local struggles can simply be shifted elsewhere; even their victories can be 'used to defuse and depoliticize – that is, domesticate – the crucial significance of the local effort' (Allman 1999:6).

This task of creating spaces of orientation is one which calls for a radical and collective notion of democratic responsibility which generates and is sustained by an entirely different time order. It requires a full acknowledgement of four different dimensions of our life – employed work, social reproduction work, personal self-development and political activism – across which everyone's time would be distributed in a proportional way in a more comprehensively just society. Such a transformative vision must be a fully integrated one, which 'takes as its point of departure the division of labour and the time dedicated to each. In other words, it seeks to alter our society's time regime in a fundamental way' (Haug 2010:224). Haug envisions an alternative and more socially just model, in which time would be generated by *all* citizens across four interwoven areas of labour, related to four key dimensions of human life: production, reproductive work, personal learning and development, and political activism. Everyone, she argues powerfully, should be responsible for putting their time to use in all four dimensions, without gendered or other oppressive inequalities. This is a transformation that would not only see educational and other human service work – the work of social reproduction – fully valued and recognized, but would unlock its confinement to a feminized, and therefore often oppressed, space in which clock time grinds against process time, and process time subordinates women's needs to the needs of others. As in any dialectical relationship, in which opposing categories cannot exist without each other, the negation of one necessarily also entails the negation of its negation. In a transformed society, all time, including the time dedicated to social reproduction work, would be generated differently: a time beyond the binary of clock versus process time would emerge. Securing this compass through educational work is a politics of recognizing the competing time orders at work; studying the political economy of time in depth and critically; and engaging more explicitly in time politics at every available opportunity of our lifetime. It is a responsibility we cannot afford to shirk.

Acknowledgements

The research reported here was funded by: Australian Research Council, Discovery Project DP0986413; UK Economic and Social Research Council, grant no. RES-000-22-2588; and the Jenny and Antti Wihuri Foundation, Finland.

Our thanks are due to the research participants and other research team members.

This chapter is based on: Colley, H., Henriksson, L., Niemeyer, B. and Seddon, T. (2013) Competing time orders in human service work: towards a politics of time, *Time & Society*, 21(3): 371–394, published by SAGE.

References

Allman, P. (1999) *Revolutionary Social Transformation: Democratic Hopes, Political Possibilities and Critical Education*, West Connecticut: Bergin & Garvey.

Chadderton, C. and Colley, H. (2012) 'School to work transition services: marginalising 'disposable' youth in a state of exception', *Discourse*, 33(3): 329–343.

Colley, H. (2012) 'Not learning in the workplace: austerity and the shattering of *illusio* in public service work', *Journal of Workplace Learning*, 24(5): 317–337.

Davies, K. (1994) 'The tensions between process time and clock time in care-work: the example of day nurseries', *Time and Society*, 3(3): 277–303.

Esping-Andersen, G. (1990) *The Three Worlds of Welfare Capitalism*, Bristol: Polity.

FINLEX (2010) Sähköinen säädöskokoelma (Electronic collection of statutes). Online. Available at: http://www.finlex.fi/fi/laki/kokoelma/2010/ (accessed 5 May 2013).

Goffman, E. (1969) *Asylums*. Penguin Books: London.

Harvey, D. (1990) *The Condition of Postmodernity: An Enquiry into the Origins of Cultural Change*, Cambridge, MA: Blackwell.

Harvey, D. (2006) *The Limits to Capital*, 2nd edn, London: Verso.

Haug, F. (2010) 'A politics of working life', in T. Seddon, L. Henriksson and B. Niemeyer (eds) *Learning and Work and the Politics of Working Life* (pp. 217–225), London: Routledge.

Heikkinen, A. (2002) 'Transforming VET policies and professionalism: a view from Finland', in W. Nijhof, A. Heikkinen and L. Nieuwenhuis (eds) *Shaping Flexibility in Vocational Education and Training* (pp. 207–225), Dordrecht: Kluwer Academic Publishers.

Henriksson, L. (2008) 'Reconfiguring Finnish welfare service workforce: inequalities and identity', *Equal Opportunities International* 27(1): 49–63.

Henriksson, L., Wrede, S. and Burau, V. (2006) 'understanding professional projects in welfare state; revival of old professionalism?', *Gender, Work and Organization*, 13(2): 174–192.

Heydebrand, W. (2003) 'The time dimension in Marxian social theory', *Time and Society* 12(2/3): 147–188.

ME (Ministry of Education) (2010) *Ammatillisten aineiden opettajien sekä rehtoreiden kelpoisuusvaatimuksia selvittäneen työryhmän loppuraportti. (Closing report of the working group on the eligibility standards of vocational teachers and principals.)* Working papers and reports 5, Helsinki: Ministry of Education.

Mészáros, I. (2008) *The Challenge and Burden of Historical Time: Socialism in the Twenty-First Century*, New York: Monthly Review Press.

Newman, S., Niemeyer, B., Seddon, T., Devos, A., Henriksson, L. and Joseph, C. (2014) Special issue: Global transformations and educational work: remaking the idea of a teaching occupation, *Globalization, Societies and Education*, 12.

Niemeyer, B. (2007) 'Is there a pedagogy of social inclusion? Critical reflections on European policy and practice in school-to-work transition', in H. Colley, P. Boetzelen, B. Hoskins and T. Parveva (eds) *Social Inclusion for Young People: Breaking Down the Barriers* (pp. 83–97), Strasbourg: Council of Europe.

Niemeyer, B. (2011) 'Ordnung im Zwischenraum!-?', Vortragsmanuskript des Fachtags Berufliche Förderpädagogik, Osnabrück, 24 March 2011.

Niemeyer, B. (2012) 'The impacts of European social inclusion policy on national educational systems', in P. Gonon and S. Stolz (eds) *Challenges and Reforms in Vocational Education. Aspects of Inclusion and Exclusion*, Bern: Peter Lang.

Niemeyer, B. and Frey-Huppert, C. (2009) Berufsorientierung an allgemeinbildenden Schulen in Deutschland im Überblick. Eine Bestandsaufnahme im Auftrag der Hans-Böckler-Stiftung; Düsseldorf.

Postone, M. (1993) *Time, Labor and Social Domination*, Cambridge: Cambridge University Press.

Seddon, T., Henriksson, L. and Niemeyer, B. (eds) (2010) *Learning and Work and the Politics of Working Life*, London: Routledge.

Seitter, W. (2010) 'Zeitformen (in) der Erwachsenenbildung: eine historische Skizze', *Zeitschrift für Pädagogik* 56(3): 305–316.

Sennett, R. (1998) *The Corrosion of Character: The Personal Consequences of Work in the New Capitalism*, New York: W. Norton.

Shaikh, A.M. and Tonak, E.A. (1994) *Measuring the Wealth of Nations: The Political Economy of National Accounts*, Cambridge: Cambridge University Press.

Stacey, M. (1984) 'The division of labour revisited', in P. Abrams, R. Deem, J. Finch and P. Rock (eds) *Development and Diversity: British Sociology, 1950–1960* (pp. 172–190), London: George & Allen.

Tronto, J. (2010) 'Creating caring institutions: politics, plurality, and purpose', *Ethics and Social Welfare*, 4(2): 158–171.

Waerness, K. (1984) 'The rationality of caring', *Economic and Industrial Democracy*, 5(2): 185–211.

Wrede, S., Henriksson, L., Höst, H., Johansson, S. and Dybbroe, B. (eds) (2008) *Care Work in Crisis. Reclaiming the Nordic Ethos of Care*, Lund: Studentlitteratur.

Ylijoki, O.-H. and Mäntylä, H. (2003) 'Conflicting time perspectives in academic work', *Time and Society*, 12(1): 55–78.

Chapter 15

Professional learning for planetary sustainability

Thinking through Country

Margaret Somerville

Introduction

As we enter the second decade of the twenty-first century, scientists and governments alike acknowledge the urgency of addressing escalating planetary problems. The latest report of the Intergovernmental Panel for Climate Change has moved on from providing evidence that global warming is a serious international issue to addressing how we might respond to the disasters that will inevitably result (IPCC 2012). In this chapter, I explore the question of how to prepare professional practitioners for their ethical responsibilities to planetary sustainability. I set the chapter in the time of the Anthropocene, the new geological age of human-induced changes to planetary processes, and ask: How can we re-think professional learning in relation to our responsibilities to the planet, and to the more-than-human world?

I outline my own professional learning to 'think through country' from my collaborative research with Australian Aboriginal researcher Chrissiejoy Marshall as a possible framework for planetary sustainability. This framework is used as a lens to examine a series of projects about teacher education and teacher professional learning designed to develop new curriculum and pedagogies through participatory action research, and in community discussions about professional learning needs. These projects have drawn on professional networks of educators and sustainability practitioners in order to map what is currently a new and unexplored field of research.

International moves to put sustainability education on the global agenda have their origins in the Brundtland Report, 'Our Common Future', of 1987. The Brundtland Report (Brundtland and Khalid 1987) generated the United Nations Decade of Education for Sustainable Development 2005–2014. Sustainable development is defined in terms of an ethics of intergenerational justice, as development that meets the needs of the present without compromising the ability of future generations to meet their own needs. Less frequently cited is the moral responsibility to communities and nations whose environments and quality of life become further impoverished under neoliberal conditions of globalization and wealth concentration. The Report emphasizes the necessity to integrate social, cultural, economic and environmental considerations as distinct from earlier models of environmental education, opening the way for a different approach. Education for Sustainable Development has become widely seen as 'a new improved version of Environmental Education', most visibly at the national policy level of many countries (Jickling and Wals 2008:4).

Half-way through this decade, however, intensified concerns about the impact of human induced climate change have increased the sense of urgency to address global planetary problems (Kagawa and Selby 2010). Formal, non-formal and informal education have an important role to play but there is little empirical research to guide the process. The most crucial need identified in the field and the research literature is the preparation of sustainability literate teachers and teacher educators (Nolet 2009).

Many environmental education and sustainability theorists have argued that the goals of education for sustainability cannot be realized using the same ontologies and epistemologies – ways of being and knowing – with which we currently operate. They maintain that a fundamental re-orientation of education systems is required (Tilbury 2004; Sterling 2005; Nolet 2009). Even more so, it is proposed that 'in the face of runaway climate change nothing short of a lived paradigm shift is needed' in which interdisciplinary approaches enable a reclaiming of local, everyday and indigenous knowledges (Kagawa and Selby 2010:241).

The Anthropocene

Paul Crutzen and co-workers proposed the 'Anthropocene' as 'a new phase in the history of both humankind and of the Earth, when natural forces and human forces became intertwined, so that the fate of one determines the fate of the other' (Zalasiewicz *et al.* 2010:2231). While the International Geological Society contemplates the validity of the proposal, what is more interesting is the way in which scholars from across a number of disciplines are taking up this term as a provocation to new structures of thought. A group of social scientists in Australia, for example, has developed a manifesto as a call for new ways of thinking and knowing, and for innovative forms of action (Yeatman *et al.* 2010). They claim that by naming human agency, this term opens the possibility for emergent responses to more sustainably connect nature and culture, economy and ecology, and the natural and human sciences, in order to address escalating planetary problems (Yeatman *et al.* 2010).

Clare Colebrook in her recent book, *Extinction: Framing the end of the species*, names the core of this new paradigm as the new ways of thinking provoked by a contemplation of the end of the species. Comparing this shift to the way that Darwin's concept of evolution represented an epistemic shift in our thinking through the introduction of a past before human existence, Colebrook names the Anthropocene as an epochal shift in which we must contemplate a future beyond human existence. She names the 'discovery' of climate change as an epochal event in which we must recognize the prospect of the mass extinction of species, including the human species itself.

It is as though what is facing extinction is not only the human species but also a certain mastery or image of the species (the species sense of its mastery and its capacity to master itself): climate change is not only change of the climate but a change in the very way in which we think about climates and rates and modes of change. Extinction is not only extinction of the species but also an extinguishing of the human animal's sense of humanity.

(Colebrook 2010:15)

Recognizing our mutual entanglement in the fate of the planet in the era of the Anthropocene articulates the need to 're-orient the entire terrain of thinking', to open up our exploration of what new knowledge formations, the concept of life might require, in the twenty-first century. It requires us to develop new concepts of the human, new figures of life, and new understandings of what counts as thinking. This new thinking is emergent and is especially new in the area of professional learning.

What new ways of being, thinking and doing can we bring to our professional practice and how do we go about learning these? In relation to my professional practice as a teacher, educator and researcher, how can we translate the harsh realities of planetary sustainability into our ethical responsibilities to bring hope and meaning to the next generation of children who will inherit this world? This question demands something vastly more than current superficial concepts of sustainability education.

Thinking through Country

For over twenty years, I have been involved in collaborative research with Australian Aboriginal peoples and communities (Somerville and Perkins 2010; Somerville 2013a). My interest began as a young wife and mother relocating to the desert in Central Australia when my husband was appointed to a teaching position on a government settlement. My experiences of ceremony with old Pintubi women who had only been in contact with white society for a few years stayed with me, inchoate, embodied experiences, until a recent project in collaboration with U'Alayi researcher Chrissiejoy Marshall. It was during the final process of writing a self through this project that I realized that the concept of 'place', that I had worked with since my first collaborative project with Aboriginal people, had become a practice of *Thinking Through Country*. A fundamental re-orientation had occurred which allowed me to understand those early experiences in the desert for the first time. I wrote a self becoming-other in thinking through country as a way to articulate this new terrain of thought (Somerville 2013a). In the following, I trace the steps of my professional learning in order to articulate the grounds of possibility for an ethical practice of deep sustainability learning.

Chrissiejoy Marshall came to me as a newly enrolled doctoral student and struggled with an ambivalent desire to conform to Western academic language and knowledge structures. Liberated by my encouragement from years of working with doctoral students and their alternative knowledge frameworks, she slowly and painstakingly developed a radical alternative methodology for her research. Although researching the development of a training package in conflict resolution and now living in Sydney, she realized that in order to make any knowledge claims at all she had to 'think through country', the specific country of the Narran Lake where she grew up. She produced a DVD for the presentation of her methodology at doctoral school that she called 'Calling up Blackfella Knowing through Whitefella Magic'.

In her presentation, Chrissiejoy created a carefully orchestrated performance in conversation with her non-Indigenous audience using her paintings, oral storytelling, U'Alayi and Erinbinjori language, and multiple acts of translation. Chrissiejoy's performance was pedagogical in the sense that it was designed to teach her non-Indigenous audience the deepest understandings from Aboriginal culture about a new way of thinking. This new way of thinking was not performed from an essentialized image of the noble savage in communication with nature. It was constituted within the struggle between Erinbinjori and U'Alyai languages, knowledges and histories, and Western academic thought expressed in English. The translation was made possible by multimodal forms of representation, including new digital technologies. We further developed this methodology in combination with my 'postmodern emergence' (Somerville 2007) for a collaborative research project about water in the Murray–Darling Basin.

The fate of the Murray–Darling Basin, a large artesian basin spanning five states in south-eastern Australia, had attracted international attention due to its severe ecological decline after 13 years of drought. Described as 'the food basket of the nation', the Basin produces 40 per cent of the country's agricultural output, in ways that are now recognized as unsustainable. Large numbers of professional practitioners have been involved in numerous strategies and reviews but 20 years after the launch of a new strategy of integrated catchment management (MDBC 2001), water quality and ecosystem health were continuing to decline. Failure to involve Aboriginal communities was identified as a major issue, but the discourses and practices of natural resource management failed to take account of profound paradigm differences in Aboriginal onto-epistemologies (Ward *et al.* 2003).

We named our new methodology 'Thinking through Country'. Our project began with the Narran Lake and continued to travel with the flow of the waterways throughout the Murray–Darling Basin. At the end of five years of research with Indigenous artists throughout the Basin, I revisited Chrissiejoy's DVD, analysing each segment in detail and responding with the question: How can I learn to think through country as a white settler woman in contemporary urban Australia? (Somerville 2013a, 2013b). In the following I trace that learning in the hope of articulating some principles that can be applied to a deep knowledge of sustainability practice.

Beginning with Country

Chrissiejoy framed the performance of her methodology with a composite painting of all of the parts of the whole fitted together like a jigsaw puzzle. In the accompanying script she named each of these parts through her own understanding of the components of a methodology of country comprising conceptual framework, ontology, epistemology, methodology and representation. Beginning in the centre top of the jigsaw painting, she named the central framing component 'A mudmap of Country', which I understand as a representation of a conceptual framework.

> Starting in the centre top of the painting this jigsaw piece is viewed as a mud map of the Noongahburrah country. The black lines are the rivers within, and marking the boundaries of this Country, and the black orb in the centre represents the Narran Lake, where I was raised, and which has always been the most significant and sacred site for Noongahburrabah, Murriburrah, Ngunnaburrah, and all the other peoples of the nation that spoke the U'Alayi language as well as several other nations of Aboriginal people within bordering countries
>
> (Immiboagurramilbun[1] 2008)

Like many of us in contemporary urban societies, Chrissiejoy had long been physically displaced from the place of her growing up. We recorded her childhood memories of the Narran Lake, whilst sitting in her house in Sydney's densely populated western suburbs. It was as if we travelled through time and space back to her childhood by the lake. I came to know the Narran Lake in all of its cycles and its seasons through Chrissiejoy's powerful body memories.

> I don't remember a time without the Lake. There were times when it dried back but they were quite rare. It was always full and in season there'd be thousands and thousands of birds. You'd wake up in the morning to birds getting a fright, taking off and making a terrible clatter. Then going to sleep of a night time, listening to all the birds, that lulled chatter that you hear of an evening.
>
> (Immiboagurramilbun 2008)

In this sense, 'country' as a conceptual framework is not a generalized notion like 'the environment' or 'nature', but a specific material location of long term intimate, everyday embodied attachment. This embodied attachment is carried across time and space as a continuing framework for thought and action. I have frequently used this same process of recording childhood place attachments in different sites of professional learning. Participants are asked to close their eyes and return to a significant place of their childhood and evoke their memory through all of their senses. The response has been profound and connects people to place as an entirely different starting point than the abstract concept of sustainability.

Me, myself and I: an onto-epistemology

In dwelling deeply in the in-between of Chrissiejoy's multimodal representations I came to understand thinking through country as a complex onto-epistemology. The elements of this connected being-and-knowing are introduced in the section of Chrissiejoy's DVD labelled 'Me, myself and I'. This is portrayed in the second segment of the jigsaw painting as represented by four black swans on a blue background of water. Chrissiejoy explains that the first two swans are for her mother, and the second two represent the water people, the Noongahburrah clan of her grandfather's people. The swans are designated as *Mulgury*, an Erinbinjori language word signalling their collective meaning as creatures of the '*Niddeerie*'. The concepts of Mulgury and Niddeerie have been simplistically and reductively translated as 'totem' and 'dreamtime' but Chrissiejoy is careful to provide a fuller and more complex understanding of these core concepts.

> At the beginning all was Mulgury.[2] Only creative power and intent. Through the intent and power of our Creator, Mulgury reproduces into form to carve the beings and shapes of the world where the water meets the sky and earth sings the world to life. The pattern of life is Mulgury and Mulgury is traced in the Niddrie [the framework of the ancient laws within Niddeerie] of Mudri [person]. Every tracing, every rock, tree, plant, landform, the water, fish, reptile, bird, animal and Mudri is in the sacred relationship, through Niddeerie.[3] The pattern, shape and form of Mulgury is life, and all is a continuing tracing of Mulgury.
>
> (Ticalarnabrewillaring 1961, translated by Immiboagurramilbun[4] 2008)

In the face of these complexities, all I can do is to suspend understanding but continue to hold the meaning of the space opened up by these words. The sense of unknowing is important in this learning, as in all new knowledge generation (Somerville 2007). I sense that form and meaning are created simultaneously with the fabric of the earth and all its creatures, including humans. I respond to the word 'tracing' and its evocation of mark-making in returning to the visual representation of black swans on the blue surface of the lake. I understand that Chrissiejoy's mother *is* swan, and that collectively Noongahburrah people are swan. Swan belongs to the time and place of the creation of the land and people of *Terewah*, the language name for the Narran Lake which means home of the black swan. The creation of the lake and its creatures did not happen once in the beginning of time, but each time swan is evoked in language and ceremony, swan and the lake come into being again and again in past, present and future. Those who carry that identity are both swan and place. Country, swan and person are together an ontological reality. In learning this new knowledge from a position of unknowing a space is opened up in which I can become, not more of myself, but other-to-myself as part of this deep learning.

Learning Country through story

Stories are the ways that this knowledge of country is shared and learned. The methodology for this complex knowledge is represented in the jigsaw painting through a depiction of the creation story of the Narran Lake. Simple versions of creation stories are told to introduce young children to the complex cosmology of country in their daily lives.

> The first stories are almost beyond my memory. I grew up knowing the stories so I'm guessing that I was told as a very, very small child. When you first get told about the creation of the Lake and Guriya and how all that connects it's a very simplistic story, it was just simply that this huge animal was, you know, kept the kids away from the water holes because, 'look out Guriya'll get you'. It was a story to keep you safe and then later on it gets deeper and deeper, so it's the same story but it just gets more detailed. As a tiny, tiny child you probably didn't even understand really that it was Guriya that created the Lake, it was more about he swallowed people and if you went too close to the water, the deep water, he might be still there, he might get you. Later on you get told about the creation story and then further on than that you get told about how they killed him and how he is now called upon as the spirit to make things grow.
>
> (Immiboagurramilbun 2008)

A practical methodology of Country: place-based learning

Place-based experiences in everyday life are crucial to this learning. The methodology of creation story telling is expanded into a practical approach to learning country through immersion in the everyday life of the world around them. This is expressed in a vibrant painting called 'Finding and knowing place of self and others within Country' that shows the winding green tendrils of new growth and a scatter of fat white witchetty grubs, a prized food source.

> As children we spent much time following the life cycle of the grub, as we did with all other animals, birds, insects and plant life. We would learn when they mated, how the mother prepared for her babies, we watched the young grubs grow and we knew how to know when they reached maturity. You can imagine the depth of knowledge gained from this kind of learning. It not only gave knowledge about the insect itself, but also about everything that is connected to it, the type of conditions most favoured. We learned what happened when floods or drought hit the area, what the grub needed for survival and what other animals and birds fed on the grub itself. In addition, we were shown how it all connected to us
>
> (Immiboagurramilbun 2008).

The methodology of country is a practical action related to the inherited assignation of a living creature to individuals and groups through kinship structures. All living things which supply resources to sustain human life are part of this kinship system so it can equally be a wild yam, a witchetty grub, a honey ant or a kangaroo. Chrissiejoy says that:

> As an Aboriginal person you are given a Mulgury at birth and it comes with the responsibility for that animal or plant and is part of you and you of it. Part of that obligation is to learn all about your Mulgury and everything that is connected to it. If your Mulgury was the Kangaroo, you would learn that you are related to the trees, the insects, the birds, the grass, the wind, the rain and all the things which occur and surround a kangaroo's life. You would spend years observing and learning about the life of your Mulgury – what it needs to survive and how it assists in the survival of other species. Most importantly, you would learn how all those things connect to yourself – how they all become your brothers and sisters, part of your family and about the responsibility which goes with that.
>
> (Immiboagurramilbun 2008)

In response to each of the elements of Chrissiejoy's thinking through country I wrote from my own location as a contemporary white woman in the post-industrial location of Latrobe Valley Victoria. It was also in this place that I had become involved in a long-term collaboration with the Commercial Road Primary School, Morwell (Somerville 2007). My relationship with the visionary teacher who established a programme of integrated place-based learning with children in this depressed post-industrial location continued over several years as I observed his pedagogical practices and began to integrate teacher education students into the school. Eventually a colleague and I developed a three-year participatory action research study to integrate teacher education and teacher professional learning into the Morwell River wetlands programme (Somerville and Green 2012). In the following, I apply the elements outlined above to the analysis of this participatory action research study.

Pedagogies for teacher education and professional learning for sustainability

Country

The Morwell River itself is an interesting phenomenon. Over 50 years ago it was diverted into a pipe to make way for the expansion of an open cut coal mine. Aboriginal artefacts on display in the reception area of the power station tell the story of a time when people sang, danced, camped and ate by the river. The open cut mine was be extended again. In this move, as reported in the local paper, we have an 'improved river and an improved road'; the river was once again diverted to expand the coal mine. This time it was liberated from its pipe and returned, according to the planning map, to a river's meandering curves. The Morwell River Wetlands is an artificial wetlands, constructed by an international power company.

The school has a special relationship with the wetlands and has plotted its evolution through the frogs, birds, fish, native trees, shrubs and grasses, and other creatures large and small who have come to inhabit the place. Regular visits to the wetlands are integrated into a programme of place-based learning across all grades and all subject areas. The visionary teacher who led this programme came from a family of beekeepers, reminding me of the learning that Chrissiejoy talked about with the witchetty grubs: 'It not only gave knowledge about the insect itself, but also about everything that is connected to it, the type of conditions most favoured'. When the visionary teacher was about to retire and the programme was threatening to fold, we developed a collaborative participatory action research study involving two grade 3/4 teachers, the deputy principal, the principal, the lead teacher, the environmental officer from the power company, 80 grade 3/4 students, 50 teacher education students and ourselves as teacher educators.

Teacher education and teacher professional learning programme

The teacher education students participated in a series of five weeks of specially designed learning tasks leading up to a group exercise to design activities for the grade 3/4 primary school children at the Morwell River Wetlands. The visionary teacher and the environmental officer provided lectures about the history of the wetlands and the programme in the school. The teachers supported the development of learning activities by the students as part of their professional learning. They explained how the place-based learning in the wetlands was to be integrated into a thematic unit of study on 'Adaptation'.

During the 12-week semester, we traced the trajectory of their learning as evidenced in their/the students' online posts, their written plans for the wetlands learning activities, and our observations of the activities in practice in the wetlands recorded in field journals. The teachers participated in two focus groups, a most significant finding from which was their belief that it would be these teacher education students who would lead sustainability education for the next generation of children. They had observed the teacher education students through the process of their learning and conducting the activities in the wetlands and saw that they were immersed in a transformative process that would continue to inform their practice throughout their teaching.

There were two outstanding peaks in the trajectory of teacher education student learning related to particular pedagogical practices that we developed. The first was a session in which we introduced the students to the memory work technique to elicit their early body/place memories. The second was their learning through the activities they designed and implemented in the wetlands.

Body/place memory work

The teacher education students were divided into small groups of six to eight and the instructions for this pedagogical exercise were to recall an embodied place memory, to tell it to the others, each taking a turn while the others listened in silence, and then to assist each other to move further into the sensory experience of these memories – smell, sound, touch, movement, and other senses that may not even have a name. They were then to write this memory to express that one small specific body memory of a particular place.

> When I was around four or five I remember vividly, trying to skip stones across a small creek whilst on a four wheel drive trip with my dad. Dad and I used to frequent the bush exploring tracks, rivers and creeks in our four wheel drive. I do remember one track in particular which crossed the same creek many times. Each time I would beg my dad to stop and let me throw rocks into the water. Some I could skip across the top, while others I would throw hard into the water, for a mighty splash. I remember the noise these larger rocks would make when entering the water, just like it was yesterday. I can see the shallow creek coming up to my ankles, the cold water flowing over my feet, with the sun shining through a small gap in the canopy onto my face, keeping me warm. My dad over to the left picking up and throwing larger rocks that I couldn't lift into the water, with me geeing him on, splosh there's that noise again. I remember this so clearly, my dad and I in a carefree time just having fun and not worrying about anything else in the world.
>
> (Teacher education student, individual post)

The memory work exercise was a powerful experience for these students just as it was for Chrissiejoy when she paused and travelled through time and space to the Narran Lake of her childhood. The movement from body/place memory into language was fundamental to this introductory learning activity and it happened first through telling the memory orally to each other in a collective process structured for this purpose. More significantly the movement from oral telling into written language brought these experiences, that are not usually available for pedagogical work, into the public domain. It is this process of 'naming the world' as not separate from the self but as a self-coming-into-being-with-the-world that mirrors the onto-epistemology of Chrissiejoy's 'Me, myself and I'. It was the basis for all that followed as students built on this in an iterative process, moving out to explore the pedagogical possibilities of the world of the campus around them and finally designing an activity for the children in the wetlands.

Designing place-based learning in Country

The design of the learning activity incorporated each of the stages of learning and knowing they had achieved before. One group, for example, went down to a small wetlands in the campus grounds to explore what might be found that could then be incorporated into their learning activity. This group gave the following account of the process.

> We took a walk down to the lake [on campus] to see what might interest children. On the way we discovered poo, yabby holes and listened to birds. So our focus changed. We took pictures of different types of poo, recorded the birds, took pictures of the birds, and took pictures of the yabby holes.
>
> From this we thought of many activities that could be of interest to the learners.
>
> - Senses, mind map; close your eyes what do you feel, think, smell, hear then draw from their thought patterns;
> - Water, man-made structure; what lives in the water; uses of water; classroom research on what lives in static water.
> - Yabby hole, what type of animal makes this hole; from the size of the hole can we tell how big the animal is; other animals that live in holes; what role does the size of the hole mean in relation to the size of the animal; what other habitats are there and who uses them; create, build, draw, make habitats that are relevant animals.
> - Poo, what animal did this poo; can we tell how big an animal is from the size of the poo; can we dissect the poo and then know what the animal ate; what is the water concentration to rough matter.
>
> (Teacher education student group post, July 2011)

Students learned this place from a position of unknowing and in the process became other-to-themselves. The process was most unlike the usual methods of lesson planning. It was grounded in the pre-service teachers' newly learned body experience of this specific place in all of its intimate material sensory detail. The 'Country' of this place includes poo, yabby holes, the sound of birds, the elements of water and earth, as redolent with pedagogical potential. The pre-service teachers are sensing, feeling, thinking, dwelling in the place to imagine the student place-makings that their activities might generate. They planned to engage the children in the same way, to 'create, build, draw, make habitats that are relevant to animals'. In order to do this the teacher/learner had to think themselves into country, into being the animal they are learning, just as Chrissiejoy described a practical methodology of learning everything that is related to the kangaroo as Mulgury, in all its intimate detail.

I recorded the day with 50 pre-service teachers and 80 children at the wetlands in a journal entry called 'Blue' to capture my sense of how children and pre-service teachers together drew from 'the chaos of the earth' (Grosz 2008). I began to think about the extensive structures that enabled the pedagogical possibilities of the day – the drawn out negotiations of timetables, scheduling, curriculum, themes, lesson plans as 'the frame' that enables this to happen (Somerville and Green 2012). Chaos, like the state of Niddrie, is the condition of the universe: 'In the beginning is chaos, the whirling, unpredictable movement of forces, vibratory oscillations that constitute the universe' (Grosz 2008:5). The frame allows philosophy, art and science, to draw strength, force and material from it 'for a provisional and open-ended cohesion, temporary modes of ordering, filtering' (Grosz 2008:8).

Child-becoming-frog: Mulgury

The journal entry 'Blue' was prompted by two boys looking up at the colour of the sky with a blue paint sample in their hands to see if it matched the sky's blue colour. At the same time a flock of wild ducks flew overhead moving in and out of perfect formation, black lines of flight against a blue, blue sky. Ultimately, however, it was the return to the signature element of the wetlands, the frog that became the focus of this entry.

> [Two pre-service teachers] called us over to tell us about the kids having discovered a brown frog hiding under a piece of wood placed there for habitat. Many kids are all around showing different things, but it is one girl, Gemma, who attracts my attention with the quality of her attention. [The pre-service teacher] gently lifts up the wood and underneath is a small stripy brown frog half buried in moist brown soil amidst a flurry of ants. We ask Gemma 'Why doesn't the frog hop away?' and Gemma tells us that it is well camouflaged, an idea discussed in 'adaptation', but it is what expands on this that is interesting.
>
> Gemma says that she thinks the frog is aware that we are there because it moves it legs and digs itself a little further into the dark moist ground. As she says this she makes small movements with her hands to mimic the frog digging. But it isn't scared of us, she says, because it knows that it is the same colour as the ground and we won't be able to see it. The frog is not worried by the ants, she tells us, because if the ants were aggressive to it they would be biting it, and the frog would jump away. If the frog was eating the ants it would not be there under the rock living there with them.
>
> (Somerville, journal entry, August 2011).

While I have observed and written about becoming-frog before (Somerville 2007; Somerville *et al.* 2011), I have not observed this process as a pedagogical outcome of a designed activity before. It is the process of the pre-service teachers' immersion with the child in the nature of frog in this place. It is not the general place or the generalized learning of frog but it is frog that is part of country, the constructed wetlands, the artificially placed wood, the colour of the earth, the colour of the frog, the quality of the frog's movements, and its skin, the ants that inhabit that small place with the frog, the children and teacher are all part of this moment of learning country.

Conclusion

The visionary teacher who had designed the project to require the teacher education students to plan the wetlands activity was carrying out his responsibility to hand on his knowledge to the next generation of teachers. He was inspired that his work was expanded in the repertoire of activities that the teacher education students developed. The teachers learned by scaffolding the teacher education students and observing them in their first round of activity to give them feedback for the next round. Many, but not all of the teacher education students were transformed, and the school students drew amazing maps with images and text of their learning. As teacher educators we learned that our professional learning was collective, relational, inspirational and challenging, often moving beyond our comfort zones. We learned too of the difficulties for students when they were placed in schools where their ideas and practices of sustainability learned in country were rejected: 'We don't do sustainability in this school', they would say. We mapped sustainability initiatives in schools and communities across the Gippsland region and identified a small number of schools where our students could be placed in the following year of the study.

We recognized that a deep learning of sustainability requires a depth of practice in country that produces its own ethics of recognition. This involved a sense that we are part of a planet of life forms that is precious and vulnerable and that our ways of being and knowing the world shift as we learn to name the world differently and the world in turn names us.

Acknowledgements

I would like to acknowledge my life-long love for my friend, colleague, mentor and guide, Immiboagurramilbun (Chrissiejoy Marshall) for our collaboration in developing thinking through country.

Notes

1   Chrissiejoy has asked that her Aboriginal name, Immiboagurramilbun, be used in the text where it refers to her Aboriginal knowledges. She has similarly asked that the term 'Aboriginal' be used rather than 'Indigenous' and that her own spellings of language names be maintained.
2   Spirit. In a footnote in her Glossary Immiboagurramilbun explains that 'Mulgury' is typically translated as 'totem', derived from American Indian cultural practices. Like most translations of complex Aboriginal concepts she believes this is inappropriate and reductive.
3   Niddeerie is past, present and future and it is with us always, often referred to as 'dreaming' but this is not a word Immiboagurramilbun relates to in her world.
4   Ticalarnabrewillaring is Immiboagurramilbun's Erinbinjori grandmother's name, and the date of translation, 1961, indicates the depth of translating of these ideas by Immiboagurramilbun, which is Chrissiejoy's Erinbinjori name.

References

Brundtland, G.H. and Khalid, M. (1987) *Our Common Future: The Brundtland report*, Oxford: Oxford University Press.

Colebrook, C. (2010) *Extinction: Framing the end of the species*.

Grosz, E. (2008) *Chaos, Territory, Art: Deleuze and the framing of the earth*, New York: Columbia University Press.

Immiboagurramilbun (Marshall, C.) (2008) Thinking through Country. DVD adapted from Marshall, C., Talking up Blackfella Knowing through Whitefella Magic, for Bubbles on the Surface Exhibition 3, Switchback Gallery, Gippsland, Victoria.

IPCC (Intergovernmental Panel on Climate Change) (2012) *Managing the Risks of Extreme Events and Disasters to Advance Climate Change Adaptation – Special Report*, New York: Cambridge University Press. Online. Available at: http://www.ipcc.ch/pdf/special-reports/srex/SREX_Full_Report.pdf (accessed February 2013).

Jickling, B. and Wals, A. (2008) 'Globalization and environmental education: Looking beyond sustainable development'. *Journal of Curriculum Studies*, 40: 1–21.

Kagawa, F. and Selby, D. (2010) *Education and Climate Change: Living and learning in interesting times*, London and New York: Routledge.

MBDC (Murray–Darling Basin Ministerial Council) (2001) 'Integrated Catchment Management in the Murray–Darling Basin 2001–2010: Delivering a sustainable future', Murray–Darling Basin Commission.

Nolet, V. (2009) 'Preparing sustainability-literate teachers', *Teachers College Record*, 111(2): 409–442.

Somerville, M. (2007) 'Postmodern emergence', *International Journal of Qualitative Studies in Education*, 20(2): 225–243.

Somerville, M. (2010) 'A place pedagogy for "global contemporaneity"', *Journal of Educational Philosophy and Theory*, 42(3): 326–334.

Somerville, M. (2013a) *Water in a Dry Land: Place learning through artwork and story*, New York and London: Routledge.

Somerville, M. (2013b) Water in a Dry Land website. http://www.innovativeethnographies.net/water-in-a-dry-land (accessed May, 2013).

Somerville, M. and Green, M. (2012) 'Place and sustainability literacy in schools and teacher education', Joint Australian Association for Research in Education and Asia-Pacific Educational Research Association Conference, Sydney: AARE. Online. Available at: http://www1.aare.edu.au/papers/2012/Margaret%20Somerville%20Paper.pdf#zoom=85 (accessed 31 May 2013).

Somerville, M. and Perkins, T. (2010) *Singing the Coast: Place and identity in Australia*, Canberra, ACT: Aboriginal Studies Press.

Somerville, M., Davies, B., Power, K., Gannon, S. and de Carteret, P. (2011) *Place Pedagogy Change*, Rotterdam: Sense Publishing.

Sterling, S. (2005) Memorandum from Dr. Stephen Sterling. Environmental Education: Follow Up to Learning the Sustainability Lesson. *Fifth Report of Session 2004–05. House of Commons Environmental Audit Committee* (Appendix 39: Memorandum from Dr. Stephen Sterling), London: The Stationery Office (TSO).

Tilbury, D. (2004) Rising to the challenge: Education for sustainability in Australia. *Australian Journal for Environmental Education*, 20(2): 103–114.

Ward, N., Reys, S., Davies, J. and Roots, J. (2003) 'Scoping study on Aboriginal involvement in natural resource management decision making and the integration of Aboriginal cultural heritage considerations into relevant Murray–Darling Commission programs', Murray–Darling Basin Commission.

Yeatman, A., Rose, D., Mathews, F., Roelvink, G., Poltera, J., Cameron, J., Weir, J., Graham, J., Rigby, K., Gibson, K., Anderson, K., Dombroski, K., Kato, K., Iveson, K., Instone, L., Somerville, M., Fincher, R., Wearne, S. and van Dooren, T. (2010) *Manifesto for Living in the Anthropocene*, Georges River, 8 February, 2010.

Zalasiewicz, J., Williams, M., Steffen, W. and Crutzen, P. (2010) 'The new world of the anthropocene', *Environmental Science and Technology*, 44(7): 2228–2231.

Index

Abbot, A. 69
Aberton, H. 164–5
Aboriginal peoples 215–16, 220
Accident and Emergency departments 16–19
action research 213, 221
activity theory 122, 160
actor–network theory (ANT) 42–4, 47–9, 53–7, 100, 121, 173
Adler, P. 126
advertising industry 127
'agencement' 55
agency, concept of 47, 161–3
'agential cuts' (Barad) 162, 167
agile methods 32–5
Airbus crash (2009) 157–8
Allman, P. 209–10
Anderson, B. 55–6, 60–2
Anthropocene age 213–15
apprenticeship 85–90, 94–7; in engineering 114; in expansive environments 89–90, 95–6; in Germany 206–7; medieval concept of 94; as a model of learning 86–9, 96–7; professional 85, 96
'assemblage' concept 43–7, 55–7, 118, 122, 162, 167
Australia 52, 57, 63, 214–25
autonomy, professional 126

Bahcall, J.K. 100–1, 107
Bai, H. 162
Baker, T. 120
Barad, K. 52, 77, 162–3, 167–8
Bauman, Z. 131–3
Bechky, B. 19, 127
Beck, J. 130–1, 157–8
Becker, H.S. 39

Bennett, J. 158–62
Berg, M. 46
Bernstein, B. 130, 144
Birra-Li Project 145
Bjorkeng, K. 194–6
'border resources' between core and margin of a practice 21
Boud, D. 85–6
'boundary objects' 129
Bourdieu, Pierre 68
Bovaird, Tony 143
Boyle, D. 165
Bradley, B. 55
Braidotti, R. 162–3
bricolage, sociomaterial 112, 119–22
Brown, J.S. 86–7
Bruegger, U. 28
Brundtland Report (1987) 213–14
Bucciarelli, L.L. 113
Button, G. 12

call centre operators 20–1
Callon, Michel 39, 44–8, 161
Campbell Collaboration 25
Canada 184
Caputo, J. 167
Carolan, M. 62
Centre for the Advancement of Inter-professional Education (CAIPE) 146
child protection services 157
climate change 213–15
clinical nurse developers 29, 34
clinical practice 41, 46
clock time 199–200, 203–10
Clot, Y. 69
Cochrane Collaboration 25
co-configuration of production 128, 137
co-construction of knowledge 54

cognitivist approaches to professional learning 54
Colebrook, Clare 214–15
Colley, H. 160
community participation in development of public services 165–6
computer engineering 31–5
Connexions 204–6
Connolly, Peter 157
Cook, S.D.N. 86–7
Cooper, R. 57
co-production: building capacity for 150; core elements of 142; definition of 165; in healthcare 140–51; in policing 165–7; resurgence in the 1990s and early 2000s 142; 'strong' and 'weak' forms of 141–8, 151; studies of 143–50
Cotter, R. 77
Cribb, A. 160
Crutzen, Paul 214
Cullen, J. 77
cultural theory of learning (Hodkinson) 41–2
Cunliffe, A.L. 77
curriculum: conceptualisation of 174–5; sociomaterial 171–4, 181
Cyclone Nargis 61–2

Daniels, H. 28
Darwin, Charles 214
Davies, K. 200
Deleuze, G. 55, 158–9
DEMOS 142, 144
dentistry see endodontic practice
diffraction 67–8, 77–8
digital technologies 122
distributed knowledge and cognition 26, 113, 122, 151
Doane, G. 186, 195
doctors' learning in transition 38–41, 44, 48; characteristics of 40
Dopson, S. 28
dying patients, treatment of 45–6

Edwards, A. 28, 160
Edwards, R. 42, 44, 62
electrocardiograms (ECGs) 13–19
endodontic practice 100–10
Engeström, Y. 128
engineering: heterogeneous 121; ideology of 121
engineering knowledge 112–14, 119–21

epistemic communities 160
epistemic objects 27–35; in computer engineering 31–4; in nursing 29–31
epistemic practices 26–35
ethical labour 160
European Social Fund 207
Evetts, J. 86
evidence-based practice 31
Ewenstein, B. 28
'expansive–restrictive continuum' of learning 89, 96
expert communities and cultures 27, 31, 35
expert knowledge 146–7

Fenwick, T. 42–4, 47, 86, 88, 96, 186; co-editor
film crews 127
FInland 201–4
Fish, Stanley 68
focus-group discussions 102
Fox, A. 92
Franzak, J.K. 70
Freidson, E. 69
front-end change activities 148–50

Gainsburg, J. 113, 120
geographers and geography teachers 58–60
Germany 206–8
Gherardi, S. 185–6
Goodwin, C. 99
Governance International 142–3
Grabher, G. 127
Grosz, E. 223–4
Guattari, F. 55
Guile, D. 133–5

Hager, P. 186
Hall, R. 128–30
Haraway, D. 77
Hardy, I. 54–5
Harris, M. 165
Harrison, P. 60–2
Hassard, J. 42
Haug, F. 209–10
healthcare 140–51
Heath, C. 12
Heidegger, Martin 68
Henderson, K. 113–14
Hodkinson, P. 41
Hollan, J.D. 99

Ibarra, H. 79
InfoLab 115–17
Intergovernmental Panel on Climate
   Change (IPCC) 213
Internet relay chat (IRC) 121
interprofessional education (IPE) 146
interprofessional work and learning
   125–38; case study of 128–30; growth
   of 126–7; and professional formation
   133–7
'Interview to the Double' (ITTD) 67,
   71–8
intra-activity and intra-actions
   162, 167

Jensen, C.B. 161–2
Jensen, K. 28, 32, 86
Journal of Education and Work 1
journeymen 94

Kant, Immanuel 199
Keevers, L. 78
Knorr Cetina, Karin 26–8, 31, 35
'knotworking' (Engeström) 128
knowing-in-practice 3, 11–15, 167, 185,
   195; as a practical accomplishment
   12–13
'knowing what' and 'knowing how'
   112, 136
knowledge *about* practice and knowledge
   in practice 40
knowledge circulation 34–5
knowledge-in-action 27
knowledge objects 27–9, 33–5
knowledge practice 55–6
knowledge processes 26
knowledge society 26
Kostulski, K. 69
Kretzschmar, R.M. 172

Lahn, L. 28
Latour, Bruno 42, 118, 168
Lattuca, L.R. 54–5
Lave, J. 41, 94
Law, J. 42–3, 53, 55, 121
Leander, K.M. 55
learning: definition of 54; *situated*
   or *sociocultural* approach to 55
Learning Assemblages study 54, 57
Lee, Alison 140–2, 145–6, 151
Levi-Strauss, C. 119
Liverpool Care Pathway (LCP) 45–8

'logics of choice' and 'logics of care' 47
Lorimer, H. 53

McDowell, J. 135
McFarlane, C. 55–6
McGivern, G. 28
McIntyre, A. 78
Macknight, V. 56
Marková, I. 102–3
Markus, H. 68
Marshall, Chrissiejoy 213–22
Marx, Karl 199
materiality in professional practice 3–4,
   7, 55, 114, 122, 158, 161–2, 166–7,
   172–4, 181, 186
May, L. 159
Mead, G.H. 68
medical records 46–7
mental health care 163–5
mentoring 78
Michael, M. 63
Midler, C. 127
midwives, study of 72–9
mobility of professionals 94–5
Mol, A. 42–3, 47
'moments of translation' (Callon)
   44, 46
Mørk, B.E. 28
Morwell River wetlands 220–5
Mulcahy, D. 48
multi-agency practice and multi-
   professional team work 160
multiple nature of professional knowledge
   69–72, 78–9
Murphy, K. 102
Murray–Darling Basin 216

Narran Lake 216–19, 222
National Health Service (NHS)
   constitution 48
Needham, C. 167
'NEET' (not in education, employment
   or training) category of young people
   204, 207
Nelson, R.E. 120
Nerland, M. 32, 86; *co-editor*
networks 43–8
Nicolini, D. 72
non-representational theory (NRT) 53–7
Nordic welfare system 201–2
Norway 29–30
Nurius, P. 68

nursing 35, 160, 184–96; epistemic
    objects in 29–31; study of self-
    employment in 187–96

occupational communities 88
Oddone, I. 71
organisational culture 96
Orlikowski, W.J. 3, 118–19, 161, 185–6
Orr, J. 119–20
Osberg, D. 54
Ostrom, E. 147

participation in the practices of social
    groups 54–5, 60
'participational' metaphor for learning 2–3
'pedagogies of reflection' (Guile) 133
pelvic examination 171–3, 176–82
Pickering, A. 62
Pinard stethoscopes 76–9
place-based learning 219–20
policing 165–7
policy on the delivery of public services
    198–200
post-modern professions 79
Postone, M. 200
practice-based knowledge and learning
    12, 53, 112–14, 150–1, 185–6
'practice' turn in research 3, 85–6
practices, definition of 185
preparedness, concept of 40, 48
present-to-hand philosophy 68
Pries, L. 119
'Principal Investigator' (PI) role 91–5
process management 126, 137
process time, concept of 199–210
'productive system' concept 87–92
professional formation 133–8
professional learning, definition of 54–6
'professional patients' 171–2, 175–6, 182
professional responsibility 157–68, 209;
    and the curriculum 174–5; dilemmas
    of 163–7; distribution of 165; emphasis
    on individuals 158–61; in medicine
    171–82; sociomaterial conception of
    159–63, 182
professionalism 67–70, 131–2; new forms
    of 160
professionals, definition of 2
'projectification' of production 126–7,
    137
public services, development of 165–6,
    198–200

Raelin, J. 77
'rationality of caring' 201–4
ready-to-hand practitioners 68
reconceptualisation: of practice-based
    education 150–1; of professional practice
    148–9; of the service user 145–6
recontextualisation: concept of 125,
    134–6; types of 137–8
reflection 58, 72, 77, 133–4
reflective learning 77
reflective practitioners 63
relational view of knowledge 56, 63, 158
relativism 68
Renault (company) 127
representational view of knowledge
    54–8, 62
research in relation to professional
    practice 25
risk culture 157–8
Rosengarten, M. 63
Rossiter, C. 149

Saussure, F. de 43
Scanlon, L. 70
scapegoating 157, 168
Schatzki, Theodore 68, 151, 171–6, 181
Schön, D. 133, 136
Scott, S.V. 118
security passes 42–3
'see-through bodies' 180–2
Shoesmith, Sharon 157
situated practices 12–13, 41
Slade, B. 164–5
social life 173, 181
social responsibility, corporate 89
sociality 55
socialisation, professional 68, 79, 85
sociocultural perspectives on learning 41
sociomaterialty 2–4, 7, 12, 26, 39–44, 48,
    112–14, 118–22, 151, 158–63, 167–8,
    186; case study of 115–17; central
    premise of 161; and the curriculum
    171–4, 181; in nursing work 185; and
    professional responsibility 159–63, 182;
    and social life 173; and time 198–9
software development projects 31–4
Solbrekke, T.D. 158, 161
Sorensen, E. 54, 56
'space of reasons' (McDowell) 135–7
standard-setting agencies 25
Streeck, W. 96–7
Stronach, I. 160

Suchman, L. 12, 71
Sugrue, C. 161
surgical microscopes 100–10
sustainability 213–14, 217, 225
sustainable development, definition of 213

talk *in* practice and talk *about* practice
    19–20
teacher professional learning 43, 52–63,
    160, 213; 'more-than-representational'
    account of 53, 56–7
telecardiology 13–22; core of 15–19, 22;
    margins of 19–22
telemedicine 11
Teunissen, P.W. 39
Thrift, Nigel 53, 56, 61
time orders 199–201, 209–10;
    researching of 201
Tobias, S. 86
tools, use of 99–100, 109–10, 119–21

Treleaven, L. 78
Trevelyan, J. 113, 121

university researchers 90–5
university teaching 133–5

Varcoe, C. 186, 195
Vygotsky, L.S. 69, 99–100

Waerness, K. 201
Weddle, A.B. 99
Wenger, E. 41, 88, 94
Westerman, M. 39
White, S. 52
Whyte, J. 28
Williams, Rosalind 121
workplace curriculum 88

Yeatman, Anna 141
Young, M.F.D. 130–1